SOCIAL SECURITY LEGISLATION
SUPPLEMENT 2004

General Editor
David Bonner, LL.B., LL.M.

Commentary by
David Bonner, LL.B., LL.M.
Senior Lecturer in Law, University of Leicester
Formerly Member, Social Security Appeal Tribunals

Ian Hooker, LL.B.
Lecturer in Law, University of Nottingham
Formerly Member, Social Security Appeal Tribunals

Richard Poynter B.C.L., M.A. (Oxon)
Solicitor, District Chairman,
Appeals Service, Deputy Social Security Commissioner

Mark Rowland, LL.B.
Social Security Commissioner

Robin White, M.A., LL.M.
Professor of Law, University of Leicester,
Deputy Social Security Commissioner

Nick Wikeley, M.A.
Barrister, Professor of Law, University of Southampton,
Deputy Social Security Commissioner, Deputy District Chairman, Appeals Service

David Williams, LL.M., Ph.D., C.T.A.
Solicitor, Social Security and Child Support Commissioner, Deputy Special Commissioner of Income Tax and part-time Chairman of VAT and Duties Tribunal

Penny Wood, LL.B., M.Sc.
Solicitor, District Chairman
Appeals Service

Consultant to Vol. II
John Mesher, B.A., B.C.L., LL.M.
Barrister, Professor Associate of Law,
University of Sheffield,
Social Security and Child Support Commissioner

Consultant Editor
Child Poverty Action Group

LONDON

THOMSON

SWEET & MAXWELL

2004

Published in 2004 by
Sweet & Maxwell Limited of
100 Avenue Road, Swiss Cottage,
London NW3 3PF
(http://www.sweetandmaxwell.co.uk)
Typeset by Interactive Sciences Ltd, Gloucester
Printed in England by
MPG Books Ltd, Bodmin, Cornwall

No natural forests were destroyed to make this product.
Only farmed timber was used and re-planted.

A catalogue record for this book is
available from the British Library

ISBN 0 421 881 402

All rights reserved. Crown Copyright Legislation is reproduced under the terms of Crown Copyright Policy Guidance issued by HMSO.

No part of this publication may be reproduced or transmitted, in any form or by any means, or stored in any retrieval system of any nature without prior written permission, except for permitted fair dealing under the Copyright, Designs and Patents Act 1988, or in accordance with the terms of a licence issued by the Copyright Licensing Agency in respect of photocopying and/or reprographic reproduction. Application for permission for other use of copyright material including permission to reproduce extracts in other published works shall be mae to the publishers. Full acknowledgement of author, publisher and source must be given.

Application for permission for other use of copyright material controlled by the publisher shall be made to the publishers. Material is contained in this publication for which publishing permission has been sought, and for which copyright is acknowledged. Permission to reproduce such material cannot be granted by the publishers and application must be made to the copyright holder.

Commentators have asserted their moral rights under the Copyright, Designs and Patents Act 1988 to be identified as the authors of the commentary in this Volume.

©

2004

CHILD POVERTY ACTION GROUP

The Child Poverty Action Group (CPAG) is a charity, founded in 1965, which campaigns for the relief of poverty in the United Kingdom. It has a particular reputation in the field of welfare benefits law derived from its legal work, publications, training and parliamentary and policy work, and is widely recognised as the leading organisation for taking test cases on social security law.

CPAG is therefore ideally placed to act as Consultant Editor to this 4-volume work—**Social Security Legislation 2003 and Supplement 2003/2004**. CPAG is not responsible for the detail of what is contained in each volume, and the authors' views are not necessarily those of the CPAG. The Consultant Editor's role is to act in an advisory capacity on the overall structure, focus and direction of the work.

For more information about CPAG, its rights and policy publications or training courses, its address is 94 White Lion Street, London N1 9PF (telephone: 020 7837 7979—website: *www.cpag.org.uk*).

PREFACE

This is the combined Supplement to the 2003 edition of the four volume work, *Social Security Legislation*, which was published in September 2003.

Part I of this Supplement contains new legislation (this time only Regulations), presented in the same format as in the main volumes. This will enable the reader to note very quickly wholly new sets of legislation. This year this Part is taken up with yet more material on Tax Credits, with the establishment of the Department for Constitutional Affairs, presaging the abolition of the Lord Chancellor, and with yet another set of Work-Focused Interview provisions.

Parts II, III, IV and V contain updating material—a separate Part for each volume of the main work—which amends the legislative text and key aspects of the commentary so as to be up to date as at November 24, 2003. Part VI, the final section of the Supplement, gives some information on significant changes coming into force between November 24, 2003—the date to which this Supplement is up to date—and mid-April 2004, the date to which the 2004 edition of the main work will be up to date. It also contains the April 2004 benefit rates.

As always we welcome comments from those who use this Supplement. Please address them to the General Editor, David Bonner, at the Faculty of Law, The University, Leicester LE1 7RH.

David Bonner
Ian Hooker
Richard Poynter
Mark Rowland
Robin White
Nick Wikeley
David Williams
Penny Wood
February 1, 2004

CONTENTS

	Page
Preface	v
Using the Updating Material in this Supplement	viii
Pages of Main Volumes Affected by Material in this Supplement	ix
Table of Abbreviations	xv
Table of Cases	xix
Table of Commissioner's Decisions	xxi
Table of European Materials	xxiii
Table of Statutes	xxv
Table of Statutory Instruments	xxxvii
Table of Social Security Commissioners' Decisions	li
Part I: New Legislation	1
Part II: Updating Material Vol. 1: Non Means Tested Benefits	33
Part III: Updating Material Vol. II: Income Support, Jobseeker's Allowance, Tax Credit and the Social Fund	71
Part IV: Updating Material Vol. III: Administration, Adjudication and the European Dimension	131
Part V: Updating Material Vol. IV: Tax Credits and Employer Paid Social Security Benefits	189
Part VI: Forthcoming Changes and Up-rating of Benefits	203

USING THE UPDATING MATERIAL IN THIS SUPPLEMENT

The amendments and updating contained in Parts II–V of this Supplement are keyed in to the page numbers of the relevant main volume of *Social Security Legislation 2003*. Where there have been a significant number of changes to a provision, the whole section, subsection, paragraph of regulation, as amended, may well be reproduced with square brackets indicating the material inserted or omitted by the amendment. Other changes may be noted by an instruction to insert or substitute new material or to remove a word or phrase or provision. The date the change takes effect, and the legislation making the change, is also noted. Where explanation is needed of the change, or there is updating to existing annotations but no change to the legislation, you will also find commentary in this Supplement. The updating material explains new statutory material, takes on board Commissioners' or courts' decisions, or gives prominence to points which now seem to warrant more detailed attention.

This Supplement amends the text of the main volumes of *Social Security Legislation 2003* to be up to date as at November 24, 2003.

PAGES OF MAIN VOLUMES AFFECTED BY MATERIAL IN THIS SUPPLEMENT

Main volume page affected	Relevant paragraph in supplement
VOLUME I	
54–57	2.001
66	2.002
86–87	2.003
101–102	2.005
135	2.006
140–141	2.007
141	2.009
144	2.010
145	2.011
162	2.012
163	2.013
193–202	2.014
235–236	2.017
299	2.018
392	2.019
392–393	2.020
393	2.022
451	2.023
456	2.024
456	2.026
457	2.027
458	2.028
459	2.029
459–460	2.030
462–464	2.031
517	2.032
529	2.033
532	2.034
545–546	2.035
549–550	2.036
558	2.037
653	2.038
653	2.039
687–688	2.040
694–695	2.041
697–698	2.042
700	2.043
701–702	2.044
706	2.045
727–729	2.047

Pages of Main Volumes Affected by Material in this Supplement

Main volume page affected	Relevant paragraph in supplement
733	2.049
735–736	2.050
752–755	2.051
766	2.052
770–772	2.053
772	2.054
775	2.055
777	2.056
780	2.057
871	2.058
878–879	2.059
881	2.060
900	2.061
916	2.062
916–918	2.064
925–928	2.065
943–950	2.067
943	2.079
949	2.080
950	2.081
958	2.082
981	2.083

VOLUME II

Main volume page affected	Relevant paragraph in supplement
xiv	3.001
5	3.002
19	3.003
51	3.004
52	3.004–3.005
53	3.006
127	3.007
121–123	3.008
157	3.009
181	3.010
184	3.011
187	3.012
192	3.013
194	3.014
234	3.015
245	3.016
250	3.017

Pages of Main Volumes Affected by Material in this Supplement

Main volume page affected	Relevant paragraph in supplement
252	3.018
260	3.019
299	3.020
300	3.021
329	3.022
330	3.023
335	3.024
344	3.025
355	3.026
376	3.027
390	3.028
422–423	3.029
425	3.030
431	3.031
432	3.032
440	3.033
447	3.034
459	3.035–3.036
460	3.038
466–467	3.038
472	3.039
475	3.040–3.042
476–477	3.043
476	3.044
478	3.045
479	3.046
480	3.047
492	3.048
503	3.049
505	3.050–3.051
507	3.052
511	3.053
513	3.054
514	3.055
528	3.056
537	3.057
538	3.058
538–539	3.059
546	3.060
555	3.061
556	3.062
569	3.063
570	3.064–3.065
573–574	3.066
575–578	3.067
577	3.068
583–584	3.069

Pages of Main Volumes Affected by Material in this Supplement

Main volume page affected	Relevant paragraph in supplement
587	3.072–3.073
590	3.074
591	3.075
594	3.076
600	3.077
606	3.078
607	3.079
617	3.080
622	3.081
625	3.082
634–635	3.083
642	3.084
660	3.085
661	3.086–3.087
667	3.088
668	3.089
672–673	3.090
673–674	3.092
676	3.093
677	3.094
677	3.095
680	3.096
683	3.097–3.098
684	3.099
685	3.100–3.101
686	3.102
687–688	3.103
691	3.104–3.105
692	3.106
693	3.107–3.108
694	3.109–3.110
696–697	3.111
722–723	3.112
739–740	3.113
755	3.114
758	3.115
759	3.116
764	3.118
778	3.119
783	3.120
787	3.121
854	3.122
943–945	3.123
946	3.124
947	3.125
948	3.126
951	3.127

Pages of Main Volumes Affected by Material in this Supplement

Main volume page affected	Relevant paragraph in supplement
952	3.128
965	3.129
1017	3.130
1018	3.131
1023	3.132
1050	3.133
1052	3.134
1066	3.135
1071	3.136
1072	3.137
1078	3.138–3.139
1089	3.140
1097	3.141
1098–1099	3.142
1102	3.143
1103	3.144
1104	3.145
1106	3.146
1109	3.147
1110	3.148
1111	3.149
1114	3.150
1126	3.151
1132	3.152
1135	3.153
1139–1140	3.154
1142	3.155
1143	3.156
1153	3.157
1171	3.158
1180	3.159
1181	3.160
1185	3.161–3.162
1187	3.163
1192	3.165
1198	3.166
1218–1219	3.167
1223	3.168
1234	3.169
1235	3.170
1237–1238	3.171
1240	3.172
1241	3.173
1242	3.174
1243	3.175
1244	3.177
1245–1246	3.178

Pages of Main Volumes Affected by Material in this Supplement

Main volume page affected	Relevant paragraph in supplement
1246	3.179–3.180
1249	3.181
1258	3.182
1262	3.183
1265	3.185
1266	3.186
1266–1267	3.187
1267	3.188
1270	3.189
1278	3.190
1282	3.191
1289	3.192
1293	3.193

VOLUME III

Main volume page affected	Relevant paragraph in supplement
23	4.001
29	4.002
29–30	4.006
30	4.008
34–36	4.008a
41	4.009
45–49	4.010
52–53	4.011
111–112	4.012
134–136	4.013
141	4.014
155–158	4.015
165–166	4.016
170	4.017
175	4.018
186–187	4.019
198–199	4.020
204	4.021
207	4.022
210	4.023
216	4.024
219–220	4.025
224	4.026
228	4.027–4.028
233–234	4.029
236	4.030
251	4.031

Pages of Main Volumes Affected by Material in this Supplement

Main volume page affected	Relevant paragraph in supplement
276–278	4.032
338–341	4.033
344–347	4.034
353–354	4.036
354	4.037
355	4.044
376–378	4.045
383–384	4.046
387	4.047
389–390	4.048
391	4.049–4.050
395–397	4.051
415	4.052
416–418	4.054
421–422	4.055
426	4.056
428–429	4.057
452–463	4.058
463–467	4.062
469–471	4.068
498	4.069
511	4.070
513	4.071
518	4.072
524–525	4.073
527–534	4.074
534–540	4.076
584	4.079
595	4.080
600–605	4.081
616–617	4.082
624	4.083
626	4.084
642	4.085
662	4.086
694–695	4.087
700–701	4.088
702–703	4.089
703–704	4.090
706–707	4.091
709–710	4.092
710	4.093
711–713	4.094
713	4.095
760	4.096
906	4.098–4.099
1019	4.100

Pages of Main Volumes Affected by Material in this Supplement

Main volume page affected	Relevant paragraph in supplement
1022	4.101
1029	4.102
1038	4.103
1047	4.105
1059	4.106
1080	4.107

VOLUME IV

Main volume page affected	Relevant paragraph in supplement
21	5.001
164	5.002
169	5.003
173	5.004
179	5.005–5.006
190	5.007
209	5.008
213	5.009
259	5.010
267	5.011
364	5.012
377	5.013
378	5.014
386	5.015
391	5.016
393	5.017
408	5.018
411	5.019
411–412	5.020
412	5.021–5.022
414	5.023
415	5.024
415–417	5.025
417	5.026
432	5.027
436	5.028
441	5.029
437	5.030
447	5.031
456–458	5.032
464	5.033
479	5.034
498	5.035–5.036
515	5.037

TABLE OF ABBREVIATIONS USED IN THIS SERIES

Adjudication Regulations	Social Security (Adjudication) Regulations 1986
All E.R.	All England Law Reports (Butterworths)
AO	Adjudication Officer
AOG	HMSO, *Adjudication Officers Guide*
Attendance Allowance Regulations	Social Security (Attendance Allowance) Regulations 1991
Blue Books	HMSO, *The Law Relating to Social Security*, Vols 1–11
CBA 1975	Child Benefit Act 1975
CAO	Chief Adjudication Officer
CPAG	Child Poverty Action Group
CSO	Child Support Officer
Claims and Payments Regulations 1979	Social Security (Claims and Payments) Regulations 1979
Claims and Payments Regulations 1987	Social Security (Claims and Payments) Regulations 1987
C.M.L.R.	Common Market Law Reports
Commissioners Procedure Regulations	Social Security Commissioners (Procedure) Regulations 1999
Computation of Earnings Regulations 1978	Social Security Benefit (Computation of Earnings) Regulations 1978
Computation of Earnings Regulations 1996	Social Security Benefit (Computation of Earnings) Regulations 1996
DAT	Disability Appeals Tribunal
Decisions and Appeals Regulations 1999	Social Security and Child Support (Decisions and Appeals) Regulations 1999
Dependency Regulations	Social Security Benefit (Dependency) Regulations 1977
DLA	Disability Living Allowance
DMA	Decision-making and Appeals
DMG	HMSO, *Decision-Makers Guide*
Disability Working Allowance Regulations	Disability Working Allowance (General) Regulations 1991
DPTC	Disabled Person's Tax Credit
DWA	Disability Working Allowance
E.C.R.	European Court Reports

Table of Abbreviations used in this Series

EHRR	European Human Rights Reports
Eur. L. Rev.	European Law Review
Family Credit Regulations	Family Credit (General) Regulations 1987
General Benefit Regulations	Social Security (General Benefit) Regulations 1982
HASSASSAA 1983	Health and Social Services and Social Security Adjudication Act 1983
Hospital In-Patients Regulations	Social Security (Hospital In-Patients) Regulations 1975
Income Support Regulations	Income Support (General) Regulations 1987
IB Regulations	Social Security (Incapacity Benefit) Regulations 1994
I.L.J.	Industrial Law Journal
IWA	Social Security (Incapacity for Work) Act 1994
IW (General) Regulations	Social Security (Incapacity for Work) (General) Regulations 1995
IW (Transitional) Regulations	Social Security (Incapacity for Work) (Transitional) Regulations 1995
Invalid Care Allowance Regulations	Social Security (Invalid Care Allowance) Regulations 1976
JSA Regulations	Jobseeker's Allowance Regulations 1996
JSA (Transitional) Regulations	Jobseeker's Allowance (Transitional) Regulations 1996
J.S.W.L.	Journal of Social Welfare Law
JSWFL	Journal of Social Welfare and Family Law
JSSL	Journal of Social Security Law
MAT	Medical Appeal Tribunal
Maternity Benefit Regulations	Social Security (Maternity Benefit) Regulations 1975
Medical Evidence Regulations	Social Security (Medical Evidence) Regulations 1976
Ogus, Barendt and Wikeley	A. Ogus, E. Barendt and N. Wikeley, *The Law of Social Security* (4th ed., Butterworths, 1995)
Overlapping Benefits Regulations	Social Security (Overlapping Benefits) Regulations 1979
Overpayments Regulations	Social Security (Payments on account, Overpayments and Recovery) Regulations 1988
Persons Abroad Regulations	Social Security Benefit (Persons Abroad) Regulations 1975
Persons Residing Together Regulations	Social Security Benefit (Persons Residing Together) Regulations 1977

Table of Abbreviations used in this Series

Prescribed Diseases Regulations	Social Security (Industrial Injuries) (Prescribed Diseases) Regulations 1985
Recovery of Benefits Act	Social Security (Recovery of Benefits) Act 1997
Recovery of Benefits Regulations	Social Security (Recovery of Benefits) Regulations 1997
RMO	Regional Medical Officer
SDA	Severe Disablement Allowance
Severe Disablement Allowance Regulations	Social Security (Severe Disablement Allowance) Regulations 1984
SMP	Statutory Maternity Pay
SSA 1975	Social Security Act 1975
SSA 1980	Social Security Act 1980
SSA 1985	Social Security Act 1985
SSA 1986	Social Security Act 1986
SSA 1988	Social Security Act 1988
SSA 1989	Social Security Act 1989
SSA 1998	Social Security Act 1998
SS (No. 2) A 1980	Social Security (No. 2) Act 1980
SSAT	Social Security Appeal Tribunal
SSHBA	Social Security and Housing Benefits Act 1982
SS (MP) A 1977	Social Security (Miscellaneous Provisions) Act 1977
SSP	Statutory Sick Pay
SSPA 1975	Social Security Pensions Act 1975
SSCBA 1992	Social Security Contributions and Benefits Act 1992*
SSAA 1992	Social Security Administration Act 1992*
SSCPA 1992	Social Security Consequential Provisions Act 1992
USI Regulations	Social Security (Unemployment, Sickness and Invalidity Benefit) Regulations 1983
WFTC	Working Families' Tax Credit
White Paper	Jobseeker's Allowance, Cm. 2687 (October, 1994)
Widow's Benefit and Retirement Pensions Regulations	Social Security (Widow's Benefit and Retirement Pensions) Regulations 1979
Wikeley, Annotations	N. Wikeley, Annotations to Jobseekers Act 1995 (c.18), Currnet Law Statutes Annotated (1995)
W.L.R.	Weekly Law Reports

* Where the context makes it seem more appropriate, these could also be referred to as Contributions and Benefits Act 1992, Administration Act 1992

TABLE OF CASES

Appleby v Chief Adjudication Officer, judgment, June 29, 1999, CA 2.071
Bland v Chief Supplementary Benefit Officer [1983] 1 W.L.R. 262; [1983] 1 All
E.R. 537; (1983) 127 S.J. 53, CA 4.028
Chief Adjudication Officer v Faulds [2000] 1 W.L.R. 1035; [2000] 2 All E.R. 961;
2000 S.C. (H.L.) 116; 2000 S.L.T. 712; 2000 S.C.L.R. 713; [2000] I.C.R.
1297; (2000) 97(22) L.S.G. 46; 2000 G.W.D. 17–703; *The Times*, May 16,
2000; *Independent*, June 19, 2000, HL 2.014
Chief Adjudication Officer v Foster [1993] A.C. 754; [1993] 2 W.L.R. 292; [1993]
1 All E.R. 705; [1993] C.O.D. 259; (1993) 137 S.J.L.B. 36; *The Times*,
February 1, 1993; *Independent*, February 2, 1993; *Guardian*, January 29, 1993,
HL 4.105
Cockburn 2.007, 2.008
Collins v Secretary of State for Work and Pensions (Case C–138/02) 4.098
Cooke v Secretary of State for Social Security; sub nom. Cooke v Social Security
Commissioner [2001] EWCA Civ 734; [2002] 3 All E.R. 279; *Daily Telegraph*,
May 1, 2001, CA 4.028
EC Commission v French Republic 4.099
Fawcett Properties Ltd v Buckingham CC [1961] A.C. 636; [1960] 3 W.L.R. 831;
[1960] 3 All E.R. 503; (1961) 125 J.P. 8; 59 L.G.R. 69; (1961) 12 P. & C.R.
1; 104 S.J. 912, HL 2.070
Ferguson v Secretary of State for Work and Pensions [2003] EWCA Civ 536,
CA 3.122
George Mitchell (Chesterhall) Ltd v Finney Lock Seeds Ltd [1983] 2 A.C. 803;
[1983] 3 W.L.R. 163; [1983] 2 All E.R. 737; [1983] 2 Lloyd's Rep. 272; [1983]
Com. L.R. 209, HL 4.026
Hooper v Secretary of State for Work and Pensions; Withey v Secretary of State for
Work and Pensions; Naylor v Secretary of State for Work and Pensions; Martin
v Secretary of State for Work and Pensions; sub nom. R. (on the application of
Hooper) v Secretary of State for Work and Pensions [2003] EWCA Civ 813;
[2003] 3 All E.R. 673; [2003] 2 F.C.R. 504; 14 B.H.R.C. 626; (2003) 100(29)
L.S.G. 35; *The Times*, June 28, 2003; *Independent*, June 25, 2003, CA; affirming [2002] EWHC 191; [2002] U.K.H.R.R. 785, QBD (Admin Ct) 2.002, 4.107
Hoppe v Germany (28422/95) [2003] 1 F.L.R. 384; [2003] 1 F.C.R. 176; [2003]
Fam. Law 159, ECHR 4.069
Jones v Secretary of State for Work and Pensions [2003] EWCA Civ 964, CA 3.027
Kaya v Haringey LBC [2001] EWCA Civ 677; [2002] H.L.R. 1; (2001) 98(25)
L.S.G. 46; *The Times*, June 14, 2001, CA 3.018
Lawal v Northern Spirit Ltd [2003] UKHL 35; [2003] I.C.R. 856; [2003] I.R.L.R.
538; [2003] H.R.L.R. 29; (2003) 100(28) L.S.G. 30; (2003) 153 N.L.J. 1005;
(2003) 147 S.J.L.B. 783; *The Times*, June 27, 2003, HL 4.106
Moyna v Secretary of State for Work and Pensions [2003] UKHL 44; [2003] 1
W.L.R. 1929; [2003] 4 All E.R. 162; (2003) 73 B.M.L.R. 201; *The Times*,
August 11, 2003; *Independent*, October 2, 2003, HL 2.011, 4.026
Lowther v Chatwin [2003] EWCA Civ 729; [2003] P.I.Q.R. Q5; *The Times*, August
4, 2003, CA 4.019
Lynch v Secretary of State for Work and Pensions [2003] EWCA Civ 497 .... 4.107
Mullen v Secretary of State for Work and Pensions 2002 S.C. 251; 2002 S.L.T. 149;
2002 S.C.L.R. 475; 2002 G.W.D. 3–121, 2 Div 2.014, 2.015
Ninni-Orasche v Bundesninister fur Wissenschaft und Kunst (Case C–413/01),
judgment November 6, 2003 .... 4.098

xix

Table of Cases

Nova Scotia (Workers' Compensation Board) v Martin [2003] SCC 54; October 3, 2003, Supreme Ct (Canada) 4.108

Porter v Magill [2001] UKHL 67; [2002] 2 A.C. 357; [2002] 2 W.L.R. 37; [2002] 1 All E.R. 465; [2002] H.R.L.R. 16; [2002] H.L.R. 16; [2002] B.L.G.R. 51; (2001) 151 N.L.J. 1886; [2001] N.P.C. 184; *The Times,* December 14, 2001; *Daily Telegraph,* December 20, 2001, HL 4.106

R. v Higher Education Funding Council Ex p. Institute of Dental Surgery [1994] 1 W.L.R. 242; [1994] 1 All E.R. 651; [1994] C.O.D. 147; *Independent,* September 28, 1993, QBD 4.081

R. (on the application of Carson) v Secretary of State for Work and Pensions; R. (on the application of Reynolds) v Secretary of State for Work and Pensions [2003] EWCA Civ 797; [2003] 3 All E.R. 577; [2003] Pens. L.R. 215; (2003) 100(34) L.S.G. 32; (2003) 147 S.J.L.B. 780; *The Times,* June 28, 2003, CA 4.107

R. (on the application of Nash) v Chelsea College of Art and Design [2001] EWHC Admin 538; *The Times,* July 25, 2001, QBD (Admin Ct) 4.081

R. (on the application of the National Association of Colliery Overmen, Deputies and Shotfirers) v Secretary of State for Work and Pensions [2003] EWHC 607, QBD (Admin Ct) 2.081

R. (on the application of Asha Foundation) v Millennium Commission [2003] EWCA Civ 88; [2003] A.C.D. 50; (2003) 100(11) L.S.G. 31; *The Times,* January 24, 2003, CA 4.081

R. (on the application of Sivasubramaniam) v Wandsworth County Court; R. (on the application of Sivasubramaniam) v Kingston upon Thames County Court; sub nom. Sivasubramaniam v Wandsworth County Court; R. (on the application of Sivasubramaniam) v Guildford College of Further & Higher Education [2002] EWCA Civ 1738; [2003] 1 W.L.R. 475; [2003] 2 All E.R. 160; [2003] C.P. Rep. 27; (2003) 100(3) L.S.G. 34; *The Times,* November 30, 2002, CA 4.028

Ramsden v Secretary of State for Work and Pensions [2003] EWCA Civ 32, CA 2.007, 2.016

Secretary of State for Work and Pensions v Adams [2003] EWCA Civ 796, CA 4.021

Secretary of State for Work and Pensions v Miah [2003] EWCA Civ 1111; [2003] 4 All E.R. 702; [2003] 3 F.C.R. 268; (2003) 100(38) L.S.G. 35; *The Times,* September 5, 2003; *Independent,* July 31, 2003, CA 3.013

Secretary of State for Work and Pensions v Nelligan [2003] EWCA Civ 555; [2003] 4 All E.R. 171; (2003) 100(26) L S.G. 38; (2003) 153 N.L.J. 667; *The Times,* April 23, 2003, CA 2.003

Secretary of State for Work and Pensions v Whalley [2002] EWCA Civ 166 .... 2.061, 4.029

Shire v Secretary of State for Work and Pensions [2003] EWCA Civ 1465; (2003) 100(42) L.S.G. 32; *The Times,* October 30, 2003, CA 3.033

Stanley Cole (Wainfleet) Ltd v Sheridan [2003] EWCA Civ 1046; (2003) 100(38) L.S.G. 33; *The Times,* September 5, 2003, CA 4.026

Szoma v Secretary of State for Work and Pensions [2003] EWCA Civ 1131; *The Times,* August 22, 2003, CA 1.061, 3.018

Williams v Devon CC [2003] EWCA Civ 365; [2003] P.I.Q.R. Q4; *The Times,* March 26, 2003, CA 4.016

Wilson v First County Trust Ltd (No.2); sub nom. Wilson v Secretary of State for Trade and Industry [2003] UKHL 40; [2003] 3 W.L.R. 568; [2003] 4 All E.R. 97; [2003] 2 All E.R. (Comm) 491; [2003] H.R.L.R. 33; (2003) 100(35) L.S.G. 39; (2003) 147 S.J.L.B. 872; *The Times,* July 11, 2003, HL 4.103

Wilson v Secretary of State for Trade and Industry *See* Wilson v First County Trust Ltd (No.2)

TABLE OF COMMISSIONERS' DECISIONS

C12/03–04(DLA)	4.024	CI 1714/2002	2.016
C24/02–03 (DLA)	4.025	CI 1807/2002	2.081
C50/90–00 (DLA)	4.099	CI 2286/2002	2.076
CCR/4919/01	4.017	CI 2668/2002	2.080
CCR/427/03	4.015, 4.016	CI 2746/2002	2.059
CCS/3553/2002	4.071	CI 3511/2002	2.014
CDLA 131/2001	2.009	CI 4582/2002	2.081
CDLA 3848/2001	4.024	CI 5029/2002	2.078, 2.079
CDLA 3875/01	4.074	CI 5092/2002	2.018
CDLA 1317/2002	4.027	CI 5331/2002	2.076, 2.080
CDLA 1761/02	4.081	CI 1293/2003	2.058
CDLA 2050/02	4.073	CIB 15482/1996	2.043
CDLA 2106/2002	2.012	CIB 4916/1997	2.057
CDLA 3967/2002	2.006, 4.030	CIB 6244/1997	2.043
CDLA 4331/2002	4.020, 4.024	CIB 243/1998	2.043
CDLA 2115/03	4.074	CIB 727/1998	2.052
CDLA 2462/03	4.080	CIB 2620/2000	2.051
CG 734/2003	4.107	CIB 4331/01	4.075
CG 2611/2003	2.032	CIB 313/02	4.074
CI 37/1988	2.072	CIB 2397/2002	2.041
CI 246/1988	2.073	CIB 2751/02	4.079, 4.080
CI 308/1989	2.073	CIB 3519/2002	2.049, 2.053
CI 309/1989	2.075	CIB 4598/2002	2.054
CI 550/1989	2.073	CIB 4841/2002	2.048
CI 175/90	2.075	CIB 5435/2002	2.047
CI 226/1991	2.070	CIB 5536/2002	2.055, 2.056, 2.057
CI 245/1991	2.071	CIB 399/2003	2.043
CI 43/1992	2.075	CIB 638/2003	2.001
CI 337/1992	2.042	CIB 1381/2003	2.040
CI 17/1993	2.071	CIB 1886/2003	2.042
CI 278/1993	2.016	CIB 1887/2003	2.042
CI 540/1994	2.072	CIB 3507/2003	2.044
CI 554/1994	2.015	CIS 4772/2000	3.048
CI 808/1995	2.072	CIS 852/2001	4.099
CI 2879/1995	2.074	CIS 2091/2001	3.018
CI 11874/1996	2.080	CIS 2699/2001	2.050, 3.048
CI 13238/1996	2.072, 2.073	CIS 2497/2002	3.189
CI 105/1998	2.015	CIS 4248/2001	4.079
CI 4567/1999	2.067, 2.068, 2.069	CIS 4320/2002	3.058
CI 2012/2000	2.068, 2/069	CIS 4511/2002	3.025, 4.105, 4.107
CI 226/2001	2.061	CIS 4712/2002	3.056
CI 1720/2001	2.081	CIS 788/2003	3.192
CI 1819/2001(T)	2.082	CIS 1189/2003	2.026
CI 2314/2001(T)	2.082	CIS 2208/2003	3.083
CI 2885/2001(T)	2.082	CJSA 2692/1999	3.008
CI 3596/2001	2.081	CJSA 4065/1999	4.098
CI 4708/2001	2.015, 2.016	CJSA 1501/2000	3.123
CI 5130/2001(T)	2.082	CJSA 1542/2000	3.123
CI 1/2002	2.069	CJSA 4620/2000	3.013
CI 1297/2002	4.031	CJSA 322/01	4.081
CI 1605/2002	2.061, 4.029	CJSA 3908/01	4.081

Table of Commissioners' Decisions

CJSA 2082/2002	3.008
CJSA 415.2002	3.008
CJSA 549/2003	3.023
CJSA 1134/2003	3.022
CP 5084/2001	4.107
CS 3202/02	4.079, 4.080
CSA 721/00	2.010
CSDLA 678/99	2.037
CSDLA 667/2002	2.037
CSDLA 91/2003	2.013
CSI 65/1994	2.074
CSI 371/2001	2.015
CSI 744/2002	2.060
CSIS 1009/2002	4.081
R 2/00(IB)	2.053
R(A) 2/90	4.074
R(A) 1/03	2.010
R(CR) 2/02	4.017
R(DLA) 6/01	4.028
R(DLA) 3/03	2.009
R(DLA) 5/03	4.030
R(DLA) 7/03	4.026
R(G) 1/2003	4.021
R(I) 5/76	2.071
R(I) 7/76	2.070
R(I) 8/76	2.071
R(I) 1/80	2.071
R(I) 3/80	2.071
R(I) 13/80	2.071
R(I) 13/81	2.074
R(I) 5/83	2.072
R(I) 6/83	2.071
R(I) 4/84	2.073
R(I) 2/85	2.070
R(I) 8/85	2.071
R(I) 2/92	2.073, 2.075
R(I) 5/95	2.060
R(I) 2/97	2.076
R(I) 4/99	2.077
R(I) 5/99	2.071
R(I) 5/02	4.071
R(I) 6/02	2.067, 2.068, 2.069
R(I) 2/03	4.029
R(I) 3/03	2.082
R(IB) 2/99	2.041, 2.051
R(IB) 2/99T	2.043
R(IB) 4/03	2.052
R(IS) 4/01	2.001
R(JSA) 6/02	3.123
R(JSA) 4/03	4.100
R(JSA) 6/03	3.122
R(P) 1/03	2.005
R(SB) 12/83	4.028
R(SB) 8/89	2.042
R(U) 4/83	2.001
R(U) 8/83	2.001
R(U) 3/85	2.042

TABLE OF EUROPEAN MATERIALS

Charter of Fundamental Rights of the European Union
Article 34(2) 1.056

1950 European Convention on the Protection of Human Rights and Fundamental Freedoms 1.055, 2.069, 3.025, 4.069
Article 6 .... 4.106
Article 8 ..... 3.025, 3.058, 4.109
Article 14 .... 3.025, 3.058, 4.107, 4.109
Protocol 1, Article 1 .... 3.025, 4.107

1957 Treaty establishing the European Community
Article 5 .... 1.059
Article 48 (now 39) 4.099
Article 51 (now 42) 4.099
Article 63, point 4 .... 1.054
Protocol, Article 1 .... 1.059
Protocol, Article 2 .... 1.059
Protocol, Article 3 .... 1.059

Treaty on European Union
Article 6(2) 1.055
Protocol, Article 1 .... 1.059

Protocol, Article 2 .... 1.059
Protocol, Article 3 .... 1.059
Regulation 1612/68 .... 4.099
Art.7 .... 4.098, 4.099
Art.7(2) 4.098, 4.099
Art.10(a) 4.099
Art.42 .... **4.099**
Regulation (EEC) 1408/71 .... 1.052, 1.053, 1.057, 1.058, 1.060, 1.061, 4.099
Art.69 .... 1.058
Regulation (EEC) 574/72 .... 1.052, 1.057, 1.058, 1.060
Regulation (EC)1386/2001 .... 1.057
Commission Regulation 410/2002 .... 1.057
Council Regulation 859/2003 .... 1.052
Art.1 .... **1.060**, 1.065
Art.2 .... **1.062**
Art.3 .... **1.064**
Annex **1.065**
Directive 79/7/EEC 3.189
Art.7(1)(a) **4.101**

TABLE OF STATUTES

Year	Statute	Reference
1865	Naval and Marine Pay and Pensions Act (28 & 29 Vict. c.33)	
	s.3	3.172
1868	Documentary Evidence Act (31 & 32 Vict. c.37)	1.016
1889	Commissioners for Oaths Act (52 & 53 Vict. c.10)	
	s.1(1)	1.023
1917	Air Force (Constitution) Act (7 & 8 Geo.5 c.51)	
	s.2	3.172
1947	Polish Resettlement Act (10 & 11 Geo.6 c.19)	
	s.3(1)	3.182, 4.065, 4.066
	Sch., Pt II	3.182, 4.065, 4.066
1952	Prison Act (15 & 16 Geo.6. & 1 Eliz.2 c.52)	3.163
1968	Social Work (Scotland) Act (c.49)	
	s.12B	3.082, 3.155, 5.032
1970	Taxes Management Act (c.9)	
	s.54	5.001
1971	Courts Act (c.23)	
	Pt 4	1.023
	s.28	1.020
1973	Employment and Training Act (c.50)	
	s.2	1.007, 1.008, 3.010, 3.014, 3.071, 3.077, 3.080, 3.082, 3.119, 3.152, 3.155
1974	Consumer Credit Act (c.39)	
	s.127	4.103
1974	Solicitors Act (c.47)	1.023
1975	Ministers of the Crown Act (c.26)	
	s.1	1.013
	s.2	1.013
1976	Adoption Act (c.36)	5.032
	s.57A	3.076, 3.151
1978	Adoption (Scotland) Act (c.28)	
	s.51	3.076, 3.151
1980	Reserve Forces Act (c.9)	
	s.140	3.172
	s.151	3.172
1983	Representation of the People Act (c.2)	
	s.161	1.023
1983	Mental Health Act (c.20)	3.163
1984	Mental Health (Scotland) Act (c.36)	3.163
1985	Representation of the People Act (c.50)	1.023
1985	Administration of Justice Act (c.61)	1.023
1986	Social Security Act (c.50)	
	s.51C(1)	4.056
1986	Parliamentary Constituencies Act (c.56)	
	Sch.1, para.3	1.023
1988	Income and Corporation Taxes Act (c.1)	
	327A	5.032
1988	Legal Aid Act (c.34)	1.023
1989	Prisons (Scotland) Act (c.45)	3.163
1990	Enterprise and New Towns (Scotland) Act (c.35)	
	s.2	3.071
1990	Courts and Legal Services Act (c.41)	
	Pt 2	1.023
	Pt 4	1.023
	s.113	1.023
	s.124	1.023
	s.125	1.023
1992	Social Security Contributions and Benefits Act (c.4)	3.009
	Pt II	3.043
	Pt VII	4.005
	s.30A(3)	2.038
	s.30C(3)	2.038
	s.30D(3A)	2.038
	s.30DD	2.001
	s.30DD(1)	2.001
	s.38	2.002
	s.43	2.003
	s.43(5)	2.003, 2.004
	s.52(3)	2.005
	s.56	2.017
	s.64	3.178
	s.72	2.006, 2.007, 2.009, 2.010, 2.011
	s.72(6)	2.013, 4.020

Table of Statutes

1992 Social Security Contributions and Benefits Act —*cont.*
- s.73 .... 2.012
- s.73(4) 2.013
- s.82–84 .... 2.017
- s.86 .... 2.017
- s.94(1) 2.014, 2.078
- s.104 .... 3.178
- s.105 .... 3.178
- s.114 .... **2.017**
- s.123(1)(a) 1.026
- s.123(1)(d) 1.026
- s.123(1)(e) 1.026
- s.124 .... 3.002
- s.124(1)(aa) **3.002**, 3.057, 3.072, 3.073
- s.124(1)(g) **3.002**, 3.057, 3.072, 3.073
- s.135 .... 5.013
- s.136(3) 1.026
- s.136(5)(b) 1.026
- s.137 .... 3.003
- s.137(1) 1.026
- s.142 .... 4.058
- s.171B(2) 4.078
- s.171B(3) 4.078
- s.171C(4) 4.078
- s.175(3) 1.026
- s.175(4) 1.026
- Sch.6, para.1 .... 2.018
- Sch.6, para.6(1) 2.063
- Sch.6, para.6(2) 2.063
- Sch.7, para.5 .... 2.017
- Sch.7, para.6 .... 2.017

1992 Social Security Administration Act (c.5) 3.009
- s.1 .... 2.003
- s.1(4)(ab) 4.001
- s.2A(1) 1.026
- s.2A(3)–(6) 1.026
- s.2A(8) 1.026
- s.2AA **4.002**
- s.2B 1.037, **4.006**
- s.2B(2) 1.028
- s.2B(6) 1.026
- s.2B(7) 1.026
- s.2C(2) **4.008**
- s.5 .... 4.008
- s.7A 4.035, 4.038, 4.043
- s.11 .... 4.009
- s.15A 4.010
- s.15A(1) 4.056
- s.15A(1A) 4.056
- s.71 .... 4.011
- s.124 .... 4.012
- s.179 .... 4.013
- s.189(4)–(6) 1.026
- s.189(7A) 1.026
- s.190 .... 4.014
- s.190(1)(ab) **4.014**

1992 Social Security Administration Act—*cont.*
- s.191 .... 1.026

1992 Tribunals and Inquiries Act (c.53)
- s.8(1) 1.026

1993 Pension Schemes Act (c.48)
- s.46 .... 2.005

1995 Jobseekers Act (c.18)
- s.3 .... 3.004
- s.3(1) 3.004
- s.3(1)(dd) **3.004**
- s.3A 3.005
- s.3A(1) 3.006
- s.12(1) 1.026
- s.12(4)(b) 1.026
- s.19(6)(c) 3.008
- s.19(9) 3.007
- s.35(1) 1.026
- s.36(2) 1.026
- s.36(4) 1.026

1995 Pensions Act (c.26)
- Sch.4, para.1 .... 3.003

1995 Child Support Act (c.34)
- s.10 .... 4.094

1995 Children (Scotland) Act 1995 (c.36)
- s.13 .... 3.081, 3.154

1995 Criminal Procedure (Scotland) Act (c.46) 3.163

1996 Employment Rights Act (c.18)
- s.75A 3.159
- s.75B 3.159
- s.80A 3.160
- s.80B 3.160

1996 Community Care (Direct Payments) Act (c.30) 3.082, 3.155, 5.032

1997 Social Security (Recovery of Benefits) Act (c.27)
- s.1 .... 4.015
- s.8 .... 4.016
- s.11 .... 4.017
- s.15 .... 4.018
- Sch.1 .... 4.019

1998 Social Security Act (c.14)
- s.7(4) 4.079
- s.8(2) 4.020
- s.9 .... 1.043, 4.047
- s.10 .... 1.043
- s.10(5) 4.021, 4.073
- s.12 .... 1.043, 4.022
- s.12(1) 4.023
- s.12(8) 4.024
- s.12(8)(b) 3.048
- s.13(3) 4.025
- s.14(1) 1.026
- s.14(7) 4.025
- s.14(8) 4.027
- s.14(10) 4.028

1998	Social Security Act—*cont.*	
	s.17	4.029
	s.20	2.006, 4.030
	s.20(3)	2.006
	s.26	4.073
	s.29	4.031
	Sch.6	4.033
1998	Data Protection Act (c.29)	1.023
	s.6(4)(a)	1.023
	s.6(4)(b)	1.023
	s.28	1.023
	Sch.5, para.12(2)	1.023
	Sch.6, para.2	1.023
	Sch.6, para.3	1.023
1998	Human Rights Act (c.42)	2.002, 2.069, 4.102, 4.103, 4.105
	s.1	4.102
	s.2(3)(A)	4.102
	s.4	4.103
	s.5	1.023
	s.7	4.105
	s.7(9)(A)	4.102
	s.10	1.023
	ss.14–16	4.102
	s.18	1.023
	s.19	1.023
	s.20(2)	4.102
	s.20(4)	4.102
	Sch.4	1.023
1999	Access to Justice Act (c.22)	4.028
	Pts 1–3	1.023
	Pt 7	1.023
1999	Welfare Reform and Pensions Act (c.30)	2.001, 4.043
	s.57	4.007
	s.72	4.032
	s.72(2)	4.033
	s.72(3)(aa)	**4.032**
1999	Immigration and Asylum Act (c.33)	
	s.115(9)	3.163
	s.123(9)	3.009
	s.123(9)(c)	**3.009**
2000	Representation of the People Act (c.2)	
	Sch.4	1.023
2000	Care Standards Act 2000 (c.14)	3.182
	s.2	3.115, 3.117
	s.3	3.115, 3.117
2000	Child Support, Pensions and Social Security Act (c.19)	
	Sch.7, para.6(2)	4.070
2000	Freedom of Information Act (c.36)	1.023
	s.15	1.023
2000	Freedom of Information Act—*cont.*	
	s.23	1.023
	s.24	1.023
	s.36	1.023
	s.46	1.023
	s.53	1.023
	s.65	1.023
	s.66	1.023
2001	Election Publications Act (c.5)	1.023
2001	Health and Social Care Act (c.15)	
	s.57	3.082, 3.155, 5.032
2001	Regulation of Care (Scotland) Act (asp 8)	
	s.2(3)	3.115, 3.117
	s.2(5)(a)	3.115, 3.117
	s.2(5)(b)	3.115, 3.117
2002	Carers and Direct Payments Act (Northern Ireland) (c.6)	
	s.8	5.032
2002	State Pension Credit Act (Northern Ireland) (c.14)	5.034
2002	State Pension Credit Act (c.16)	3.003, 3.009, 3.085, 3.086, 3.087, 3.093, 3.099, 3.106, 3.112, 3.113., 3.157, 4.033, 4.087, 5.034
	s.1	4.033
	s.1(2)(b)	3.003
	s.1(6)	3.003, 4.033
	s.2	4.033
	s.6	4.045, 4.055, 4.073
	s.12(1)(c)	4.058
	s.13	3.157
	s.13(3)	3.158
	s.14	3.002, 3.003, 3.004, 3.005, 3.009
	s.21	3.002
	s.115	3.085, 3.086, 3.087
	Sch.2, para.1	3.002, 3.003
	Sch.2, para.2	3.002
	Sch.2, para.4	3.003
	Sch.2, para.37	3.004
	Sch.2, para.38	3.005
	Sch.2, para.42	3.005
	Sch.3	3.002
2002	Tax Credits Act (c.21)	3.178, 5.002
	s.1(3)(d)	1.012, 5.003
	s.3(2)	5.004
	s.6	5.005
	s.7(10)	5.006
	s.15	5.007
	s.29	5.008
	s.32	5.009
	s.47	2.017

2002	Tax Credits Act—*cont.*	2003	Income Tax (Earnings and Pensions) Act (c.1) 5.010, 5.026
	s.60 .... 4.008, 4.009, 4.011, 4.012, 4.013		
	s.62(2) 1.009		Pt 2, Chap.8 .... 5.011, 5.012
	s.65(2) 1.001, 1.005		Pt 3, Chap.10 .... 5.024, 5.025
	s.67 .... 1.001, 1.005		Pt 4, Chap.6 .... 5.025
	Sch.3, para.24 .... 2.017		Pt 6, Chap.3 .... 5.026
	Sch.3, para.34 .... 2.017		Pt 7 .... 5.010, 5.023
	Sch.5, para.5 .... 1.007, 1.008		s.48 .... 5.011, 5.012
	Sch.5, para.5(2) 1.005		ss.48–61 .... 5.011
	Sch.5, para.9 .... 1.001, 1.003		s.62 .... 5.024
	Sch.6 .... 4.008, 4.009, 4.011, 4.012, 4.013		s.64 .... 5.024
			s.239(1) 5.025
2002	Employment Act (c.22)		s.239(4) 5.025
	s.49 .... 4.002		s.311 .... 5.025
	s.53 .... 4.007, 4.008, 4.014, 4.032		s.316A 5.025
			s.403 .... 5.026
	s.54 .... 4.007	2003	European Parliament (Representation) Act (c.7) 1.023
	Sch.7 .... 4.007, 4.008, 4.014		
	Sch.7, para.77 .... 4.032		
	Sch.8 .... 4.007	2003	Finance Act (c.14) 5.023, 5.032
2002	European Parliamentary Elections Act (c.24) 1.023		
			s.140 .... 5.010
2002	Adoption and Children Act (c.38) 5.032		s.175 .... 5.032
			s.176 .... 5.032
	Sch.4, para.3 .... 3.076, 3.082, 3.151, 3.155		Sch.22 .... 5.010
			Sch.36 .... 5.032

TABLE OF STATUTORY INSTRUMENTS

1965 Act of Sederunt (Rules of the Court, Consolidation and Amendment) (SI 1965/321)
    r.131 .... 3.081, 3.154
1965 Rules of the Supreme Court (SI 1965/1776)
    Ord.80 .... 3.081, 3.154
1975 Social Security (Hospital In-Patients) Regulations (SI 1975/555) 3.043
    reg.2 .... 2.023
    reg.4 .... **2.024**, 2.025
    reg.4A(1) 2.026, 2.027
    reg.5 .... 2.027
    reg.6 .... 2.024, 2.028
    reg.9(b) 2.029
    reg.9(d) 2.030
    reg.11(1) **2.030**
    reg.13 .... 2.025
    reg.17 .... 2.025
    Sch.2 .... 2.024
1975 Social Security and Family Allowances (Polygamous Marriage) Regulations (SI 1975/561)
    reg.2 .... 2.032
1976 Social Security (Medical Evidence) Regulations (SI 1976/615)
    reg.2(1)(d) 3.048
1981 County Court Rules (SI 1981/1687)
    Ord.10 .... 3.081, 3.154
1982 Social Security (General Benefit) Regulations (SI 1982/1408)
    reg.11(3) 2.059
    reg.11(6) 2.058
    reg.11(8) 2.060
    Sch.2 .... 2.058, 2.060
1985 Social Security (Industrial Injuries) (Prescribed Diseases) Regulations (SI 1985/967)
    reg.6(1) 2.061, 4.029
    reg.6(2)(b) 2.061
    reg.29 .... 2.062
    regs 30–33 .... 2.064
    Sch.1 .... 2.065, 2.067, 2.079, 2.080, 2.081, 2.082, 2.083

1987 Income Support (General) Regulations (Northern Ireland) (SI 1987/459) 1.011
    Sch.1, para.4 .... 2.020
1987 Social Fund Maternity and Funeral Expenses (General) Regulations (SI 1987/481)
    reg.5(1)(a) 3.190
    reg.7(1)(a)(i) 3.191
    reg.7(1)(e) 3.192
    reg.7A 3.193
1987 Income Support (General) Regulations (SI 1987/1967) 1.024
    reg.2(1) 1.011, 3.010, 3.011, 3.013, 3.014, 3.182, 3.186, 3.187
    reg.2(1A) 3.012
    reg.3A 3.071
    reg.13(2)(b) 3.015
    reg.17 .... 3.016
    reg.18 .... 3.017
    reg.18(1)(cc) 3.017
    reg.21 .... 3.018, 3.115
    reg.21(1B) 3.018
    reg.21(2) 3.018
    reg.21(3) 3.018, 3.182
    reg.23 .... 3.070
    reg.31(3) 3.020, 3.021, 3.090
    reg.40(1) 3.022
    reg.40(3A)–(3AB) 3.023
    reg.42(2A) 3.024
    reg.42(2C) 3.024
    reg.46 .... 3.024
    reg.51(1) 3.027
    reg.53(1ZA) 3.028
    reg.62 .... 3.029, 3.030, 3.131
    reg.62(2B)(a) 3.030
    reg.62(2B)(b) 3.030
    reg.62(2B)(cc) **3.029**, 3.030
    reg.62(2B)(e) **3.029**
    reg.66A 3.032
    reg.66A(5) **3.029**
    reg.70 .... 3.033
    reg.70(3A) 3.033
    reg.71 .... 3.034
    reg.71(1)(a)(iv) 3.034
    reg.71(1)(c) 3.034
    reg.71(1A) 3.034

Table of Statutory Instruments

1987 Income Support (General) Regulations—*cont.*
Sch.1B, para.7 .... 1.028
Sch.1B, para.14A 3.035, 3.038
Sch.1B, para.14A(1)(c) 3.038
Sch.1B, para.14B 3.036, 3.038
Sch.1B, para.14B(2)(b) 3.038
Sch.1B, para.17 .... 3.037
Sch.1B, para.24 .... 1.028
Sch.1B, para.25 .... 1.028
Sch.2 .... 3.070
Sch.2, Pt III 5.013
Sch.2, para.1(1)(e) 3.099
Sch.2, para.2A 3.039
Sch.2, para.9 .... **3.040**
Sch.2, para.9A **3.041**
Sch.2, para.10 .... 3.042
Sch.2, para.11 .... **3.044**
Sch.2, para.12 .... 3.043
Sch.2, para.12(1)(b) 3.048
Sch.2, para.12(1)(c) **3.043**
Sch.2, para.13A 3.045
Sch.2, para.13A(1) 3.045
Sch.2, para.13A(2) 3.045
Sch.2, para.14ZA 3.046
Sch.2, para.15 .... 3.047
Sch.2, para.15(2)–(3) 3.047
Sch.3 .... 3.060
Sch.3, para.4(8) 3.056
Sch.3, para.6 .... 3.049
Sch.3, para.6(1B) 3.049
Sch.3, para.8 .... 3.049
Sch.3, para.9 .... 3.057
Sch.3, para.9(1) 3.051
Sch.3, para.11(4)–(11) 3.058
Sch.3, para.12 ...... 3.052, 3.059
Sch.3, para.12(1)(a) 3.052
Sch.3, para.14 .... 3.053
Sch.3, para.14(14) **3.053**, 3.060
Sch.3, para.18(1) 3.054, 3.061
Sch.3, para.18(7)9g) 3.055, 3.062
Sch.3C 3.063
Sch.7 .... 3.043
Sch.7, para.1 .... 3.064
Sch.7, paras 1–3 .... 3.115
Sch.7, para.10A–10C 3.066
Sch.7, para.13 .... 3.065
Sch.7, para.13–13B 3.067
Sch.7, para.13B 3.068
Sch.8 .... 3.069
Sch.8, para.1 .... 3.072
Sch.8, para.1A **3.069**, 3.072
Sch.8, para.4 .... **3.070**, 3.073
Sch.9, para.9 .... **3.074**, 3.078

1987 Income Support (General) Regulations—*cont.*
Sch.9, para.15B 3.075, 3.079
Sch.9, para.25 .... 3.076
Sch.9, para.25(1A) **3.076**
Sch.9, paras 76(1) **3.077**, 3.080, 3.084
Sch.9, paras 76–78 .... 3.077, 3.080
Sch.9, para.77 ..... **3.077**, 3.080, 3.084
Sch.9, para.78 ..... **3.077**, 3.080, 3.084
Sch.10, para.7(2) 3.179
Sch.10, para.10 .... 3.083
Sch.10, para.44 .... 3.081
Sch.10, para.45 .... 3.081
Sch.10, para.66 .... 3.084, 3.156
Sch.10, para.66(1) **3.082**
Sch.10, paras 66–70 .... 3.082
Sch.10, para.67 .... **3.082**
Sch.10, para.68 .... **3.082**
Sch.10, para.69 .... **3.082**, 3.084
Sch.10, para.70 .... **3.082**, 3.084
1987 Social Security (Claims and Payments) Regulations (SI 1987/1968) 2.084, 6.002, 6.003
reg.2 .... 4.033, 6.002
reg.4 .... 4.034, 4.043
reg.4(10) **4.034**
reg.4B 4.036
reg.4D **4.037**
reg.4E **4.040**
reg.4E(2) 4.033
reg.4F **4.041**
reg.4ZC 6.002
reg.6 .... 4.044
reg.6(1ZA) **4.044**
reg.7(1A)–(1C) **4.045**
reg.13 .... 4.061
reg.13D **4.047**
reg.16 .... 4.048
reg.16A **4.049**
reg.17 .... 4.050
reg.19 .... 4.051
reg.19(2)(ff) **4.051**
reg.26B **4.052**
reg.30 .... 4.054
reg.31(1C) 4.055
reg.32 .... 4.055
reg.32(1) 4.077
reg.32(6) **4.055**
reg.32(6)(a) 4.073, 4.077
reg.32(6)(c) 4.073
reg.32ZA 6.002
reg.34A 4.056
reg.35A 4.057
reg.36(2) 3.188
Sch.9 .... 4.058
Sch.9A 4.062

Table of Statutory Instruments

1987 Social Security (Claims and Payments) Regulations —*cont.*
- Sch.9B 4.068
- Sch.9ZC 6.002

1987 Housing Benefit (General) Regulations (SI 1987/1971) 1.024
- Sch.2, Pt III 5.013
- Sch.5, para.8(2) 3.179
- Sch.5ZA, para.21A 3.179

1988 Social Security (Payments on Account, Overpayments and Recovery) Regulations (SI 1988/664)
- reg.1 .... 4.087
- reg.5 .... 4.088
- reg.7 .... 4.089
- reg.8 .... 4.090
- reg.13 .... 4.091
- reg.14 .... 4.092
- reg.15 .... 4.093
- reg.16 .... 4.094
- reg.17 .... 4.095

1988 Social Fund Cold Weather Payments (General) Regulations (SI 1988/1724)
- reg.1A **3.182**
- Sch.1 .... **3.183**
- Sch.2 .... **3.185**

1990 Community Charges (Deductions from Income Support) (No.2) Regulations (SI 1990/545)
- reg.1(2) 3.093
- reg.2 .... 3.094
- reg.3 .... 3.095
- reg.4 .... 3.096

1990 Home Guard War Widows Special Payments Regulations 3.172

1990 Naval and Marine Pay and Pensions (Special War Widows Payment) Order 3.172

1991 Social Security (Attendance Allowance) Regulations (SI 1991/2740)
- reg.7 .... 2.033
- reg.8 .... 2.034

1991 Social Security (Disability Living Allowance) Regulations (SI 1991/2890)
- reg.9 .... 2.035
- reg.9(1) 2.035
- reg.9(1A) 2.035
- reg.9(2)(c) 2.035
- reg.9(4) 2.035
- reg.9(5) 2.035

1991 Social Security (Disability Living Allowance) Regulations—*cont.*
- reg.9(7) 2.035
- reg.10 .... 2.036
- reg.10(8) 2.036
- reg.12 .... 2.037

1992 Council Tax Benefit (General) Regulations (SI 1992/1814) 1.024
- Sch.1, Pt III 5.013
- Sch.5, para.8(2) 3.179
- Sch.5ZA, para.21A 3.179

1992 Fines (Deductions from Income Support) Regulations (SI 1992/2182)
- reg.1(2) 3.097, 3.098, 3.099
- reg.2 .... 3.100
- reg.3 .... 3.101
- reg.4(1)(a) 3.102
- reg.7 .... .103
- Sch.3 .... 3.104

1993 Council Tax (Deductions from Income Support) Regulations (SI 1993/494)
- reg.1(2) 3.105, 3.106
- reg.2 .... 3.107
- reg.3 .... 3.108
- reg.4(1)(f) 3.109
- reg.5 .... 3.110
- reg.8 .... 3.111

1994 Social Security Pensions (Home Responsibilities) Regulations (SI 1994/704)
- reg.1(2) 2.019
- reg.2 .... 2.022
- reg.2(2) **2.020**
- reg.2(5) **2.021**

1994 Act of Sederunt (Rules of the Court of Session) (SI 1994/1443)
- r.43.15 .... 3.081, 3.154

1994 Social Security (Incapacity Benefit) Regulations (SI 1994/2946)
- reg.7C **2.038**
- reg.8 .... 2.039

1995 Social Security (Incapacity for Work) (General) Regulations (SI 1995/311)
- Pt III 1.028
- reg.8 .... 2.040
- reg.10 .... 1.036
- reg.13 .... 2.041
- reg.13A 2.042
- reg.13A(1)(d)(i) 2.042
- reg.15 .... 2.043
- reg.16 .... 2.044

Table of Statutory Instruments

1995 Social Security (Incapacity for Work) (General) Regulations—*cont.*
- reg.17 .... 2.046
- reg.17(2)(a) 2.045
- reg.24 .... 4.078
- reg.25(3) 2.047
- reg.27 .... 2.049
- reg.28 .... 2.050, 4.074
- reg.28(2)(a) 3.048
- Sch. 2.051
- Sch., Activity 8 .... 2.052
- Sch., Activity 13 .... 2.053
- Sch., Activity 14 .... 2.054
- Sch., Pt II, Activity 15 ..... 2.055
- Sch., Pt II, Activity 16 ..... 2.056
- Sch., Pt II, Activity 18 ..... 2.056

1996 Jobseeker's Allowance Regulations (SI 1996/207) 1.024
- reg.1(3) 3.119, 3.120
- reg.1(3F) 3.121
- reg.26 .... 3.122
- reg.81 .... 3.123
- reg.83 .... 3.124
- reg.84 .... 3.125
- reg.84(1)(d) 3.125
- reg.85 .... 3.117, 3.126
- reg.85(2A) 3.126
- reg.86A 3.125
- reg.86A(b) 3.127
- reg.86B 3.128
- reg.86B(c) 3.128
- reg.96(3) 3.092, **3.129**
- reg.131 .... 3.130, 3.131
- reg.131(3A)(cc) **3.130**
- reg.136(5) 3.132
- reg.148 .... 3.133
- reg.148A 3.134
- Sch.1 .... 3.135, 5.013
- Sch.1, column 2, para.1(1)(e) 3.099, 3.106
- Sch.1, paras 10–16 .... 3.182
- Sch.1, para.15A(2) 3.136
- Sch.1, para.17 .... 3.137
- Sch.1, para.20IA(2) 3.138
- Sch.1, para.20J 3.139
- Sch.2 .... 3.143
- Sch.2, para.6(3) 3.140
- Sch.2, para.13 .... 3.141
- Sch.2, para.17 .... 3.142
- Sch.3 .... 3.144
- Sch.5, para.1 .... 3.145
- Sch.5, para.1 .... 3.117
- Sch.5, para.2 .... 3.117
- Sch.5, paras 7–9 .... 3.146
- Sch.5, paras 15 .... 3.147
- Sch.5, paras 17A 3.148
- Sch.5A, para.1 .... 3.149
- Sch.5A, para.9 .... 3.149

1996 Jobseeker's Allowance Regulations—*cont.*
- Sch.7 .... 3.153
- Sch.7, para.26 .... 3.151
- Sch.7, paras 72–74 .... **3.152**
- Sch.8 .... 3.156
- Sch.8, para.12(2) 3.179
- Sch.8, para.42 .... 3.154
- Sch.8, para.43 .... 3.154
- Sch.8, para.59 .... **3.155**
- Sch.8, paras 59–63 .... 3.155
- Sch.8, para.60 .... **3.155**
- Sch.8, para.63 .... **3.155**

1996 Social Security (Back to Work Bonus) (No.2) Regulations (SI 1996/2570)
- reg.17 .... 3.112

1996 Social Security (Child Maintenance Bonus) Regulations (SI 1996/3195) 4.094
- reg.8 .... 3.113

1996 Health and Personal Social Services (Direct Payments) (Northern Ireland) Order
- art.15A 5.032

1998 Civil Procedure Rules (SI 1998/3132)
- r.21.11(1) 3.081, 3.154

1999 Social Security and Child Support (Decisions and Appeals) Regulations (SI 1999/991)
- reg.1(3) 3.179, 4.070, 4.071
- reg.3(9)(a) 4.072
- reg.6 .... 4.074
- reg.6(2) 4.073
- reg.6(2)(g) 4.074
- reg.7 .... 4.076
- reg.39 .... 4.079
- reg.49 .... 4.080
- reg.53(4) 4.081
- Sch.2 .... 4.082
- Sch.3A 4.083
- Sch.3B 4.084

1999 Social Security Commissioners (Procedure) Regulations (SI 1999/1495)
- reg.23 .... 4.069

1999 Tax Credits (Claims and Payments) (Amendment) Regulations (SI 1999/2572)
- reg.3(c) 4.033

1999 Social Security (Claims and Information) Regulations (SI 1999/3108) 4.055

2000	Social Security (Immigration and Asylum) Consequential Amendments Regulations (SI 2000/636)		2002	State Pension Credit Regulations (SI 2002/1792)
	reg.2(1)	3.085		Pt III 4.089
	reg.2(4)(c)	**3.086**		reg.1(2) 3.098, 3.105, 3.159, 3.160
	reg.2(7)	**3.087**		reg.2 .... 3.161
	reg.2(8)	**3.087**		reg.3 .... 3.162
	Sch., Pt I	3.085		reg.5 .... **3.163**
	Sch., Pt I, para.1	3.087		reg.10(1)(c) **3.165**
2000	Social Fund Winter Fuel Payment Regulations (SI 2000/729)			reg.15(5)(f) 3.166
				reg.15(5)(g) 3.166
				reg.15(5)(h) **3.166**
	reg.1(2)	3.186		Sch.1 .... 3.167
	reg.1(3A)	3.186		Sch.II, para.2(7) 3.169
	reg.2	**3.188**		Sch.II, para.14(2) 3.169
	reg.3(1)(b)	4.034		Sch.III, para.1(8) **3.170**
	reg.4	3.189		Sch.IV 3.171
2000	Social Security (Work-focused Interviews for Lone Parents) and Miscellaneous Amendments Regulations (SI 2000/1926)			Sch.IV, para.17 .... **3.172**
				Sch.V, para.1A **3.173**
				Sch.V, para.9A **3.174**
				Sch.V, para.13 .... **3.175**
				Sch.V, para.20(1)(d) **3.177**
				Sch.V, para.20(2) **3.178**
				Sch.V, para.20A **3.179**
		1.025		Sch.V, para.27 .... 3.180
2001	Child Support (Maintenance Calculations and Special Cases) Regulations (SI 2001/155)			Sch.VI, para.2B **3.181**
			2002	Education (Assembly Learning Grant Scheme) (Wales) Regulations (SI 2002/1857)
		3.001		
2001	Child Support (Maintenance Calculation Procedure) Regulations (SI 2001/157)			Sch. 3.029, 3.130
			2002	Child Tax Credit Regulations (SI 2002/2007)
				reg.2 .... 5.033
	reg.4	3.118	2002	Working Tax Credit (Entitlement and Maximum Rate) Regulations (SI 2002/2005)
	reg.8(2)(b)	3.114		
	reg.14	3.115		
	reg.15	3.116		reg.2 .... 5.011, 5.012
	reg.16	4.070		reg.9(3) 5.013
2001	Housing Benefit and Council Tax Benefit (Decisions and Appeals) Regulations (SI 2001/1002)			reg.9(8) 5.014
				reg.14(2)(a)(iii) 5.015
				reg.18(3) 5.016
				reg.18(4) 5.017
	reg.1(2)	3.179		reg.18(6) 5.017
2002	Fostering Services Regulations (SI 2002/57)			reg.18(7) 5.017
				reg.18(9) 5.017
	Pt II	2.019		reg.18(9)(a) 5.017
	Pt IV	2.019	2002	Tax Credits (Definition and Calculation of Income) Regulations (SI 2002/2006)
2002	Education (Student Support) Regulations (SI 2002/195)			
	reg.15	5.028		reg.2 .... 5.018
2002	Social Security (Jobcentre Plus Interviews) Regulations (SI 2002/1703) 1.024, 1.025			reg.3(1) 5.019
				reg.3(4) 5.020
				reg.3(7) 5.021
				reg.3(8) **5.022**
2002	Social Security (Electronic Communications) (Child Benefit) Order (SI 2002/1789)			reg.4 .... 5.010
				reg.4(1) 5.023
				reg.4(3) 5.024
		6.003		reg.4(5) 5.026

Table of Statutory Instruments

2002 Tax Credits (Definition and Calculation of Income) Regulations—*cont.*
- reg.7 .... 5.027
- reg.8 .... 5.028
- reg.10 .... 5.029
- reg.11 .... 5.030
- reg.12 .... 5.031
- reg.19 .... 5.010

2002 Child Tax Credit Regulations (SI 2002/2007)
- reg.3 .... 1.011

2002 Tax Credits (Income Thresholds and Determination of Rates) Regulations (SI 2002/2008) 3.035, 3.036

2002 Tax Credits (Claims and Notifications) Regulations (SI 2002/2014)
- reg.4 .... 5.034
- reg.8(2)(c). **5.035**
- reg.26 .... 5.036
- reg.33 .... **5.037**

2002 Social Security (Incapacity) (Miscellaneous Amendments) (No.2) Regulations (SI 2002/2311)
- reg.3 .... 2.039

2002 State Pension Credit (Consequential, Transitional and Miscellaneous Provisions) Regulations (SI 2002/3019)
- reg.3 .... 4.033
- reg.4 .... 4.034, 4.036, 4.037
- reg.5 .... 4.045
- reg.6 ....4.046, 4.047
- reg.7 .... 4.048, 4.049
- reg.8 .... 4.050, 4.051
- reg.9 .... 4.052
- reg.10 .... 4.054
- reg.11 .... 4.055
- reg.12 .... 4.056
- reg.13 .... 4.057
- reg.14(1) 4.058
- reg.14(2) 4.062
- reg.14(3) 4.068
- reg.24 .... 4.087, 4.088, 4.089, 4.090, 4.091, 4.092, 4.093, 4.094, 4.095
- reg.27(3) 3.118
- reg.29(2) 3.024
- reg.29(3) 3.028
- reg.29(4) 3.037
- reg.29(5)(a) 3.040
- reg.29(5)(b) 3.041
- reg.29(5)(c) 3.042
- reg.29(5)(d) 3.044
- reg.29(5)(e) 3.043
- reg.29(5)(f) 3.045

2002 State Pension Credit (Consequential, Transitional and Miscellaneous Provisions) Regulations —*cont.*
- reg.29(5)(g) 3.047
- reg.29(6)(a) 3.049
- reg.29(6)(b) 3.050
- reg.29(6)(c) 3.051
- reg.29(6)(d) 3.053
- reg.29(6)(e) 3.054
- reg.29(7)(a) 3.069
- reg.29(7)(b) 3.069
- reg.29(7)(c) 3.069
- reg.30(a) 3.140
- reg.30(b) 3.140
- reg.30(c) 3.142
- reg.31(1) 3.190, 3.191
- reg.31(2) 3.190, 3.191
- reg.31(3)–(6) 3.182
- reg.32 .... 3.098, 3.099, 3.100, 3.102, 3.103
- reg.33 .... 3.105, 3.106, 3.107, 3.108, 3.109, 3.110, 3.111
- reg.35 .... 3.093, 3.094, 3.095, 3.096
- reg.36(7A) **3.088**
- reg.36(15)–(19) 3.089

2002 State Pension Credit (Consequential, Transitional and Miscellaneous Provisions) (No.2) Regulations (SI 2002/3197)
- reg.7(1) 3.113
- reg.7(2) 3.112

2002 Education (Student Support) (No.2) Regulations (SI 2002/3200)
- reg.15 .... 5.028
- reg.15(7) 3.029, 3.030, 3.130, 5.028

2003 Social Security (Working Tax Credit and Child Tax Credit) (Consequential Amendments) Regulations (SI 2003/455)
- reg.7 .... 3.090
- reg.7(1) **3.090**
- reg.7(2) **3.090**
- reg.7(3) **3.090**
- reg.7(1) **3.091**
- reg.8(1) **3.092**
- reg.8(6) **3.092**

2003 Child Benefit and Guardian's Allowance (Administration) Regulations (SI 2003/492) 6.003
- reg.6 .... 4.096

Table of Statutory Instruments

2003 Tax Credits (Provision of Information) (Functions Relating to Health) Regulations (SI 2003/731) 1.003, 1.004
2003 Tax Credits (Definition and Calculation of Income) (Amendment) Regulations (SI 2003/732) 5.026
2003 Social Security Contributions and Benefits Act 1992 (Modifications for Her Majesty's Forces and Incapacity Benefit) Regulations (SI 2003/737) 2.038
2003 Child Benefit and Guardian's Allowance (Decisions and Appeals) Regulations (SI 2003/916)
    regs 18–20 .... 4.096
    reg.25 .... 4.070
    reg.36 .... 4.070
2003 Social Security and Child Support (Miscellaneous Amendments) regulations (SI 2003/1050)
    reg.3(1) 4.070
    reg.3(2) 4.072
    reg.3(3) 4.073
    reg.3(5)(a)–(d) 4.076
    reg.3(5)(e) 4.077
2003 Social Security (Incapacity Benefit) (Her Majesty's Forces) (Amendment) Regulations (SI 2003/1068)
    reg.2 .... 2.038
2003 Social Security (Removal of Residential Allowance and Miscellaneous Amendments) Regulations (SI 2003/1121)
    reg.2 .... 3.011, 3.016, 3.017, 3.018, 3.034, 3.039, 3.063, 3.066, 3.067, 3.074, 3.075
    reg.3 .... 3.182
    reg.4 .... 3.120, 3.124, 3.125, 3.126, 3.127, 3.128, 3.133, 3.134, 3.135, 3.144, 3.146, 3.147, 3.148, 3.149, 3.150
    reg.5 .... 3.186, 3.187
    Sch.1, para.1 .... 3.011
    Sch.1, para.2 .... 3.016
    Sch.1, para.3 .... 3.017
    Sch.1, para.4 .... 3.017
    Sch.1, para.5 .... 3.034
    Sch.1, para.6 .... 3.039
    Sch.1, para.7 .... 3.063
    Sch.1, para.8 .... 3.066, 3.067

2003 Social Security (Removal of Residential Allowance and Miscellaneous Amendments) Regulations—*cont.*
    Sch.1, para.9(a) 3.074
    Sch.1, para.9(b) 3.075
    Sch.2, para.1 .... 3.120
    Sch.2, para.2 .... 3.124
    Sch.2, para.3 .... 3.125
    Sch.2, para.4 .... 3.126
    Sch.2, para.5 .... 3.127
    Sch.2, para.6 .... 3.128
    Sch.2, para.7 .... 3.133
    Sch.2, para.8 .... 3.134
    Sch.2, para.10 .... 3.144
    Sch.2, para.11 ..... 3.135, 3.146, 3.147, 3.148
    Sch.2, para.12 ...... 3.149, 3.150
2003 Social Security (Hospital In-Patients and Miscellaneous Amendments) Regulations (SI 2003/1195)
    reg.2 .... 2.023, 2.024
    reg.2(4) 2.026
    reg.2(5) 2.027
    reg.2(6) 2.028
    reg.2(7) 2.029
    reg.2(8) 2.030
    reg.2(9) 2.031
    reg.3 .... 3.012, 3.045, 3.064, 3.065, 3.068
    reg.3(4) 3.055
    reg.6 .... 3.121, 3.136, 3.138, 3.145, 3.147, 3.149
    reg.6(4) 3.142
    reg.9 .... 3.089
2003 Fines (Deductions from Income Support)(amendment) Regulations (SI 2003/1360)
    reg.2(a) 3.097
    reg.2(b) 3.101
    reg.2(c) 3.104
2003 Tax Credits (Employer Penalty Appeals) Regulations (SI 2003/1382) 5.001
2003 Social Fund Maternity and Funeral Expenses (General) Regulations (SI 2003/1570)
    reg.2 .... 3.193
2003 State Pension Credit (Decisions and Appeals Amendments) Regulations(SI 2003/1581)
    reg.2 .... 4.082

xxxv

2003 Social Security (Claims and Payments and Miscellaneous Amendments) Regulations (SI 2003/1632)
    reg.2 .... 4.039, 4.042, 4.044, 4.055
    reg.2(2)(a) 4.034

2003 Tax Credits (Provision of Information) (Functions Relating to Health) (No.2) Regulations (SI 2003/1650) **1.001**
    reg.1 .... **1.002**
    reg.2 .... **1.002**

2003 Social Security Amendment (Students and Income-related Benefits) Regulations (SI 2003/1701)
    reg.2(1) 3.029, 3.031, 3.130, 3.132
    reg.2(3)(c) 3.029, 3.031
    reg.2(3)(d) 3.130, 3.132
    reg.3(1)(a) 3.029, 3.130
    reg.3(1)(b) 3.029, 3.130
    reg.3(2)(c) 3.029
    reg.3(2)(d) 3.130

2003 Social Security (Working Tax Credit and Child Tax Credit) (Consequential Amendments) (No.3) Regulations (SI 2003/1731)
    reg.2(2) 3.020
    reg.2(3)(a) 3.035, 3.036
    reg.2(3)(b) 3.035, 3.036
    reg.4 .... 3.129
    reg.5 .... 4.083
    reg.6 .... 3.090
    reg.6(3) 3.092

2003 Social Fund Winter Fuel Payment (Amendment) Regulations (SI 2003/1737)
    reg.2 .... 3.188

2003 State Pension Credit Act 2002(Commencement No.5) and Appointed Day Order (SI 2003/1766) 3.157, 3.128
    art.2 .... 4.010

2003 Social Security Pensions (Home Responsibilities) Amendment Regulations (SI 2003/1767)
    reg.2(2) 2.019
    reg.2(3) 2.020
    reg.2(4) 2.021

2003 Secretary of State for Constitutional Affairs Order (SI 2003/1887) 1.013, 4.102
    art.1 .... **1.014**
    art.2 .... **1.015**
    art.3 .... **1.016**
    art.4 .... **1.017**, 1.018, 1.019, 1.023
    art.5 .... **1.018**, 1.019
    art.6 .... **1.019**
    art.7 .... **1.020**, 1.021
    art.8 .... **1.021**
    art.9 .... **1.022**
    Sch.1 .... **1.023**

2003 Social Security Amendment (Students and Income-related Benefits) (No.2) Regulations (SI 2003/1914)
    reg.2(1) 3.031, 3.130, 3.132
    reg.2(2)(c) 3.031
    reg.2(2)(d) 3.130, 3.132

2003 National Minimum Wage Regulations 1999 (Amendment) Regulations (SI 2003/1923) 3.007

2003 Social Security Amendment (Students and Income-related Benefits) (No.2) regulations (SI 2003/1941)
    reg.2(1) 3.029
    reg.2(2)(c) 3.029

2003 Tax Credits (Provision of Information) (Function Relating to Employment and Training) Regulation (SI 2003/2041) 1.005
    reg.1 .... **1.006**
    reg.2 .... **1.007**

2003 Child Benefit and Guardian's Allowance (Administration) (Amendment No.3) Regulations (SI 2003/2107)
    reg.6 .... 4.096

2003 Tax Credits Act 2002 (Child Tax Credit) (Transitional Provisions) Order (SI 2003/ 2170) 1.009, 5.003
    art.1 .... **1.010**
    art.2 .... **1.011**
    art.2(1) 1.012
    art.2(2) 1.012

Table of Statutory Instruments

2003 Social Security (Industrial Injuries) (Prescribed Diseases) Amendment (No.2) Regulations (SI 2003/2190)
- reg.2(2) 2.062
- reg.2(3) 2.064
- reg.3 .... 2.065, 2.083

2003 Social Fund Winter Fuel Payment (Amendment) (No.2) Regulations (SI2003/2192)
- reg.2 .... 3.188

2003 Social Security (Attendance Allowance and Disability Living Allowance) (Amendment) Regulations (SI 2003/2259)
- reg.2 .... 2.033, 2.034
- reg.3 .... 2.035, 2.036

2003 Social Security (Incapacity) (Miscellaneous Amendments) Regulations (SI 2003/2262)
- reg.2 .... 4.085
- reg.3 .... 2.039
- reg.4 .... 2.045

2003 State Pension Credit (Transitional and Miscellaneous Provisions) Amendment Regulations (SI 2003/2274)
- reg.2(2) 3.159, 3.160
- reg.2(3) 3.161
- reg.2(4) 3.162
- reg.2(5) 3.163
- reg.2(6) 3.165
- reg.2(7) 3.166
- reg.2(8) 3.167
- reg.2(9) 3.168, 3.169
- reg.2(10) 3.170
- reg.2(11)(a)–(e) 3.171
- reg.2(11)(f) 3.172
- reg.2(12)(a) 3.173
- reg.2(12)(b) 3.174
- reg.2(12)(c) 3.175
- reg.2(12)(d) 3.177
- reg.2(12)(e) 3.178
- reg.2(12)(f) 3.179
- reg.2(12)(g) 3.180, 3.181
- reg.3(a) 3.088
- reg.3(b) 3.088
- reg.5(2) 4.073
- reg.5(3) 4.076
- reg.5(4) 4.084
- reg.6 .... 3.085, 3.086, 3.087

2003 Social Security (Miscellaneous Amendments) (No.2) Regulations (SI 2003/2279)
- reg.2(2) 3.010

2003 Social Security (Miscellaneous Amendments) (No.2) Regulations —cont.
- reg.2(3) 3.046
- reg.2(4)(a)(i) 3.076
- reg.2(4)(a)(ii) 3.076
- reg.2(4)(b) 3.077
- reg.2(4)(c) 3.077
- reg.2(5)(a) 3.081
- reg.2(5)(b) 3.081
- reg.2(5)(c) 3.082
- reg.2(5)(d) 3.082
- reg.3(2) 3.119
- reg.3(3) 3.137, 3.139
- reg.3(4)(a)(i) 3.151
- reg.3(4)(b) 3.152
- reg.3(4)(c) 3.152
- reg.3(5)(a) 3.154
- reg.3(5)(b) 3.154
- reg.3(5)(c) 3.155

2003 Social Security (Third Party Deductions and Miscellaneous Amendments) Regulations (SI 2003/2325)
- reg.2 .... 4.064
- reg.3(a) 3.018
- reg.3(b) 3.018

2003 Income Support (General) Amendment Regulations (SI 2003/2379)
- reg.2(1) 3.042, 3.043, 3.044
- reg.2(2) 3.042
- reg.2(3) 3.044
- reg.2(4) 3.043

2003 Social Security (Incapacity Benefit Work-focused Interviews) Regulations (SI 2003/2439) 1.024
- reg.1 .... **1.027**
- reg.2 .... **1.028**, 1.044
- reg.3 .... **1.029**, 1.030, 1.034, 1.037
- reg.4 .... **1.030**, 1.034
- reg.4(1) 1.036
- reg.5 .... **1.033**
- reg.6 .... 1.029, 1.030, 1.031, **1.034**
- reg.6(1) 1.035
- regs 6–8 .... 1.030
- reg.7 .... 1.029, 1.031, **1.035**
- reg.8 .... 1.031, **1.036**
- reg.9 .... **1.037**
- reg.9(4) 1.030, 1.035, 1.038, 1.039, 1.043
- reg.10 .... **1.038**
- reg.11 .... **1.041**
- reg.12 .... **1.043**, 4.022
- reg.13(a) 3.077
- reg.13(b) 3.082

xxxvii

2003	Social Security (Incapacity Benefit Work-focused Interviews) Regulations —cont.		2003	Social Security (Electronic Communications) Carer's Allowance Order (SI 2003/2800) 6.002
	reg.16(a)	3.152		art.2 .... 6.002
	reg.16(b)	3.155		art.2(1) 6.002
	reg.17	4.086		art.2(2) 6.002
	Sch.	**1.044**		art.2(3) 6.002
	Sch., Pt 1 .... 1.028,	**1.044**		art.2(4) 6.002
	Sch., Pt 2 .... 1.028,	**1.047**		art.3 .... 6.002
2003	Social Fund Cold Weather Payments (General) Amendment Regulations (SI 2003/2605)			art.4 .... 6.003
			2003	Tax Credits (Miscellaneous Amendments No.2) Regulations (SI 2003/2815)
	reg.2	3.183		reg.3 .... 5.018
	reg.3	3.185		reg.4(2) 5.019
	Sch.1	3.183		reg.4(3) 5.020
	Sch.2	3.185		reg.4(4) 5.021
2003	Income Support (General) (Standard Interest Rate Amendment) Regulations (SI 2003/2693)			reg.4(5) 5.022
				reg.5(2) 5.023
				reg.5(3) 5.024
	reg.2	3.052		reg.5(4) 5.025, 5.026
2003	Child Support (Miscellaneous Amendments) (No.2) Regulations (SI 2003/2779)			reg.6 .... 5.027
				reg.8(2) 5.029
				reg.8(2) 5.029
				reg.9(2) 5.030
				reg.10 .... 5.031
	reg.5(2)(a)	3.114		reg.11 .... 5.032
	reg.5(2)(b)	3.114		reg.13 .... 5.011, 5.012
	reg.5(3)(a)	3.115		reg.14(2) 5.013
	reg.5(3)(b)	3.115		reg.14(3) 5.014
	reg.5(3)(c)	3.115		reg.15 .... 5.015
	reg.5(3)(d)	3.115		reg.16(2) 5.016
	reg.5(3)(e)	3.115		reg.16(3) 5.017
	reg.5(4)(a)	3.116		reg.16(4) 5.017
	reg.5(4)(b)	3.116		reg.17 .... 5.033
	reg.5(4)(c)	3.116		reg.18 .... 5.034
	reg.5(4)(d)	3.116		reg.20 .... 5.035
	reg.5(4)(e)	3.116		reg.21 .... 5.036
	reg.6(3)	3.118		reg.22 .... 5.037

PART I

NEW LEGISLATION

NEW REGULATIONS

Tax Credits

Tax Credits (Provision of Information) (Functions Relating to Health) (No. 2) Regulations 2003

(S.I. 2003 No. 1650)

Made	*25th June 2003*
Laid before Parliament	*26th June 2003*
Coming into force	*17th July 2003*

ARRANGEMENT OF REGULATIONS

1. Citation, commencement and extent 1.001
2. Prescribed functions relating to health

The Commissioners of Inland Revenue, in exercise of the powers conferred upon them by sections 65(2) and 67 of, and paragraph 9 of Schedule 5 to the Tax Credits Act 2002 hereby make the following Regulations:

Citation, commencement and extent

1.—(1) These Regulations may be cited as the Tax Credits (Provision of Information) (Functions Relating to Health) (No. 2) Regulations 2003 and shall come into force on 17th July 2003. 1.002

(2) These Regulations do not extend to Northern Ireland.

Prescribed functions relating to health

2.—(1) The function specified in paragraph (2) is prescribed for the purposes of paragraph 9 of Schedule 5 to the Tax Credits Act 2002 (provision of information by the Board of Inland Revenue for health purposes). 1.003

(2) The function specified in this paragraph is the conduct, by a person providing services to the Secretary of State and the Scottish Ministers, of a survey of the mental health of persons in Great Britain who are under the age of 17 on 1st September 2003.

(3) Nothing in these Regulations limits the operation of the Tax Credits (Provision of Information Relating to Health) Regulations 2003.

General Note

1.004 These regulations supplement the Tax Credits (Provision of Information) (Functions Relating to Health) Regulations 2003 (S.I. 2003 No. 731) [main volume IV, pp. 577–578], on which see the General Note to those regulations at para 2.514 of Vol IV.

(S.I. 2003 No. 2041)

Tax Credits (Provision of Information) (Function Relating to Employment and Training) Regulations 2003

(S.I. 2003 No. 2041)

Made	6th August 2003
Laid before Parliament	8th August 2003
Coming into force	29th August 2003

ARRANGEMENT OF REGULATIONS

1. Citation, commencement and extent
2. Prescribed function relating to employment and training

1.005

The Commissioners of Inland Revenue, in exercise of the powers conferred upon them by sections 65(2) and 67 of, and paragraph 5(2) of Schedule 5 to, the Tax Credits Act 2002, hereby make the following Regulations:

Citation, commencement and extent

1.—(1) These Regulations may be cited as the Tax Credits (Provision of Information) (Function Relating to Employment and Training) Regulations 2003 and shall come into force on 29th August 2003.

(2) These Regulations do not extend to Northern Ireland.

1.006

Prescribed function relating to employment and training

2.—(1) The function specified in paragraph (2) is prescribed for the purposes of paragraph 5 of Schedule 5 to the Tax Credits Act 2002 (provision of information by the Board of Inland Revenue for employment and training purposes).

(2) The function specified in this paragraph is the operation of the Employment Retention and Advancement Scheme, that is to say the scheme for assisting persons to improve their job retention or career advancement, established by the Secretary of State under section 2 of the Employment and Training Act 1973.

1.007

GENERAL NOTE

These regulations, made under para. 5 of Sched. 5 to the Tax Credits Act 2002, enable information relating to tax credits, child benefit or guardian's allowance to be provided by the Board of Inland Revenue to the Secretary of State for the purposes of the operation of the Employment Retention and Advancement Scheme established under s.2 of the Employment and Training Act 1973.

1.008

Tax Credits Act 2002 (Child Tax Credit) (Transitional Provisions) Order 2003

(S.I. 2003 No. 2170)

Made 21st August 2003
Coming into force 22nd August 2003

ARRANGEMENT OF ARTICLES

1.009
1. Citation and commencement
2. Transitional provision

The Treasury, in exercise of the powers conferred upon them by section 62(2) of the Tax Credits Act 2002, make the following Order:

Citation and commencement

1.010   **1.** This Order may be cited as the Tax Credits Act 2002 (Child Tax Credit) (Transitional Provisions) Order 2003 and shall come into force on 22nd August 2003.

Transitional provision

1.011   **2.**—(1) This article applies in the case of a person who throughout the period beginning on 22nd August 2003 and ending on 28th September 2003 is—
   (a) in receipt of income support;
   (b) aged not less than 60; and
   (c) responsible for a child (within the meaning of regulation 3 of the Child Tax Credit Regulations 2002).

(2) Where this article applies to a person, he shall be treated as having made a claim for child tax credit in respect of the child for whom he is responsible as mentioned in paragraph (1)(c) of this article—
   (a) on 22nd August 2003 for the purposes of enabling the Board to make an initial decision on the claim; and
   (b) on the first day of the first benefit week in relation to income support beginning on or after 29th September 2003 for all other purposes.

(3) In paragraph (2) "benefit week" has the same meaning—
   (a) in relation to a person in Great Britain, as it bears in regulation 2(1) of the Income Support (General) Regulations 1987; and
   (b) in relation to a person in Northern Ireland, as it bears in regulation 2(1) of the Income Support (General) Regulations (Northern Ireland) 1987.

(S.I. 2003 No. 2170)

GENERAL NOTE

1.012 Section 1(3)(d) of the Tax Credits Act 2002 [main volume IV p. 169] provides for the abolition of various component elements of the applicable amount for the purposes of income support and income-based jobseeker's allowance (namely the child allowances, family premium, disabled child premium and enhanced disability premium for a child or young person). This Order makes transitional provision in connection with the introduction of child tax credit, but at this stage only for pensioners formerly in receipt of the minimum income guarantee in income support. The Order thus applies to persons who were in receipt of income support, were aged not less than 60 and were responsible for a child, throughout the period beginning on August 22, 2003 and ending on September 28, 2003 (Art.2(1)). In such a case a person is deemed to have made a claim for child tax credit (a) on August 22, 2003 for the purpose of enabling a decision to be made by the Board of Inland Revenue on the claim and (b) on the first day of the first benefit week beginning on or after September 29, 2003 for all other purposes, *e.g.* as regards payment (Art.2(2)). This Order is thus associated with the introduction of state pension credit as from October 2003.

OTHER ORDERS AND REGULATIONS

The Secretary of State for Constitutional Affairs Order 2003

(S.I. 2003 No. 1887)

(Entry into force: August 19, 2003)

ARRANGEMENT OF REGULATIONS

1.013
1. Citation and commencement
2. Interpretation
3. Incorporation of the Secretary of State for Constitutional Affairs
4. Transfer of Functions to the Lord Chancellor
5. Transfer of property, rights and liabilities from the Lord Chancellor
6. Transfers from the Lord Chancellor: supplementary
7. Transfer of functions from the First Secretary of State
8. Transfer of functions from the First Secretary of State: supplementary
9. Consequential amendments

Schedule 1—Enactments conferring functions transferred by Article 4
Schedule 2—Consequential amendments (*omitted*)

Her Majesty, in pursuance of sections 1 and 2 of the Ministers of the Crown Act 1975, is pleased, by and with the advice of Her Privy Council, to order, and it is hereby ordered, as follows:

Citation and commencement

1.014
1.—(1) This Order may be cited as the Secretary of State for Constitutional Affairs Order 2003.
(2) This Order comes into force on 19th August 2003.

Interpretation

1.015
2.—(1) In this Order "instrument", without prejudice to the generality of that expression, includes in particular Royal Charters, Royal Warrants, Orders in Council, Letters Patent, judgments, decrees, orders, rules, regulations, schemes, bye-laws, awards, contracts and other agreements, memoranda and articles of association, certificates, deeds and other documents.

(2) In this Order a reference to a function of a Minister is to be read, in the case of a function which is exercisable by him jointly with another person or is otherwise shared by him with another person, as a reference to his share in that function.

(3) Any provision of this Order for the transfer of functions of the Lord Chancellor to the Secretary of State is to be read, in relation to functions exercisable by the Lord Chancellor concurrently with the Secretary of State, as providing that the functions are to cease to be exercisable by the Lord Chancellor; and references in this Order to the transfer of functions are to be read accordingly.

(4) Any reference in this Order to the functions of a Minister under an enactment includes a reference to the functions of that Minister under an instrument having effect under that enactment.

Incorporation of the Secretary of State for Constitutional Affairs

3.—(1) The person who at the coming into force of this Order is the Secretary of State for Constitutional Affairs and any successor to that person shall be, by that name, a corporation sole.

(2) The corporate seal of the Secretary of State for Constitutional Affairs shall—
  (a) be authenticated by the signature of a Secretary of State or a person authorised by a Secretary of State to act in that behalf, and
  (b) be officially and judicially noticed.

(3) Every document purporting to be an instrument made or issued by the Secretary of State for Constitutional Affairs and to be
  (a) sealed with his corporate seal authenticated in the manner provided by paragraph (2), or
  (b) signed or executed by a person authorised by a Secretary of State to act in that behalf,
shall be received in evidence and deemed to be so made or issued without further proof, unless the contrary is shown.

(4) A certificate signed by the Secretary of State for Constitutional Affairs that any instrument purporting to be made or issued by him was so made or issued shall be conclusive evidence of that fact.

(5) The Documentary Evidence Act 1868 shall apply in relation to the Secretary of State for Constitutional Affairs
  (a) as if references to orders and regulations included references to any document, and
  (b) as if the officers mentioned in column 2 of the Schedule included any officer authorised to act on behalf of the Secretary of State.

Transfer of functions from the Lord Chancellor

4.—(1) The functions of the Lord Chancellor under the enactments listed in Schedule 1 are transferred to the Secretary of State.

(2) The functions transferred by this article include functions under any provision not yet in force at the time this Order is made (and a reference in Schedule 1 to an enactment includes a reference to the

enactment as amended by an Act or subordinate legislation passed or made before that time, but not yet in force).

Transfer of property, rights and liabilities from the Lord Chancellor

1.018   **5.**—All property, rights and liabilities to which the Lord Chancellor is entitled or subject at the coming into force of this Order in connection with the functions transferred by article 4 are transferred to the Secretary of State for Constitutional Affairs.

Transfers from the Lord Chancellor: supplementary

1.019   **6.**—(1) This Order does not affect the validity of anything done (or having effect as if done) by or in relation to the Lord Chancellor before the coming into force of this Order.

(2) Anything (including legal proceedings) which, at the coming into force of this Order, is in the process of being done by or in relation to the Lord Chancellor may, so far as it relates to anything transferred by article 4 or 5, be continued by or in relation to the Secretary of State for Constitutional Affairs.

(3) Anything done (or having effect as if done) by or in relation to the Lord Chancellor in connection with anything transferred by article 4 or 5 has effect, so far as necessary for continuing its effect after the coming into force of this Order, as if done by or in relation to the Secretary of State for Constitutional Affairs.

(4) Documents or forms printed for use in connection with the functions transferred by article 4 may be used in connection with those functions even though they contain, or are to be read as containing, references to the Lord Chancellor, the Lord Chancellor's Department or an officer of the Lord Chancellor; and for the purposes of the use of any such documents or forms after the coming into force of this Order, those references are to be read as references to the Secretary of State for Constitutional Affairs, the Department for Constitutional Affairs or an officer of the Secretary of State for Constitutional Affairs (as appropriate).

(5) Any enactment or instrument passed or made before the coming into force of this Order has effect—
  (a) so far as is necessary for the purposes of or in consequence of article 4, as if references to (and references which are to be read as references to) the Lord Chancellor, the Lord Chancellor's Department or an officer of the Lord Chancellor were references to the Secretary of State, his department or an officer of his (as appropriate), and
  (b) so far as is necessary for the purposes of or in consequence of article 5, as if references to (and references which are to be read as references to) the Lord Chancellor, the Lord Chancellor's Department or an officer of the Lord Chancellor were references to the Secretary of State for Constitutional Affairs, the Department for Constitutional Affairs or an officer of the Secretary of State for Constitutional Affairs (as appropriate).

(S.I. 2003 No. 1887)

Transfer of functions from the First Secretary of State

7.—The functions of the First Secretary of State under section 28 of the Courts Act 1971 are transferred to the Secretary of State. 1.020

Transfer from the First Secretary of State: supplementary

8.—(1) This Order does not affect the validity of anything done (or having effect as if done) by or in relation to the First Secretary of State before the coming into force of this Order. 1.021

(2) Anything (including legal proceedings) which, at the coming into force of this Order, is in the process of being done by or in relation to the First Secretary of State may, so far as it relates to anything transferred by article 7, be continued by or in relation to the Secretary of State for Constitutional Affairs.

(3) Anything done (or having effect as if done) by or in relation to the First Secretary of State in connection with anything transferred by article 7 has effect, so far as necessary for continuing its effect after the coming into force of this Order, as if done by or in relation to the Secretary of State for Constitutional Affairs.

(4) Documents or forms printed for use in connection with the functions transferred by article 7 may be used in connection with those functions even though they contain, or are to be read as containing, references to the First Secretary of State, the Office of the Deputy Prime Minister or an officer of the First Secretary of State; and for the purposes of the use of any such documents or forms after the coming into force of this Order, those references are to be read as references to the Secretary of State for Constitutional Affairs, the Department for Constitutional Affairs or an officer of the Secretary of State for Constitutional Affairs (as appropriate).

(5) Any enactment or instrument passed or made before the coming into force of this Order has effect, so far as is necessary for the purposes of or in consequence of article 7, as if references to (and references which are to be read as references to) the First Secretary of State, the Office of the Deputy Prime Minister or an officer of the First Secretary of State were references to the Secretary of State, his department or an officer of his (as appropriate).

Consequential amendments

9. Schedule 2 (consequential amendments) has effect. 1.022

SCHEDULE 1

Enactments Conferring Functions Transferred by Article 4 1.023

Commissioners for Oaths Act 1889 (c. 10), section 1(1);
Courts Act 1971 (c. 23), Part 4;
Solicitors Act 1974 (c. 47);
Representation of the People Act 1983 (c. 2), except section 161;
Representation of the People Act 1985 (c. 50);
Administration of Justice Act 1985 (c. 61);
Parliamentary Constituencies Act 1986 (c. 56), except paragraph 3 of Schedule 1;
Legal Aid Act 1988 (c. 34);

Courts and Legal Services Act 1990 (c. 41), Parts 2 and 4, sections 113 and 125, and section 124 (commencement) so far as relating to any of those provisions;
Data Protection Act 1998 (c. 29), except—
  (a) sections 6(4)(a) and (b) and 28,
  (b) in Schedule 5, paragraph 12(2) so far as it relates to the resignation of the chairman or a deputy chairman, and
  (c) in Schedule 6, paragraphs 2 and 3;
Human Rights Act 1998 (c. 42), except—
  (a) sections 5, 10, 18 and 19, and
  (b) Schedule 4;
Access to Justice Act 1999 (c. 22), Parts 1 to 3, and Part 7 (supplementary) so far as relating to any provision of those Parts;
Representation of the People Act 2000 (c. 2), Schedule 4;
Freedom of Information Act 2000 (c. 36), except
  (a) sections 15, 23, 24, 36, 46, 65 and 66, and
  (b) section 53 so far as it confers functions on "the accountable person";
Election Publications Act 2001 (c. 5);
European Parliamentary Elections Act 2002 (c. 24);
European Parliament (Representation) Act 2003 (c. 7).

SCHEDULE 2

Article 9

Consequential Amendments

Public Records Act 1958 (c. 51)

1. In the Public Records Act 1958, in Part 1 of the Table at the end of paragraph 3 of Schedule 1, for "Lord Chancellor's Department" substitute "Department for Constitutional Affairs".

Courts Act 1971 (c. 23)

2.—(1) In the Courts Act 1971, in sections 27, 29 and 30 for "Lord Chancellor" in each place substitute "Secretary of State".
(2) In section 28 of that Act, for "First Secretary of State" in each place, and for "said Secretary of State", substitute "Secretary of State".
(3) In Schedule 3 to that Act—
  (a) in paragraph 2(1), for "the Lord Chancellor" substitute "he", and
  (b) in paragraph 5, for "appropriate Minister" in each place substitute "Secretary of State".

Solicitors Act 1974 (c. 47)

3. In the Solicitors Act 1974, in sections 2, 11, 12A, 14, 28, 31, 46, 47, 56 and 81A and in Schedule 1A, for "Lord Chancellor" in each place substitute " Secretary of State".

Representation of the People Act 1983 (c. 2)

4. In the Representation of the People Act 1983, section 199A is repealed.

Representation of the People Act 1985 (c. 50)

5. In the Representation of the People Act 1985, section 27(2A) is repealed.

Administration of Justice Act 1985 (c. 61)

6. In the Administration of Justice Act 1985, for "Lord Chancellor" substitute "Secretary of State" in each place—
  (a) in sections 9, 26, 38, 53 and 69,
  (b) in Schedule 3, except paragraph 3 and the second place in paragraph 4(3), and
  (c) in Schedule 4.

Parliamentary Constituencies Act 1986 (c. 56)

7. In the Parliamentary Constituencies Act 1986, section 6A is repealed.

Courts and Legal Services Act 1990 (c. 41)

8.—(1) In the Courts and Legal Services Act 1990, for "Lord Chancellor" substitute "Secretary of State" in each place—
  (a) in sections 18, 18A, 21, 22, 26, 27, 34, 35, 37, 39 to 41, 43 to 45, 48, 50(3) and (6) and 53,
  (b) in section 54, in the substituted section 23(2A) of the Solicitors Act 1974,
  (c) in sections 55, 58, 58A, 60, 69, 89, 113(1) and (8) and 125, and

(d) in Schedules 3 to 6, 8 and 9.
(2) In section 50(2) of that Act, paragraph (a) is repealed.
(3) In Schedule 9 to that Act, in paragraph 5 for "Lord Chancellor's" in each place substitute "Secretary of State's".
(4) In Schedule 19 to that Act, in paragraph 17—
 (a) for "Lord Chancellor" substitute "Secretary of State", and
 (b) for "him" substitute "the Lord Chancellor".

Data Protection Act 1998 (c. 29)

9.—(1) In the Data Protection Act 1998, for "Lord Chancellor" substitute "Secretary of State" in each place—
 (a) in sections 6(4)(c), 7 to 10, 12, 16, 17, 22, 23, 25, 26, 30, 32, 38, 51, 52, 54, 56, 64, 67 and 75,
 (b) in Schedules 1 to 4,
 (c) in Schedule 5, in Part 1 and, in Part 2, in paragraphs 13 to 15,
 (d) in Schedule 6, in paragraph 7, and
 (e) in Schedule 7.
(2) In Schedule 5 to that Act, in paragraph 12(2), at the end insert "(in the case of the chairman or a deputy chairman) or to the Secretary of State (in the case of any other member)".

Human Rights Act 1998 (c.42)

10.—(1) In sections 1 and 14 to 16 of the Human Rights Act 1998, for "Lord Chancellor" in each place substitute "Secretary of State".
(2) In sections 2(3)(a), 7(9)(a) and 20(2) and (4) of that Act, the words "the Lord Chancellor or" are repealed.

Access to Justice Act 1999 (c.22)

11.—(1) In the Access to Justice Act 1999, for "Lord Chancellor" substitute "Secretary of State" in each place—
 (a) in sections 1 to 6, 8, 9, 12 to 14, 16, 18 to 20, 23, 25 and 26,
 (b) in section 28, in the inserted section 58B of the Courts and Legal Services Act 1990,
 (c) in sections 30 and 45 to 47,
 (d) in section 50, including the amendment to paragraph 7 of Schedule 3 to the Courts and Legal Services Act 1990,
 (e) in sections 51 and 52, and(f) in Schedules 1, 3 and 8.
(2) In section 108 of that Act, in subsection (1), after "Lord Chancellor" insert "or Secretary of State".
(3) In Schedule 1 to that Act, in paragraph 15(5), for "Lord Chancellor's" substitute "Secretary of State's".
(4) In Schedule 14 to that Act, in paragraph 1(1), after "Lord Chancellor" insert "or Secretary of State".

Freedom of Information Act 2000 (c. 36)

12.—(1) In the Freedom of Information Act 2000, for "Lord Chancellor" substitute "Secretary of State" in each place—
 (a) in sections 4, 5, 7, 9, 10, 12, 13, 45, 47 and 53,
 (b) in section 69(2), in the inserted section 9A of the Data Protection Act 1998, and
 (c) in sections 75, 83 to 85 and 87.
(2) In section 46(5) of that Act, after "consult—" insert—
"(a) the Secretary of State,".
(3) In section 82(1) of that Act, the words "Lord Chancellor or the" are repealed.

Election Publications Act 2001 (c. 5)

13. In the Election Publications Act 2001, in subsections (1) and (3) of section 2, the words "or the Lord Chancellor" are repealed.

European Parliamentary Elections Act 2002 (c. 24)

14. In the European Parliamentary Elections Act 2002, section 16A is repealed.

European Parliament (Representation) Act 2003 (c. 7)

15.—(1) In the European Parliament (Representation) Act 2003, for "Lord Chancellor" substitute "Secretary of State" in each place—
 (a) in sections 3, 5, 6, 10 to 13, 17 and 18,

The Secretary of State for Constitutional Affairs Order 2003

(b) in section 21(3), in the inserted section 13(3B) of the European Parliamentary Elections Act 2002, and
(c) in section 28.
(2) Section 26 of that Act is repealed.

The Social Security (Incapacity Benefit Work-focused Interviews) Regulations 2003

(S.I. 2003 No. 2439)

(Entry into force: October 27, 2003 in respect of postcodes in Part I to Schedule
April 5, 2004 in respect of postcodes in Part II to the Schedule)

ARRANGEMENT OF REGULATIONS

1. Citation and commencement.
2. Interpretation.
3. Requirement for a relevant person entitled to a specified benefit to take part in an interview.
4. Continuing entitlement to a specified benefit dependent upon an interview.
5. The interview.
6. Waiver of requirement to take part in an interview.
7. Deferment of requirement to take part in an interview.
8. Exemptions.
9. Taking part in an interview.
10. Failure to take part in an interview.
11. Good cause.
12. Appeals.
13. Amendment to the Income Support (General) Regulations 1987 *(omitted)*.
14. Amendment to the Housing Benefit (General) Regulations 1987 *(omitted)*.
15. Amendment to the Council Tax Benefit (General) Regulations 1992 *(omitted)*.
16. Amendment to the Jobseeker's Allowance Regulations 1996 *(omitted)*.
17. Amendment to the Social Security (Jobcentre Plus Interviews) Regulations 2002 *(omitted)*.

Schedule

GENERAL NOTE

This new set of work-focused interview regulations joins the following work-focused interview regulations currently in force:

The Social Security (Work-focused Interviews for Lone Parents) and Miscellaneous Amendments Regulations 2000 (S.I. 2000 No. 1926)

The Social Security (Jobcentre Plus Interviews) Regulations 2002 (S.I. 2002 No. 1703).

All the work-focused interview regulations are designed to encourage those claiming benefit to return to work. This new scheme is introduced following the

Green Paper, *Pathways to Work. Helping People into Employment*, Cm 5690 (November 2002). A claimant already caught by the existing regulations will be exempt from an interview under the new regulations. The scheme applies to new claimants aged between 18 and 60 years of age who claims a specified benefit.

The scheme introduced by these regulations follows the pattern set by the earlier regulations but has three stages: the initial interview, a boosted interview, and a follow up stage. Claimant are obliged not just to attend an interview, but to "take part in" an interview; this involves answering specified questions, participating in discussion, and assisting the interview in the completion of an action plan. Failure to do so can result in a penalty deduction equal to 20 per cent of the applicable amount for a single adult claimant.

1.026   The Secretary of State for Work and Pensions, in exercise of the powers conferred upon him by ss.123(1)(a), (d) and (e), 136(3) and (5)(b), 137(1) and 175(3) and (4) of the Social Security Contributions and Benefits Act 1992, ss.2A(1), (3) to (6) and (8), 2B(6) and (7), 189(4) to (6) and (7A) and 191 of the Social Security Administration Act 1992 and ss.12(1) and (4)(b), 35(1) and 36(2) and (4) of the Jobseekers Act 1995 and of all other powers enabling him in that behalf, after consultation with the Council on Tribunals in accordance with s.8(1) of the Tribunals and Inquiries Act 1992 and in respect of provisions in these Regulations relating to housing benefit and council tax benefit with organisations appearing to him to be representative of the authorities concerned and after reference to the Social Security Advisory Committee, hereby makes the following Regulations:

Citation and commencement

1.027   **1.**—These Regulations may be cited as the Social Security (Incapacity Benefit Work-focused Interviews) Regulations 2003 and shall come into force on 27th October 2003.

Interpretation

1.028   **2.**—In these Regulations—

"benefit week" means any period of seven days corresponding to the week in respect of which the relevant specified benefit is due to be paid;

"interview" means a work-focused interview with a relevant person who has claimed a specified benefit and which is conducted for any or all of the following purposes—
- (c) assessing that relevant person's prospects for existing or future employment (whether paid or voluntary);
- (d) assisting or encouraging that relevant person to enhance his prospects of such employment;
- (e) identifying activities which that relevant person may undertake to strengthen his existing or future prospects of employment;
- (f) identifying current or future employment, training or rehabilitation opportunities suitable to that relevant person's needs;
- (g) identifying educational opportunities connected with the existing or future employment prospects or needs of that relevant person;

"officer" means a person who is an officer of, or who is providing services to or exercising functions of, the Secretary of State;

"personal capability assessment" means the assessment defined in Part III of the Social Security (Incapacity for Work) (General) Regulations 1995 (personal capability assessment);

"relevant decision" has the meaning given by section 2B(2) of the Social Security Administration Act 1992 (supplementary provisions relating to work-focused interviews);

"relevant person" means a person who resides in an area identified in—
- (a) Part 1 of the Schedule to these Regulations, and who makes a claim for a specified benefit on or after 27th October 2003; or
- (b) Part 2 of that Schedule, and who makes a claim for a specified benefit on or after 5th April 2004.

"specified benefit" means—
- (a) incapacity benefit;
- (b) income support where paragraph 7 (persons incapable of work) of Schedule 1B to the Income Support (General) Regulations 1987 applies;
- (c) income support where paragraph 24 or 25 (persons appealing against a decision which embodies a determination that they are not incapable of work) of Schedule 1B to the Income Support (General) Regulations 1987 applies to a person who has made a claim for a specified benefit referred to in sub-paragraph (a), (b) or (d) of this definition on or after
  - (i) 27th October 2003 where that person resides in an area identified in Part 1 of the Schedule to these Regulations; or
  - (ii) 5th April 2004 where that person resides in an area identified in Part 2 of that Schedule; or
- (d) severe disablement allowance.

Requirement for a relevant person entitled to a specified benefit to take part in an interview

3.—(1) Subject to paragraph (2) below and regulations 6 and 7, a relevant person who—
- (a) is entitled to a specified benefit; and
- (b) on the day on which he makes his claim for that specified benefit, has attained the age of 18 but has not attained the age of 60,

shall be required to take part in an interview as a condition of his continuing to be entitled to the full amount of the specified benefit which is payable to him.

(2) A relevant person who
- (a) has taken part in an interview under paragraph (1) above by virtue of
  - (i) being; or
  - (ii) having been,

  entitled to a specified benefit; and
- (b) becomes entitled to—
  - (i) another specified benefit; or
  - (ii) the same specified benefit where sub-paragraph (a)(ii) applies; and

(c) has not—
  (i) been engaged in remunerative work; or
  (ii) made a claim for a jobseeker's allowance,
  after having been entitled to the specified benefit referred to in sub-paragraph (a) above and before becoming entitled to the specified benefit referred to in sub-paragraph (b) above,
shall not be required to take part in a further interview under paragraph (1) above.

(3) An officer shall arrange for the interview referred to in paragraph (1) above to take place after the expiry of eight weeks after the date the claim for a specified benefit is made or as soon as is reasonably practicable thereafter.

Continuing entitlement to a specified benefit dependent upon an interview

4.—(1) Subject to paragraph (2) below and regulations 6 to 8 a relevant person who—
  (a) has taken part in an interview under regulation 3;
  (b) is entitled to a specified benefit; and
  (c) has not attained the age of 60,
shall be required to take part in five further interviews, each at, or as soon as is reasonably practicable after, the expiry of one month from the day he last took part in an interview, the day he was treated under regulation 6 as having complied with such a requirement to take part in an interview or, as the case may be, the day a relevant decision was made under regulation 9(4), as a condition of his continuing to be entitled to the full amount of the specified benefit which is payable to him.

(2) A relevant person who—
  (a) has taken part in one or more interviews under paragraph (1) above by virtue of—
    (i) being; or
    (ii) having been,
    entitled to a specified benefit; and
  (b) becomes entitled to—
    (i) another specified benefit; or
    (ii) the same specified benefit where sub-paragraph (a)(ii) applies; and
  (c) has not—
    (i) been engaged in remunerative work; or
    (ii) made a claim for a jobseeker's allowance,
    after having been entitled to the specified benefit referred to in sub-paragraph (a) above and before becoming entitled to the specified benefit referred to in sub-paragraph (b) above,
shall be required to continue to take part in the sequence of interviews in accordance with paragraph (1) until he has taken part in a total of five such interviews.

(3) Subject to regulations 6 and 7, where a relevant person—
  (a) has taken part in the five further interviews referred to in paragraph (1) above;

(b) is entitled to a specified benefit; and
(c) has not attained the age of 60,

he shall be required to take part in an interview as a condition of his continuing to be entitled to the full amount of the specified benefit which is payable to him where any of the circumstances specified in paragraph (6) below apply or where paragraph (7) below applies.

(4) Subject to regulations 6 and 7, where a relevant person—
(a) has had the requirement to take part in all five interviews referred to in paragraph (1) above waived in accordance with regulation 6;
(b) is entitled to a specified benefit; and
(c) has not attained the age of 60,

he shall be required to take part in an interview as a condition of his continuing to be entitled to the full amount of the specified benefit which is payable to him where any of the circumstances specified in paragraph (6) below apply or where paragraph (7) below applies.

(5) Subject to regulations 6 and 7, where—
(a) regulation 8 applies to a relevant person;
(b) the relevant person is entitled to a specified benefit; and
(c) the relevant person has not attained the age of 60,

he shall be required to take part in an interview as a condition of his continuing to be entitled to the full amount of the specified benefit which is payable to him where any of the circumstances specified in paragraph (6) below apply or where paragraph (7) below applies.

(6) The circumstances specified in this paragraph are those where— 1.032
(a) it is determined in accordance with a personal capability assessment that a relevant person is incapable of work and therefore, continues to be entitled to a specified benefit;
(b) a relevant person's entitlement to a carer's allowance ceases whilst his entitlement to a specified benefit continues;
(c) a relevant person becomes engaged or ceases to be engaged in part-time work; or
(d) a relevant person has been undergoing education, training or a rehabilitation programme arranged by an officer and that education, training or rehabilitation programme comes to an end.

(7) A requirement to take part in an interview arises under this paragraph where a relevant person has not been required to take part in an interview under paragraphs (3) to (5) above for at least 36 months from the date he last took part in an interview.

The interview

5.—(1) The officer shall inform a relevant person who is required to take part in an interview of the time and place of the interview. 1.033

(2) An officer shall conduct the interview.

(3) The officer may determine that an interview is to take place in the relevant person's home where it would, in the officer's opinion, be unreasonable to expect that relevant person to attend elsewhere because that relevant person's personal circumstances are such that attending

elsewhere would cause him undue inconvenience or endanger his health.

Waiver of requirement to take part in an interview

1.034   **6.**—(1) A requirement imposed by these Regulations to take part in an interview shall not apply where an officer determines that an interview would not be—
 (a) of assistance to the relevant person concerned; or
 (b) appropriate in the circumstances.
 (2) A relevant person in relation to whom a requirement to take part in an interview has been waived under paragraph (1) above shall be treated for the purposes of—
 (a) regulation 3 or 4; and
 (b) entitlement to a specified benefit,
as having complied with that requirement in respect of that interview.

Deferment of requirement to take part in an interview

1.035   **7.**—(1) An officer may determine, in the case of a relevant person, that the requirement to take part in an interview shall be deferred at the time the requirement to take part in an interview arises or applies because an interview would not at that time be—
 (a) of assistance to that relevant person; or
 (b) appropriate in the circumstances.
 (2) Where the officer determines in accordance with paragraph (1) above that the requirement to take part in an interview shall be deferred, he shall also determine when that determination is made, the time when the requirement to take part in an interview is to apply in the relevant person's case.
 (3) Where a requirement to take part in an interview has been deferred in accordance with paragraph (1) above, then until—
 (a) a determination is made under regulation 6(1);
 (b) the relevant person takes part in an interview; or
 (c) a relevant decision has been made in relation to that relevant person in accordance with regulation 9(4),
that relevant person shall be treated for the purposes of entitlement to a specified benefit as having complied with that requirement.

Exemptions

1.036   **8.**—A relevant person, who on the day on which the requirement to take part in an interview under regulation 4(1) arises or applies is treated as incapable of work in accordance with the provisions of regulation 10 of the Social Security (Incapacity for Work) (General) Regulations 1995 (certain persons with a severe condition to be treated as incapable of work), shall be exempt from the requirement to take part in any interview under regulation 4(1).

Taking part in an interview

1.037   **9.**—(1) The officer shall determine whether a relevant person has taken part in an interview.

(2) A relevant person shall be regarded as having taken part in an interview referred to in regulation 3 if—
  (a) he attends for the interview at the place and time notified to him by the officer;
  (b) he participates in discussions with the officer in relation to the relevant person's employability, including any action the relevant person and the officer agree is reasonable and they are willing to take in order to help the relevant person enhance his employment prospects;
  (c) he provides answers (where asked) to questions and appropriate information about—
    (i) details of and the level to which he has pursued any educational qualifications;
    (ii) his employment history;
    (iii) his aspirations for future employment;
    (iv) any vocational training he has undertaken;
    (v) any skills he has acquired which fit him for employment;
    (vi) any vocational training or skills which he wishes to undertake or acquire;
    (vii) any paid or unpaid employment he is engaged in;
    (viii) the extent to which his medical condition, in his opinion, restricts his ability to obtain or puts him at a disadvantage in obtaining employment;
    (ix) his work related abilities; and
    (x) any caring or childcare responsibilities he has; and
  (d) he assists the officer in the completion of an action plan which records the matters discussed in relation to sub-paragraph (b) above.
(3) A relevant person shall be regarded as having taken part in any one of the interviews referred to in regulation 4 if—
  (a) he attends for the interview at the place and time notified to him by the officer;
  (b) he participates in discussions with the officer—
    (i) in relation to the relevant person's employability or any progress he might have made towards obtaining employment;
    (ii) about any action the relevant person or the officer might have taken as a result of the matters discussed in relation to paragraph (2)(b) above;
    (iii) about how, if at all, the action plan referred to in paragraph (2)(d) above should be amended; and
    (iv) in order to consider any of the programmes and support available to help the relevant person obtain employment;
  (c) he provides answers (where asked) to questions and appropriate information about—
    (i) the content of any report made following his personal capability assessment, insofar as that report relates to the relevant person's capabilities and employability; and
    (ii) his opinion as to the extent to which his medical condition restricts his ability to obtain employment; and

(d) he assists the officer in the completion of any amendment of the action plan referred to in paragraph (2)(d) above in light of the matters discussed in relation to sub-paragraph (b) above and the information provided in relation to sub-paragraph (c) above.

(4) Where an officer determines that a relevant person has failed to take part in an interview and good cause has not been shown for that failure within five working days of the day on which the interview was to take place, a relevant decision shall be made for the purposes of section 2B of the Social Security Administration Act 1992.

Failure to take part in an interview

1.038
10.—(1) A relevant person in respect of whom a relevant decision has been made in accordance with regulation 9(4) shall, subject to paragraph (12) below, suffer the consequences specified in paragraph (2) below.

(2) The consequences specified in this paragraph are, subject to paragraphs (3) and (4) below, that the relevant person's benefit shall be reduced as from the first day of the next benefit week following the day a relevant decision was made, by a sum equal to 20 per cent. of the amount applicable on the date the first reduction commences in respect of a single claimant for income support aged not less than 25.

(3) Benefit reduced in accordance with paragraph (2) above shall not be reduced below ten pence per week.

(4) Where two or more specified benefits are in payment to a relevant person, a reduction made in accordance with paragraph (2) above shall be applied, except in a case to which paragraph (5) below applies, to the specified benefits in the following order of priority—

(a) income support;
(b) incapacity benefit;
(c) severe disablement allowance.

(5) Where the amount of the reduction is greater than some, but not all, of the specified benefits listed in paragraph (4) above, the reduction shall be made against the first benefit in that list which is the same as, or greater than, the amount of the reduction.

(6) For the purpose of determining whether a specified benefit is the same as, or greater than, the amount of the reduction for the purposes of paragraph (5) above, ten pence shall be added to the amount of the reduction.

1.039
(7) In a case where the whole of the reduction cannot be applied against any one specified benefit because the amount of no one benefit is the same as, or greater than, the amount of the reduction, the reduction shall be applied against the first benefit in payment in the list of priorities in paragraph (4) above and so on against each benefit in turn until the whole of the reduction is exhausted or, if this is not possible, the whole of the specified benefits are exhausted, subject in each case to ten pence remaining in payment.

(8) Where the rate of any specified benefit payable to a relevant person changes, the rules set out above for a reduction in the benefit payable shall be applied to the new rates and any adjustments to the benefits against which the reductions are made shall take effect from the

(S.I. 2003 No. 2439)

beginning of the first benefit week to commence for that relevant person following the change.

(9) Paragraph (1) above shall apply to a relevant person each time a relevant decision is made in accordance with regulation 9(4) in respect of him.

(10) Where a relevant person whose benefit has been reduced in accordance with paragraph (2) above subsequently takes part in an interview, the whole of the reduction shall cease to have effect on the first day of the benefit week in which the requirement to take part in an interview was met.

(11) For the purposes of determining the amount of any benefit payable, a relevant person shall be treated as receiving the amount of any specified benefit which would have been payable but for a reduction made in accordance with paragraph (2) above.

(12) The consequences specified in paragraph (2) above shall not apply to a person who—
- (a) brings new facts to the notice of the Secretary of State within one month of the date on which a relevant decision was notified to him and—
  - (i) those facts could not reasonably have been brought to the Secretary of State's notice within five working days of the day on which the interview was to take place; and
  - (ii) those facts show that he had good cause for his failure to take part in the interview;
- (b) is no longer required to take part in an interview as a condition for continuing to be entitled to the full amount of the specified benefit which is payable to him apart from these Regulations; or
- (c) attains the age of 60.

Good cause

11.—Matters to be taken into account in determining whether a relevant person has shown good cause for his failure to take part in an interview include—
- (a) that the relevant person misunderstood the requirement to take part in the interview due to any learning, language or literacy difficulties of the relevant person or any misleading information given to the relevant person by the officer;
- (b) that the relevant person was attending a medical or dental appointment, or accompanying a person for whom the relevant person has caring responsibilities to such an appointment, and that it would have been unreasonable, in the circumstances, to rearrange the appointment;
- (c) that the relevant person had difficulties with his normal mode of transport and that no reasonable alternative was available;
- (d) that the established customs and practices of the religion to which the relevant person belongs prevented him from attending on the day or at the time fixed for the interview;
- (e) that the relevant person was attending an interview with an employer with a view to obtaining employment;

(f) that the relevant person was pursuing employment opportunities as a self-employed earner;
(g) that the relevant person or a dependant of his or a person for whom he provides care suffered an accident, sudden illness or relapse of a physical or mental health condition;
(h) that the relevant person was attending the funeral of a relative or close friend on the day fixed for the interview;
(i) that a disability from which the relevant person suffers made it impossible for him to attend at the time fixed for the interview.

Appeals

1.043 **12.**—(1) This regulation applies to any relevant decision under regulation 9(4) or any decision made under section 10 of the Social Security Act 1998 (decisions superseding earlier decisions) superseding such a relevant decision.

(2) This regulation applies whether the decision is as originally made or as revised under section 9 of the Social Security Act 1998 (revision of decisions).

(3) In the case of a decision to which this regulation applies, the relevant person in respect of whom the decision was made shall have a right of appeal under section 12 of the Social Security Act 1998 (appeal to appeal tribunal) to an appeal tribunal.

Regs 13–17 omitted

SCHEDULE

Part 1

1.044 1. For the purposes of regulation 2 the areas are—
(a) the areas of—
Amber Valley Borough Council;
Bolsover District Council excluding the postcode districts of S43 4, NG19 7 and S80 4;
Chesterfield Borough Council;
Derby City Council;
Derbyshire Dales District Council excluding the postcode districts of S32 and S33;
Erewash Borough Council;
High Peak Borough Council excluding the postcode districts of S32 and S33;
North East Derbyshire District Council excluding the postcode districts of S12 3A, S12 3B, S12 3D, S12 3E, S12 3F, S12 3G, S12 3H, S12 3J, S12 3L, S12 3U, S12 3XA, S12 3XB, S12 3XE, S12 3XH, S12 3XL, S12 3XQ, S17 3 and S11 7;
South Derbyshire District Council;
(b) the following postcode districts—
CF31;
CF32 excluding the following parts: CF32 OP, CF32 OQ, CF32 OR, CF32 OS, CF32 OTA, CF32 OTB, CF32 OTD, CF32 OTE, CF32 OTF, CF32 OTH, CF32 OTL, CF32 OTN;
CF33 excluding the following parts: CF33 6PS, CF33 6PT, CF33 6PU, CF33 6RA, CF33 6RB, CF33 6RD, CF33 6RL;
CF34;
CF35 excluding the following parts: CF35 5AB, CF35 5AD, CF35 5AE, CF35 5AF, CF35 5AG, CF35 5AH, CF35 5AL, CF35 5AN, CF35 5AR, CF35 5AS,

(S.I. 2003 No. 2439)

CF35 5AY, CF35 5BA, CF35 5BB, CF35 5BD, CF35 5BE, CF35 5BG, CF35 5BH, CF35 5BJ, CF35 5BL, CF35 5BN, CF35 5BP, CF35 5BQ, CF35 5BW, CF35 5BY, CF35 5BZ, CF35 5DA, CF35 5DD, CF35 5DE, CF35 5DF, CF35 5DG, CF35 5DH, CF35 5DL, CF35 5DN, CF35 5DP, CF35 5DR, CF35 5DS, CF35 5DT, CF35 5DU, CF35 5DW, CF35 5DY, CF35 5EA, CF35 5EB, CF35 5ED, CF35 5EE, CF35 5EF, CF35 5EG, CF35 5HY, CF35 5RG, CF35 5RH, CF35 5S;
CF36 to CF45;
CF72 8 excluding the following parts: CF72 8JU to CF72 8JZ;
CF72 9;
CF15 7 excluding the following parts: CF15 7A, CF15 7H, CF15 7JL to CF15 7JZ, CF15 7L, CF15 7NH to CF15 7NX, CF15 7UG to CF15 7UW, CF15 7W to CF15 7Z;
FK20 8SB;
G78;
G82 5BT, G82 5EN, G82 5EP, G82 5ER to G82 5ET, G82 5EW to G82 5EZ, G82 5HB, G82 5HD to G82 5HH, G82 5HL, G82 5HN, G82 5HQ, G82 5HW, G82 5JH, G82 5JJ, G82 5JQ, G82 5JT, G82 5JU, G82 5JW to G82 5JZ, G82 5L, G82 5N, G82 5P to G82 5Q, G82 5Y;
G83 7A, G83 7B, G83 7DA, G83 7DB, G83 7DD to G83 7DH, G83 7DJ, G83 7DL, G83 7DN, G83 7DP to G83 7DU, G83 7DW, G83 7E, G83 7Y, G83 8NT, G83 8NU, G83 8NX to G83 8NZ, G83 8PA, G83 8PB, G83 8PD to G83 8PG, G83 8RA, G83 8RB, G83 8RD to G83 8RH, G83 8RQ, G83 8SZ, G83 8T, G83 8W;
G84;
PA1;
PA2 0, PA2 6 to PA2 8B, PA2 8D, PA2 8E, PA2 8H, PA2 8J, PA2 8L, PA2 8N, PA2 8P to PA2 8T, PA2 8UD, PA2 8UE, PA2 8UG, PA2 8UJ, PA2 8UL, PA2 8UQ, PA2 8UT, PA2 8UU, PA2 8UW to PA2 8UY, PA2 8W, PA2 8Y, PA2 9;
PA3 1 to PA3 4;
PA4 to PA10;
PA11 3A, PA11 3B, PA11 3D, PA11 3E, PA11 3H to PA11 3J, PA11 3L, PA11 3NA, PA11 3NB, PA11 3ND to PA11 3NG, PA11 3NL, PA11 3NN, PA11 3NP to PA11 3NR, PA11 3NT, PA11 3NU, PA11 3NW to PA11 3NZ, PA11 3PA, PA11 3PB, PA11 3PD to PA11 3PH, PA11 3PJ, PA11 3PL, PA11 3PN, PA11 3PP to PA11 3PU, PA11 3PW to PA11 3PZ, PA11 3QA, PA11 3QB, PA11 3QD to PA11 3QH, PA11 3QJ, PA11 3QL, PA11 3QN, PA11 3QP to PA11 3QT, PA11 3QW to PA11 3QZ, PA11 3RA, PA11 3RB, PA11 3RD, PA11 3RE, PA11 3RG, PA11 3RH, PA11 3RL, PA11 3RN, PA11 3RP to PA11 3RU, PA11 3RX to PA11 3RZ, PA11 3SA, PA11 3SB, PA11 3SD to PA11 3SH, PA11 3SJ, PA11 3SL, PA11 3SN, PA11 3SP to PA11 3SU, PA11 3SW to PA11 3SZ, PA11 3T, PA11 3Y;
PA12;
PA13 4A, PA13 4B, PA13 4D, PA13 4E, PA13 4H, PA13 4J, PA13 4L, PA13 4N, PA13 4PA, PA13 4PB, PA13 4PD to PA13 4PH, PA13 4PJ, PA13 4PL, PA13 4PN, PA13 4PP to PA13 4PU, PA13 4PW to PA13 4PZ, PA13 4Q to PA13 4T, PA13 4W, PA13 4Y, PA13 4Z;
PA14 5, PA14 6A, PA14 6B, PA14 6D, PA14 6E, PA14 6H, PA14 6J, PA14 6L, PA14 6N, PA14 6PA, PA14 6PB, PA14 6PD to PA14 6PH, PA14 6PJ, PA14 6PL, PA14 6PN, PA14 6PP to PA14 6PT, PA14 6PW, PA14 6Q to PA14 6TA, PA14 6TD, PA14 6TE, PA14 6TG, PA14 6TH, PA14 6TJ, PA14 6TL, PA14 6TN, PA14 6TP, PA14 6TR, PA14 6TS, PA14 6U, PA14 6WA, PA14 6WD to PA14 6WF, PA14 6X, PA14 6YA, PA14 6YB, PA14 6YD to PA14 6YH, PA14 6YJ, PA14 6YL, PA14 6YN, PA14 6YP to PA14 6YU, PA14 4YW to PA14 6YZ;
PA15;
PA16;
PA18 to PA33;
PA34 4, PA34 5A, PA34 5B, PA34 5D, PA34 5E, PA34 5H to PA34 5J, PA34 5N to PA34 5P, PA34 5QA, PA34 5QD, PA34 5QE, PA34 5R to PA34 5T, PA45 5UG to PA34 5UJ, PA34 5UL, PA34 5UN, PA34 5UQ, PA34 5Y;
PA35 to PA37;

1.045

1.046

25

PA38 4BA, PA38 4BB, PA38 4BD, PA38 4BE, PA38 4BG, PA38 4BH, PA38 4BJ, PA38 4BL, PA38 4BN, PA38 4BQ, PA38 4DB, PA38 4DD to PA38 4DH, PA38 4DJ, PA38 4DL, PA38 4DN, PA38 4DP to PA38 4DR;
PA41 to PA49;
PA60 to PA78.

PART 2

2. For the purposes of regulation 2 the areas are—
(a) the areas of—
Basildon District Council;
Braintree District Council;
Castle Point District Council;
Chelmsford Borough Council;
Colchester Borough Council;
Epping Forest District Council;
Harlow District Council;
Maldon District Council;
Mendip District Council;
Rochford District Council;
Sedgemoor District Council;
Southend on Sea Borough Council;
South Somerset District Council;
Taunton Deane Borough Council;
Tendring District Council;
Thurrock Borough Council;
Uttlesford District Council;
West Somerset District Council;
(b) the following postcode districts—
BB1–BB12;
BB18;
DH2 1AH, DH2 1AJ, DH2 1AL, DH2 1AW, DH2 1BQ, DH2 1UT, DH2 1XF, DH2 1XG, DH2 1XG;
DH3 1A, DH3 1B, DH3 1D, DH3 1E, DH3 1H, DH3 1J, DH3 1L, DH3 1N, DH3 1P, DH3 1Q, DH3 1RD, DH3 1RF, DH3 1RG, DH3 1RH, DH3 1RJ, DH3 1RL, DH3 1RN, DH3 1RP to DH3 1RS, DH3 1RW, DH3 1X, DH3 2AG, DH3 2AH, DH3 2AJ, DH3 2AL, DH3 2AP, DH3 2AR to DH3 2AU, DH3 2AW to DH3 2AZ, DH3 2BA, DH3 2BB, DH3 2BD, DH3 2BE, DH3 2BG, DH3 2BH, DH3 2BL, DH3 2BQ, DH3 2D, DH3 2EA, DH3 2EH, DH3 2EJ, DH3 2EL, DH3 2EN, DH3 2EP, DH3 2ER, DH3 2ET, DH3 2EW to DH3 2EZ, DH3 2H, DH3 2J, DH3 2L, DH3 2N, DH3 2P, DH3 2Q, DH3 2RA, DH3 2RE, DH3 2RH, DH3 2RN, DH3 2RR, DH3 2RT, DH3 2RY, DH3 2RZ, DH3 2S, DH3 2T;
DH9 0RY, DH9 0RZ, DH9 0SA;
NE8;
NE9 5, NE9 6, NE9 7A, NE9 7B, NE9 7D, NE9 7E, NE9 7H, NE9 7J, NE9 7L, NE9 7NA, NE9 7NB, NE9 7ND, NE9 7QA, NE9 7QB, NE9 7QD to NE9 7QF, NE9 7SP, NE9 7T, NE9 7UA, NE9 7UB, NE9 7UD, NE9 7UP, NE9 7US to NE9 7UU, NE9 7UX, NE9 7UY, NE9 7W, NE9 7XA, NE9 7XB, NE9 7XD to NE9 7XH, NE9 7XJ, NE9 7XL, NE9 7XN, NE9 7XP to NE9 7XU, NE9 7XY, NE9 7YA, NE9 7YB, NE9 7YD to NE9 7YH, NE9 7YJ, NE9 7YL, NE9 7YN, NE9 7YP, NE9 7YS;
NE10;
NE11;
NE15 8NR;
NE16 3, NE16 4, NE16 5A, NE16 5B, NE16 5D, NE16 5EB, NE16 5ED to NE16 5EF, NE16 5EH, NE16 5EL, NE16 5EN, NE16 5EP to NE16 5EU, NE16 5EW, NE16 5EX, NE16 5H, NE16 5J, NE16 5L, NE16 5N, NE16 5P to NE16 5U, NE16 5W to NE16 5Z, NE16 6AA, NE16 6AB, NE16 6AD, NE16 6AE, NE16 6BE, NE16 6BG, NE16 6NU, NE16 6NX, NE16 6PA, NE16 6PB, NE16 6PD to NE16 6PG;

NE17 7AA, NE17 7AB, NE17 7AD to NE17 7AH, NE17 7AJ, NE17 7AN, NE17 	1.050
7AP, NE17 7AQ, NE17 7AR, NE17 7AS, NE17 7AW, NE17 7AZ, NE17 7BA,
NE17 7BB, NE17 7BD, NE17 7BP, NE17 7BS to NE17 7BU, NE17 7BX to NE17
7BZ, NE17 7D, NE17 7E, NE17 7HA, NE17 7HB, NE17 7HD, NE17 7HE,
NE17 7HS, NE17 7HU, NE17 7HX to NE17 7HZ, NE17 7J, NE17 7L, NE17
7QE, NE17 7TE, NE17 7TF to NE17 7TH, NE17 7TJ, NE17 7TL;
NE36 0E, NE36 0H, NE36 0J, NE36 0L, NE36 0N, NE36 0P to NE36 0U, NE36
0W, NE36 0Y, NE37 3JB;
NE39 1, NE39 2;
NE40;
NE41 8JD, NE41 8JE, NE41 8JG, NE41 8JH, NE41 8JJ, NE41 8JL, NE41 8JN,
NE41 8JQ, NE41 8JW;
NE42 5NL, NE42 5NN, NE42 5NP, NE42 5NR, NE42 5NW;
NE82;
NE85 2NE;
NE98 1B, NE98 1X, NE98 1YL;
OL12 8AA to ZZ;
OL13;
SR5 1RP;
SR6 7A, SR6 7B, SR6 7D, SR6 7E, SR6 7H, SR6 7J, SR6 7L, SR6 7NA, SR6 7ND
to SR6 7NH, SR6 7NJ, SR6 7NN, SR6 7NP to SR6 7NT, SR6 7NW, SR6 7NZ,
SR6 7P to SR6 7T, SR6 7W to SR6 7Y.

European Community Law

Council Regulation (EC) No 859/2003 of 14 May 2003 extending the 	1.052
provisions of Regulation (EEC) No 1408/71 and Regulation (EEC) No
574/72 to nationals of third countries who are not already covered by
those provisions solely on the ground of their nationality.

[2003] OJ L124/1

GENERAL NOTE

As the Preamble makes clear, for some years, there has been concern that 	1.053
nationals of countries other than EEA countries and Switzerland ("participating
countries") were at a disadvantage in that there was no provision for the co-
ordination of the social security rules of two or more participating countries for
the benefit of third country nationals who had lawfully lived and worked in the
European Union. This regulation seeks to ameliorate their circumstances by
extending, with effect from June 1, 2003, the provisions of Regulation 1408/71
to such third country nationals where they have had contact with two or more
participating countries.

THE COUNCIL OF THE EUROPEAN UNION,
Having regard to the Treaty establishing the European Community and in 	1.054
particular Article 63, point 4 thereof,
Having regard to the proposal from the Commission,[1]
Having regard to the opinion of the European Parliament,[2]
Whereas:

[1] OJ C 126 E, 28.5.2002, p. 388
[2] Opinion of 21 November 2002

1.055 (1) As its special meeting in Tampere on 15 and 16 October 1999, the European Council proclaimed that the European Union should ensure fair treatment of third-country nationals who reside legally in the territory of its Member States, grant them rights and obligations comparable to those of EU citizens, enhance non-discrimination in economic, social and cultural life and approximate their legal status to that of Member States' nationals.
(2) In its resolution of 27 October 1999,[3] the European Parliament called for prompt action on promises of fair treatment for third-country nationals legally resident in the Member States and on the definition of their legal status, including uniform rights as close as possible to those enjoyed by the citizens of the European Union.
(3) The European Economic and Social Committee has also appealed for equal treatment of Community nationals and third-country nationals in the social field, notably in its opinion of 26 September 1991 on the status of migrant workers from third countries.[4]
(4) Article 6(2) of the Treaty on European Union provides that the Union shall respect fundamental rights, as guaranteed by the European Convention on the Protection of Human Rights and Fundamental Freedoms signed in Rome on 4 November 1950 and as they result from the constitutional traditions common to the Member States, as general principles of Community law.

1.056 (5) This Regulation respects the fundamental rights and observes the principles recognised in particular by the Charter of Fundamental Rights of the European Union, in particular the spirit of its Article 34(2).
(6) The promotion of a high level of social protection and the raising of the standard of living and quality of life in the Member States are objectives of the Community.
(7) As regards the conditions of social protection of third-country nationals, and in particular the social security scheme applicable to them, the Employment and Social Policy Council argued in its conclusions of 3 December 2001 that the coordination applicable to third-country nationals should grant them a set of uniform rights as near as possible to those enjoyed by EU citizens.

1.057 (8) Currently, Council Regulation (EEC) No 1408/71 of 14 June 1971 on the application of social security schemes to employed persons and their families moving within the Community,[5] which is the basis for the coordination of the social security schemes of the different Member States, and Council Regulation (EEC) No 574/72 of 21 March 1972, laying down the procedure for implementing Regulation (EEC) No 1408/71,[6] apply only to certain third-country nationals. The number and diversity of legal instruments used in an effort to resolve problems in connection with the coordination of the Member States' social security schemes encountered by nationals of third countries who are in the same situation as Community nationals give rise to legal and administrative complexities. They create major difficulties for the individuals concerned, their employers, and the competent national social security bodies.
(9) Hence, it is necessary to provide for the application of the coordination rules of Regulation (EEC) No 1408/71 and Regulation (EEC) No 574/72 to third-country nationals legally resident in the Community who are not currently covered by the provisions of these Regulations on grounds of their nationality and who satisfy the other conditions provided for in this Regulation; such an

---

[3] OJ C 154, 5.6.2000, p. 63
[4] OJ C 339, 231.12.1991, p. 82
[5] OJ L149, 5.7.1971, p. 2; Regulation last amended by Regulation (EC) No 1386/2001 of the European parliament and of the Council (OJ L187, 10.7.2001, p. 1)
[6] OJ L74, 27.3.1972, p. 1; Regulation last amended by Commission Regulation (EC) No 410/2002 (OJ L62 5.3.2002, p. 17).

extension is in particular important with a view to the forthcoming enlargement of the European Union.

(10) The application of Regulation (EEC) No 1408/71 and Regulation (EEC) No 574/72 to these persons does not give them any entitlement to enter, to stay or to reside in a Member State or to have access to its labour market.

(11) The provisions of Regulation (EEC) No 1408/71 and Regulation (EEC) No 574/72 are, by virtue of this Regulation, applicable only in so far as the person concerned is already legally resident in the territory of a Member State. Being legally resident is therefore a prerequisite for the application of these provisions.

(12) The provisions of Regulation (EEC) No 1408/71 and Regulation (EEC) No 574/72 are not applicable in a situation which is confined in all respects within a single Member State. This concerns, inter alia, the situation of a third country national who has links only with a third country and a single Member State.

(13) The continued right to unemployment benefit, as laid down in Article 69 of Regulation (EEC) No 1408/71, is subject to the condition of registering as a job-seeker with the employment services of each Member State entered. Those provisions may therefore apply to a third-country national only provided he/she has the right, where appropriate pursuant to his/her residence permit, to register as a job-seeker with the employment services of the Member State entered and the right to work there legally.

(14) Transitional provisions should be adopted to protect the persons covered by this Regulation and to ensure that they do not lose rights as a result of its entry into force.

(15) To achieve these objectives it is necessary and appropriate to extend the scope of the rules coordinating the national social security schemes by adopting a Community legal instrument which is binding and directly applicable in every Member State which takes part in the adoption of this Regulation.

(16) This Regulation is without prejudice to rights and obligation arising from international agreements with third countries to which the Community is a party and which afford advantages in terms of social security.

(17) Since the objectives of the proposed action cannot be sufficiently achieved by the Member States and can therefore, by reason of the scale or effects of the proposed action, be better achieved at Community level, the Community may take measures in accordance with the principle of subsidiarity enshrined in Article 5 of the Treaty. In compliance with the principle of proportionality as set out in that Article, this Regulation does not go beyond what is necessary to achieve these objectives.

(18) In accordance with Article 3 of the Protocol on the position of the United Kingdom and Ireland annexed to the Treaty on the European Union and to the Treaty establishing the European Community, Ireland and the United Kingdom gave notice, by letters of 19 and 23 April 2002, of their wish to take part in the adoption and application of this Regulation.

(19) In accordance with Articles 1 and 2 of the Protocol on the position of Denmark annexed to the Treaty on the European Union and to the Treaty establishing the European Community, Denmark is not taking part in the adoption of this Regulation and is not therefore bound by or subject to it,

HAS ADOPTED THIS REGULATION:

Article 1

Subject to the provisions of the Annex to this Regulation, the provisions of Regulation (EEC) No 1408/71 and Regulation (EEC) No 574/72 shall apply to nationals of third countries who are not already covered by those provisions solely on the ground of their nationality, as well as to members of their families and to their survivors, provided they are legally resident in the territory of a Member State and are in a situation which is not confined in all respects within a single Member State.

GENERAL NOTE

1.061   This short article enfranchises third country nationals into the scheme for the co-ordination of social security found in the two principal regulations where they are not already within that scheme. Some third country nationals are already covered by the rules in Regulation 1408/71, namely, stateless persons, refugees and members of families and survivors of Community nationals in the circumstances set out in Regulation 1408/71.

The condition for third country nationals is that they are "legally resident" in the territory of a Member State. This phrase is not defined, but will have to be applied by national authorities in accordance with their immigration laws. The most likely way forward will be that Member States will regard as legally resident all those whose immigration status is compliant with national requirements. But see for discussion of a slightly different phrase in a different context, *Szoma v Secretary of State for Work and Pensions*, Court of Appeal, Judgment of July 30, 2003, [2003] EWCA Civ 1131 in which the Court of Appeal ruled that, under United Kingdom social security regulations and in the context of asylum seekers, "persons subject to immigration control are not lawfully present in the United Kingdom." (para.34). Leave to appeal to the House of Lords is being sought in this case.

Note too that the extension of Regulation 1408/71 to third country nationals only relates to the co-ordination of schemes within the participating countries, and so has no application where the third country national has only had contact with the social security system of one Member State. So, for example, the regulation does not apply where an Australian national is living and working in the United Kingdom, and has had no contact with the social security system of any other Member State.

Article 2

1.062   1. This Regulation shall not create any rights in respect of the period before 1 June 2003.
2. Any period of insurance and, where appropriate, any period of employment, self-employment or residence completed under the legislation of a Member State before 1 June 2003 shall be taken into account for the determination of rights acquired in accordance with the provisions of this Regulation.
3. Subject to the provisions of paragraph 1, a right shall be acquired under this Regulation even if it relates to a contingency arising prior to 1 June 2003.

1.063   4. Any benefit that has not been awarded or that has been suspended on account of the nationality or the residence of the person concerned shall, at the latter's request, be awarded or resumed from 1 June 2003, provided that the rights for which benefits were previously awarded did not give rise to a lump-sum payment.
5. The rights of persons who prior to 1 June 2003, obtained the award of a pension may be reviewed at their request, account being taken of the provisions of this Regulation.
6. If the request referred to in paragraph 4 or paragraph 5 is lodged within two years from 1 June 2003, rights deriving from this Regulation shall be acquired from that date and the provisions of the legislation of any Member State on the forfeiture or lapse of rights may not be applied to the persons concerned.

7. If the request referred to in paragraph 4 or paragraph 5 is lodged after expiry of the deadline referred to in paragraph 6, rights not forfeited or lapsed shall be acquired from the date of such request, subject to any more favourable provisions of the legislation of any Member State.

GENERAL NOTE

This article deals with the temporal effect of the extension of the system of co-ordination to third country nationals. Rights may not be acquired prior to June 1, 2003, but periods of insurance or residence before that date may be taken into account in determining entitlement to a right accruing after June 1, 2003. So, periods of contribution prior to June 1, 2003 may be taken into account in determining whether there is entitlement to a benefit payable with effect from June 1, 2003 or later.

1.064

Article 3

This Regulation shall enter into force on the first day of the month following its publication in the Official Journal of the European Union.
This Regulation shall be binding in its entirety and directly applicable in the Member States in accordance with the Treaty establishing the European Community.
Done at Brussels, 14 May 2003.

ANNEX

SPECIAL PROVISIONS REFERRED TO IN ARTICLE 1

I. GERMANY

In the case of family benefits, this Regulation shall apply only to third-country nationals who are in possession of a residence permit meeting the definition in German law of the "Aufenthaltserlaubnis" or "Aufenthaltsberechtigung".

1.065

II. AUSTRIA

In the case of family benefits, this Regulation shall apply only to third-country nationals who fulfil the conditions laid down by Austrian legislation for permanent entitlement to family allowances.

PART II

UPDATING MATERIAL
VOLUME I

NON-MEANS TESTED BENEFITS

pp.54–57, *annotation to Social Security Contributions and Benefits Act 1992, s.30DD: reduction for pension payments*

2.001

Reduction can only come into play where a pension payment is "payable to" the person entitled to incapacity benefit. So, in *CIB 638/2003,* Commissioner Turnbull held that, where under a court order part of the claimant's occupational pension was paid over by the pension trustees to his former spouse, that part of the pension so paid over was not "payable to" the claimant, it could not be taken into account in effecting a reduction, and the remainder which was payable to him fell below the threshold so that no reduction of incapacity benefit could be made. The Commissioner did not find helpful decisions on abatement of unemployment benefit (*R(U)4/83* and *R(U)8/83*) since the statutory wording there referred to payments which "fall to be made to him". Nor was a decision on income support (*R(IS)4/01*) in point since the issue there was whether the payments constituted part of the claimant's "income". He noted that the "earmarking" provisions in financial settlements on divorce had been operative for some four years before s.30DD was inserted by the Welfare Reform and Pensions Act 1999. He thought

> "it reasonable to infer that it would have been apparent to the framers of s.30DD that one of the common situations in which it would fall to be applied was that where an earmarking order had been made. I think that there is some argument for saying that, if it had been intended that sums which by such an order are required to be paid to W should be treated for the purposes of s.30DD(1) as nevertheless payable to H, the opportunity would have been taken expressly so to provide" (para. 15).

p.66, *annotation to Social Security Contributions and Benefits Act 1992, s.38: non-statutory payments to widowers*

2.002

The case of *Hooper v Secretary of State for Work and Pensions* [2003] EWCA Civil 813, [2003] 3 All E.R. 673 has now been considered in the Court of Appeal, and the claimant's appeal allowed in part. Leave has been given, however, for both parties to appeal to the House of Lords and the final outcome remains uncertain.

The Court of Appeal upheld the trial judge's ruling that the 1992 legislation was incompatible with the non discrimination provisions of the Human Rights Act 1998 once the latter act came into force October 4, 2000, but they held also, that the failure to make non-statutory discretionary payments of an amount equal to those that would have been paid as a Widow's payment, and Widowed mother's allowance to a widow from that date, was discriminatory. One claimant was, therefore, entitled to a payment of £1000 equal to a Widow's payment. In principle he and others would also have been entitled to sums in respect of Widowed mother's allowance but for the fact that they were, at the relevant time, in receipt of Income Support and were not, for the present at least, shown to have suffered any loss. A failure to receive a payment equivalent to Widow's pension was held to be not compensatable because the payment of pension to a widow in respect of a death occurring after 1995 was held to be unjustifiably generous in favour of the widow and to make an equally irrational payment to a widower was not regarded as "just satisfaction". Nor did the Court think that the policy followed by the department in making friendly settlements in favour of pre-1998 Act claimants only after they had succeeded in showing that their claim was admissible in the European Court of Human Rights, could be regarded, in itself, as being an independent violation of convention rights. For further comment see Volume III (main volume).

2.003 **pp.86–87,** *annotation to Social Security Contributions and Benefits Act 1992, s.43: priority between pensions when claimant is entitled to more than one pension*

In *Secretary of State for Work and Pensions v Nelligan* [2003] EWCA Civ 555, [2004] 4 All E.R. 171 the application of s.43(5) is explained. The claimant had retired in 1986 at the age of 60 and claimed for, and received, her Category A pension. When her husband retired some six years later he too received a Category A pension. The claimant could then have claimed a Category B pension, and had she done so, would have received more than her existing pension. The claimant did not realise this until a further eight years later when she made a claim for the extra payment to be backdated for that period. The Court of Appeal's decision limits the extent of backdating to three months, the maximum period permitted under the Claims and Payments Regulations.

Section 43(5) operates, they explain, only to declare priority between pensions when the claimant is entitled to them both. Under s.1 of the SSA 1992 the claimant was not entitled to the Category B pension until she had made a claim for it. And therefore there was nothing for s.43(5) to act upon earlier.

2.004 While such interpretation would seem to make the bracketed words in this section almost useless, they are reinvigorated by a provision in the Claims and Payments Regulations that permits a claim for one pension to be treated as a claim for another as well. Thus a pensioner may claim only a Category A pension, but if they are at the same time entitled to a Category B, the claim can be treated as made for both, and under s.43(5) the claimant will be paid the greater amount. Unfortunately this provision could not aid the claimant in the present case because the claimant must qualify for both pensions at the time the claim for one of them is made; in this case when she claimed the Category A pension in 1986 that was the only pension to which she was entitled because her husband had then not retired.

pp.101–102, *annotation to Social Security Contributions and Benefits Act 1992, s.52, special provision for surviving spouses, calculation of additional pension in a Category A Pension*

2.005 The operation of s.52(3) is examined in *R(P) 1/03*. The case concerned the calculation of the additional pension and the treatment of a guaranteed minimum pension derived from an occupational pension scheme which, under s.46 of the Pension Schemes Act, had to be deducted from that entitlement. The claimant contended that this deduction should be made from the additional pension derived only from her own earnings as an intermediate stage in calculating the pension. The Secretary of State, on the other hand, contended that the GMP deduction fell to be made only at the end of the calculation process. The difference was significant in this case (some £35 per week) because it meant that the claimant avoided the cap (the "prescribed maximum") in s.52(3). The tribunal had found in favour of the claimant—her argument had the advantage that it seems natural to attach the GMP deduction only to the additional pension element to which it related. But Commissioner Williams allowed the Secretary of State's appeal. He finds the wording of s.46 clear, it provides for a deduction to be made from the pension to which the claimant is entitled, and this could only mean the deduction is made from the rate of Category A or Category B pension as finally determined. To have decided otherwise created other anomalies in the legislation.

p.135, *annotation to Social Security Contributions and Benefits Act 1992, s.72: conduct of tribunal in determining disability*

A tribunal which must determine whether the claimant is so severely disabled as to qualify for the care component, must reach its conclusion in accordance with the restrictions imposed upon it by s.20(3) of the SSA 1998. This section prevents the tribunal from making a physical examination of the claimant and it precludes a physical test for the purposes of the mobility component of DLA. It does not, however, prevent the tribunal from reaching a conclusion based upon their observation of the claimant's physical abilities, or based upon his response to questions that test what he is capable of doing and, except in relation to mobility, it does not prevent the tribunal asking the claimant to carry out a simple physical task, *e.g.,* to pick an object up from the floor. The claimant may refuse, but in that case the tribunal may draw an inference from his refusal provided that in doing so they make due allowance for any reason he may give for that refusal. (See *CDLA/3967/2002* and commentary to Section 20 in Volume III [main volume].) 2.006

pp.140–141, *annotation to Social Security Contributions and Benefits Act 1992 s.72, attention in connection with bodily functions*

The Court of Appeal gave further consideration to this phrase in *Ramsden v Secretary of State for Work and Pensions* [2003] EWCA Civ 32, R(DLA) 2/03. The claimant, aged twelve, was faecally incontinent as a result of spina bifida, but for psychological reasons did not wear incontinence pads. He soiled himself once or twice a day and required attention from his mother in cleaning him up in a bath and shower, and also cleaning up the clothes, towels, bedding, carpets, furniture and other surfaces that had been fouled. On a renewal claim the AO refused to renew and that decision was upheld by a tribunal. The tribunal took into account the washing of the claimant, and the rinsing of his soiled clothing, bedding, etc, but specifically excluded any time spent in laundering the clothing etc as required, in their view, by the decision in 2.007

Cockburn. The tribunal made no overt reference to the time spent cleaning carpets, furniture, and other surfaces, though, in the proceedings that followed, it was assumed that that time, too, was excluded on the basis that it was not sufficiently closely connected with the child's bodily function. A Commissioner upheld the tribunal decision.

2.008 The Court of Appeal, in allowing the appeal, reviewed thoroughly the speeches in *Cockburn*. That case, they concluded, recognised that certain acts of attendance performed by way of cleaning-up after an incident of incontinence could qualify as acts of attendance for the purpose of this benefit. Potter, L.J., giving the first judgement continued:

> "Within the constraints of the requirement that such cleaning-up should take place in the presence or the vicinity of the applicant, I consider that steps taken for the **immediate** removal of soiling from clothes, towels or bed linen or adjacent surfaces are apt to qualify under this head. In a case of faecal incontinence which results in the soiling of clothes, towels or bed linen, or the dropping or smearing of faeces on carpets or furniture, it is at the very least in the interests of hygiene that such occurrences be rectified immediately as a part and parcel of the cleaning-up operation necessary following the incident of incontinence giving rise to such soiling. If that is done, then, even if the operation concerned is one of thorough washing rather than merely 'rinsing', the criteria of immediacy and intimacy are sufficiently satisfied and the time spent in cleaning-up should be taken into account when assessing whether or not the attention given amounts to a significant portion of the day".

The court returned the case to a fresh tribunal to consider whether the attention amounted to "a significant portion of the day". On that point, too, they take a flexible view of what is meant by "significant".

p.141, *annotation to Social Security Contributions and Benefits Act 1992, s.72: attention in connection with bodily functions, Asbergers Syndrome*

2.009 The decision of Commissioner Howell in *CDLA 131/01* has now been reported as *R(DLA) 3/03*.

p.144, *annotation to Social Security Contributions and Benefits Act 1992, s.72: attention in connection with bodily functions, pre-lingually deaf*

2.010 The decision of Commissioner Parker in *CSA 721/00* has now been reported as *R(A) 1/03*. This lends approval to the views expressed there.

p.145, *annotation to Social Security Contributions and Benefit Act 1992, s.72: significant portion of the day*

2.010a Several points on the meaning of this phrase are also resolved in *Ramsden v Secretary of State for Work and Pensions* [2003] EWCA Civ 32, R(DLA) 2/03. First, this case determines that the meaning of the word "day" is to be consistent with the day remaining as a residue of 24 hours when the "night" has been accounted for as in *R. v National Insurance Commissioner Ex p. Secretary of State for Social Services* [1974] 1 W.L.R. 1290; in other words it is the period between the time when the household becomes active in the morning and when its members finally retire to bed at night. The decision in CDLA/1463/99 is thus overruled and those in CDLA/5419/99 and R(DLA) 8/02 are preferred. While this undoubtedly is the better interpretation of the section it does seem to work unjustly in the case of a claimant who requires some, though not significant, attention, during the day and one, far more disruptive, event at night, because unless the night time attention is prolonged or repeated, it appears that that attention cannot be accounted for at all. On the other hand, of course, by limiting the time period of day it does become easier for the claimant to show that his day time attention is significant as a proportion of that period.

The Court of Appeal also endorses the view that the phrase "significant portion" should be interpreted so as to make a "broad determination" of the question. Lord Justice Potter, giving the leading judgment, accepts that the task for the tribunal is principally a mathematical exercise involving comparison of the aggregate of time spent in giving attention, with the day as a whole. But he continues,

"However it is also likely to be affected by the total time available in the day, by the extent to which the relevant tasks become a matter of routine, and the concentration and intensity of the activity comprised in those tasks. Thus while in broad terms it seems to me that a period of one hour, made up of two half-hour periods [of] concentrated activity, would reasonably be regarded as a significant portion of a day, in different circumstances there may well be room for a different view."

This passage is followed by one in which Potter, L.J. expressly approves the reasoning in CSDLA/29/94 in which Commissioner Walker puts forward the view that the day, and the "significant portion" of it, must be assessed from the position of the attender. Combining this with the decision of the Court of Appeal it would seem now possible to argue that, for an attender with an especially long and busy day, the time spent attending does become significant when it might not be for someone who was otherwise largely idle. For the busy attender, the time spent attending is significant because without it their day might seem already full. Or, again, if the tasks required are arduous and physically or mentally demanding the time spent becomes significant because the effect of those tasks may be to exhaust the attender—for him or her their "day" (in then sense of what is achievable) would be largely used up. On the other hand if the tasks become routine and can be fitted in to the attender's regular daily pattern of life they will offer less inconvenience and may become a less than significant part of their "day".

2.010b

As to the "one-hour" rule of thumb used by many tribunals, this case makes clear that there is no such minimum period—CDLA 58/93 must to that extent be overruled. While, no doubt, tribunals may still choose to centre their thinking around a total time period of an hour, it is now clear that they must reach their decision on the basis of their own common sense and judgment of what is significant and explain that in their reasoning.

p.146, *annotation to Social Security Contributions and Benefits Act 1992, s.72: the cooking test*

2.011   The decision in *Moyna v Secretary of State for Work and Pensions* [2003] 4 All E.R. 162 in the House of Lords, has allowed the appeal and restored the decision of the Commissioner. The Commissioner's decision had been that a claimant who could not cook a main meal on one to three days of the week could still be regarded as capable of cooking for the purposes of the s.72 cooking test. In his view a tribunal which had so found could not be said to have made an error of law. The Court of Appeal allowed an appeal on the basis that the test should be more precise and that someone who was unable to prepare a meal on a regular and not infrequent basis could not be said to be capable of cooking—to say so, in their view, was to make an error of law. The House of Lords disagree. They reaffirm the view of Commissioner that the test is a more general one of overall impression and to reach a decision on it with which others may disagree, cannot be said to be an error of law.

But this does leave us in some difficulty, for if the tribunal had found initially that Mrs Moyna was not capable of cooking then, it would seem, that too would have been a decision that was properly made and could not be reviewed as an error of law. This does nothing to assist tribunals hearing appeals in the case of claimants whose abilities fluctuate within the nine month period for qualification. The House of Lords make clear that the test is not one of frequency (only the claim form for the benefit introduces the matter of the number of days on which the claimant is unable to cook a meal) and they make clear also that it never has been the case that a claimant's inability to cook must be total throughout the qualifying period, but beyond that their Lordships leave it to the good sense of tribunals to decide whether a claimant is capable of cooking, by "taking 'a broad view' of the matter and making a judgment". It is, they say "an exercise in judgment rather than in arithmetical calculation of frequency".

p.162, *annotation to Social Security Contributions and Benefits Act 1992, s.73: claimant who would not walk on unfamiliar routes with supervision not disqualified*

2.012   A person qualifies for mobility component at the lower rate under paragraph (d) even though they may never undertake to walk on unfamiliar routes. The test is hypothetical in the sense that the claimant is entitled if they could not walk that route without guidance or supervision—it matters not that they would not walk there anyway. In *CDLA/ 2106/2002* the tribunal had found that the claimant (to whom they had already refused M.A. at the higher rate) would not have gone walking on unfamiliar routes (or seemingly on familiar routes) because of the danger of falling. It seems that the claimant must have said that the provision of supervision would have made no difference to her because the chairman went on to remark "There is no point in making an award if its purpose is frustrated". The Commissioner allowed the appeal remarking that the element of an award being frustrated is provided for in subs. (8), but that provision requires that the claimant be *unable* to benefit from locomotion not merely that he chooses not to.

p.163, *annotation to Social Security Contributions and Benefits Act 1992, s.73(4): child requiring substantially more guidance and supervision than another person at his age*

Subsection (4) imposes the same conditions upon a claim made in respect of child as those provided for in s.72(6). A recent decision of Commissioner Parker (*CSDLA/91/2003*) applies the same reasoning to the conditions for mobility as that adopted for the care component. When guidance and supervision is required it must be substantially more than would be required for a child of that age of normal physical and mental development. In judging what is substantially more, account must be taken of both the quality and the quantity of the supervision. Thus where all children might need to be accompanied on a certain route, a disabled child who required support, or restraint, or encouragement, or even constant surveillance should qualify. 2.013

pp.193–202, *annotation to Social Security Contributions and Benefits Act 1992, s.94(1): caused by accident, the accident/process distinction*

The "accident/process" distinction continues to pose problems for decision makers and appellate bodies, including Commissioners and Courts, the more so since it is accepted that a series of accidents (as "accident" is understood in *CAO v Faulds*) constitutes "accident" (within the scheme) rather than "process" (outside the scheme unless the case can be covered by the Prescribed Diseases Regulations). 2.014

In *CI 3511/2002*, Commissioner Fellner considered the case of an ambulance technician incapacitated because of work-related stress. The single person tribunal erred in law by holding that the claimant was entitled to an industrial accident declaration because this was a case of accident by process. Commissioner Fellner held that the case fell on the "process" side of the line—there was no identifiable accident or series of accidents. In doing so she considered the decision of the Court of Session Second Division in *Mullen v Secretary of State for Work and Pensions* [2002] S.L.T. 149, a Scottish case, not binding on her but merely of persuasive value. There that court held that a former assistant care officer incapacitated by back pain brought about through lifting patients had suffered a series of accidents over a seven-year period, and had thus suffered injury caused by accident, even though it was not possible to identify the date of each of the accidents or to state which of them, if not all, caused or contributed to the back condition. It considered that "process" was in contrast typical of cases where a condition (it gave as examples pneumoconiosis or asbestosis) develops gradually and imperceptibly over a period of time.

2.015 Commissioner Fellner distinguished *Mullen* on the basis that there were there specific and identifiable physical injuries each of which could be described as an accident. Instead she followed another persuasive Scottish authority, *CSI 371/2001* (not available on the Commissioners' website) which had placed on the process side of the line a case where a civil servant had suffered stress and anxiety because of excessive workload and a number of incidents of friction with his line manager, whom he saw as unreasonable. The tribunal had not there been prepared to find that the claimant's appreciation of excessive workload was the sort of triggering event that had enabled success in *CI 554/1992* (main volume, pp.198–199), one of the rare cases where mental injury through stress resulted from accident. As Commissioner Fellner noted, on balance, stress illnesses are more likely to arise through process rather than accident (para.14). It is, therefore, fortunate that the Industrial Injuries Advisory Council is soon to publish a position paper on whether, and in what circumstances, work-related stress and its effects might be added to the list of prescribed industrial diseases (*Annual Report 2002, http://www.iiac.org.uk/annrep/intro2002.shtm*).

However, as Commissioner Howell made clear in *CI 4708/2001*, work related stress can arise through accident where one can identify an event which produced a pathological change for the worse in the claimant's condition. Referring the tribunal to which he remitted the case to *CI 105/1998* (main volume, p.197), he further emphasised that

"in the light of present more up-to-date knowledge about the way people can suffer breakdowns and stress reactions to particular events, it should no longer be taken to be the law, if ever it was, that words alone can never give rise to an 'accident' for this purpose" (para.11).

2.016 Note also that, as emphasised by Commissioner Rowland in *CI 1714/2002*, it is not necessary for the claimant to identify when the accident took place more precisely than necessary for the determination of the claim, so that there "the summer of 1978" sufficed (para.10). The key point is rather that the tribunal should be satisfied that an accident occurred (see also *CI 278/1993* [main volume, p.198]), and on this aspect it is important to note that the law does not require corroboration of the claimant's evidence if the tribunal believe that evidence (para.11).

As always where fine distinctions need to be made, it is not easy to reconcile all the cases. As Commissioner Howell put it in *CI 4708/2001*, it is a difficult and invidious line for decision-makers and tribunals to have to draw (paras 6, 11). Indeed *Mullen* sits uneasily with Scottish decisions that brain damage suffered over the course of a football career through repeatedly heading the old style leather football constituted injury through process rather than a series of identifiable accidents. The Industrial Injuries Advisory Council is to examine that among the whole area of sports injuries (*Annual Report 2002, ibid.*).

pp.235–236, Social Security Contributions and Benefits Act 1992, s.114 amendment

With effect from April 6, 2003, s.114(4) is amended by the Tax Credits Act 2002, s.47 and Sch.3, paras 24 and 34 to read as follows:

2.017

"(4) The provisions in question are section 56, 82 to 84, 86 and paragraphs 5 and 6 of Schedule 7 to this Act."

p.299, annotation to Social Security Contributions and Benefits Act 1992, Sch.6, para.1: assessment of disablement—the limits of comparison

As Commissioner Fellner rightly noted in a deafness case, CI 5092/2002

2.018

"It must not be forgotten that the comparison under Schedule 6 is simply with another person of the same age and sex, and that individual hobbies and preferences are not to be taken into account. Thus, this claimant's complaints of loss of pleasure in particular kinds of music and in birdsong, and having to have the TV volume high, are relevant only in so far as other men of his age might be able to have, or not to be burdened with, these things. His being a radio ham, as he told the tribunal, would not be relevant" (para.17).

p.392, Home Responsibilities Regulations 1994: insertion of definition of "foster parent" into reg.1(2)

With effect from September 1, 2003, reg.2(2) of the Social Security Pensions (Home Responsibilities) Amendment Regulations 2003 (SI 2003/1767) inserted after the definition of "child benefit" the following definition:

2.019

" "foster parent" means a person approved as—
(a) a foster parent in accordance with the provisions of Part IV of the Fostering Services Regulations 2002 (approval of foster parents); or
(b) a foster carer in accordance with the provisions of Part II of the Fostering of Children (Scotland) Regulations 1996 (approval of foster carers);"

pp.392–393, Home Responsibilities Regulations 1994: amendment of regulation 2 (preclusion from regular employment)

With effect from September 1, 2003, regulation 2(3) of the Social Security Pensions (Home Responsibilities) Amendment Regulations 2003 (SI 2003/1767) amended regulation 2(2) to read—

2.020

"(2) The conditions specified in this paragraph are—
(a) that child benefit awarded to him was payable in respect of a child under the age of 16;

(b) that—
: (i) as a person to whom paragraph 4 of Schedule 1 to the Income Support (General) Regulations 1987 applies he is not required to be available for employment, and
: (ii) income support is payable to him;

[(c) that he was a foster parent.]"

2.021 With effect from the same date, regulation 2(4) of those amending regulations amended regulation 2(5) by inserting sub-paragraph (aa):

"(5) Except where paragraph (6) below applies, paragraph (1) above shall not apply in relation to any year—
: (a) if the person in question is a woman who has made or is treated as having made an election in accordance with regulations having effect under section 19(4) of the Act and that election had effect at the beginning of that year; or
: [(aa) in the case of a person who satisfies the condition in paragraph (2)(c) above in respect of the year 2003–04 or any subsequent year, if he does not furnish such information as the Secretary of State may from time to time require which is relevant to the question of whether in that year he was precluded from regular employment by responsibilities at home within the meaning of these Regulations; or]"
: (b) in the case of a person who satisfies the conditions in paragraph (3) above in respect of any year preceding 2002–2003, if he does not furnish such information as the Secretary of State may from time to time require which is relevant to the question of whether in that year he was precluded from regular employment by responsibilities at home within the meaning of these Regulations; or
: (c) in the case of a person who satisfies the conditions in paragraph (3) above in respect of the year 2002–2003 or any subsequent year, if he does not, within the period of three years immediately following the end of that year, furnish such information as the Secretary of State may from time to time require which is relevant to the question of which is relevant to the question of whether, in that year, he was precluded from regular employment by responsibilities at home within the meaning of these Regulations."

p.394, *annotation to Home Responsibilities Protection Regulations 1994, reg.2*

2.022 The effect of the amendments to regulation 2, set out above in the update to pp.392–393, is to provide that home responsibilities protection shall be available to a person who is to be taken to have been precluded from regular employment by responsibilities at home in respect of the year 2003–04 and any subsequent year throughout which he was an approved foster parent.

p.451, *Hospital In-Patients Regulations 1975, reg.2 amendment*

With effect from May 21, 2003 the definition of "38% of basic pension" is omitted: The Social Security (Hospital In-Patients and Miscellaneous Amendments) Regulations 2003, SI 2003/1195, reg.2.

2.023

p.456, *Hospital In-Patients Regulations 1975, insertion of new reg.4 and annotation*

With effect from May 21, 2003 (or the first pay day following that day), a new reg.4 is inserted by The Social Security (Hospital In-Patients and Miscellaneous Amendments) Regulations 2003, SI 2003/1195, reg.2, into the regulations as follows,

2.024

"Circumstances in which personal benefit is to be adjusted.

4. Where a person
   (d) receives, or has received, free in-patient treatment continuously for a period of more than 52 weeks; and
   (e) satisfies the conditions for the receipt of a personal benefit which is specified in Schedule 2 to these regulations,
for any part of the period after the 52nd week the weekly rate of that benefit shall be adjusted in accordance with regulation 6."

GENERAL NOTE

This and the related amendments make major changes to the rules on the reduction in benefit for those in hospital. The general pattern across the affected benefits is that there are two stages of reduction. The first operated after six weeks followed by a further reduction at 52 weeks. These amendments remove the reduction which occurs after six weeks. There is now only one reduction which takes effect after 52 weeks.

2.025

Regulation 4 is re-drafted so as only to refer to 52 week reductions; and reg. 5 is omitted. The effect is that those without a dependant will now have their benefit reduced after 52 weeks to 20 per cent of basic retirement pension rate.

As regards adult dependency additions, reg.11 is amended to refer only to a reduction after 52 weeks.

There is no change to the rule in reg.13 relating to child dependency additions which provides for a reduction after 12 weeks to such rate (if any) as the claimant is actually spending on the child.

The special rules in reg.17 on persons admitted to hospital from care accommodation, the general effect of which was that they were subject to the 52 week rate of reduction either immediately in the case of persons from local authority homes or after six weeks in the case of persons from private sector homes, is abolished. So in future such persons will receive their full benefit for the first 52 weeks like everyone else.

p.456, *Hospital In-Patients Regulations 1975, reg.4A amendment*

With effect from May 21, 2003 (or the first pay day following that day), reg.2(4) of The Social Security (Hospital In-Patients and Miscellaneous Amendments) Regulations 2003 (SI 2003/1195) amends reg.4A(1) by omitting the words "5 or".

2.026

45

p.457, *Hospital In-Patients Regulations 1975, reg.5 omitted*

2.027   With effect from May 21, 2003 (or the first pay day following that day), reg.2(5) of The Social Security (Hospital In-Patients and Miscellaneous Amendments) Regulations 2003 (SI 2003/1195) omits reg.5.

p.457, *Hospital In-Patients Regulations 1975, reg.6 amendment*

2.028   With effect from May 21, 2003 (or the first pay day following that day), reg.2(6) of The Social Security (Hospital In-Patients and Miscellaneous Amendments) Regulations 2003 (SI 2003/1195) amends reg.6 by substituting "4" for "4(d)2 in both places where it occurs.

p.459, *Hospital In-Patients Regulations 1975, reg.9 amendment*

2.029   With effect from May 21, 2003 (or the first pay day following that day), reg.2(7) of The Social Security (Hospital In-Patients and Miscellaneous Amendments) Regulations 2003 (SI 2003/1195) amends reg.9(b) by substituting "52" in place of "6".

pp.459–450, *Hospital In-Patients Regulations 1975, reg.11: insertion of new para.(1)*

2.030   With effect from May 21, 2003 (or the first pay day following that day), reg.2(8) of The Social Security (Hospital In-Patients and Miscellaneous Amendments) Regulations 2003 (SI 2003/1195), inserts new reg.11(1) as follows,

"(1) Subject to paragraph (3), in a case to which regulation 9(d) applies, for any part of a period of continuous free in-patient treatment which the dependant receives after the 52nd week of such continuous treatment, the weekly rate of dependency benefit payable to the beneficiary shall be adjusted so that 20% of the basic pension is payable."

The same provisions substitute "(1)" for "(1)(b)" in paragraph (3).

pp.462–464, *Hospital In-Patients Regulations 1975, reg.17*

2.031   With effect from May 21, 2003 (or the first pay day following that day), reg.2(9) of The Social Security (Hospital In-Patients and Miscellaneous Amendments) Regulations 2003 (SI 2003/1195) omits paragraphs (2), (3) and (6), and, in paragraph (4) omits the words "(or is regarded under this regulation as having received)".

p.517, *Polygamous Marriages Regulations 1975, reg.2: insertion of an annotation*

GENERAL NOTE

2.032   In *CG/2611/2003* the Commissioner was determining an appeal in relation to a claim for widow's benefit in respect of a man who married three times. It seems that that the husband, a Bangladeshi, entered into his first marriage in Bangladesh in the early 1960s. In 1968 he married the claimant in Bangladesh in accordance with Muslim law. Some time in the 1970s the husband took a third wife in Bangladesh. At the time of the husband's death, there was some uncertainty about the status of the first marriage, but the second and third marriages were still subsisting. The second wife claimed widow's benefit. The Secretary of State's argument was that the claim to widow's benefit must be disallowed because the husband had contracted polygamous marriages, at least two of which subsisted at his death, and the claimant was not the husband's only wife at the date he died. Under the Polygamous Marriages Regulations 1975, the claim could only succeed if, at the material time, the marriage was, in fact, monogamous.

The tribunal had concluded that at the time of the marriage to the claimant, the husband was domiciled in the United Kingdom. The Commissioner casts doubt on the correctness of that conclusion but refers the matter back to a fresh tribunal for determination. Were it to be correct, then the marriage contracted with the claimant would have been void by the law of the husband's domicile.

The decision highlights the need for the most careful (and consistent) findings of fact in these complex cases. The place of domicile of the husband at the dates of each of the marriages he contracts will be of fundamental importance in determining the validity of those marriages and consequently the application of the Polygamous Marriages Regulations 1975 to any claim for benefit.

p.529, *Attendance Allowance Regulations 1991: amendment of reg.7 to remove disqualification where care may be paid for from public or local funds*

With effect from October 6, 2003 reg.7 was amended by reg.2 of the Social Security (Attendance Allowance and Disability Living Allowance) (Amendment) Regulations 2000 (SI 2003/2259) as follows: 2.033

(a) in paragraph (1)
  (i) omit the words "Except in the cases specified in paragraphs (2) and (3) and";
  (ii) insert "or" at the end of subparagraph (a);
  (iii) omit "or" at the end of subparagraph (b) and omit subparagraph (c).
(b) omit paragraphs (3) and (4).

p.532, *Attendance Allowance Regulations 1991: amendment of reg.8 to remove disqualification in certain cases where care is paid for from person's own resources*

With effect from October 6, 2003, reg.8 was amended by reg.2 of the Social Security (Attendance Allowance and Disability Living Allowance) (Amendment Regulations) 2003 (SI 2003/2259) as follows: 2.034

(a) in paragraph (6)
  (i) omit subparagraph (a) and the word "and" which follows it;
  (ii) in subparagraph (b)(i) omit the words "his own resources" where they first appear, and substitute "the resources of the person for whom it is provided";

(iii) at the end of subparagraph (b)(i) insert "or".

pp. 545–546, *Disability Living Allowance Regulations 1991, amendment of reg. 9 to remove disqualification where care may be paid for from public or local funds*

2.035   With effect from October 6, 2003 reg.9 was amended by reg.3 of the Social Security (Attendance Allowance and Disability Living Allowance) (Amendment) Regulations 2003 (SI 2003/2259) as follows:

"(a) in paragraph (1)
   (i) omit the words "paragraphs (1A) to (4)" and substitute "paragraphs (1A) to (2A)";
   (ii) after subparagraph (a) insert "or";
   (iii) omit the word "or" after subparagraph (b) and omit subparagraph (c);
(b) in paragraph (1A) omit the words "and (c)" and the words "or may be";
(c) in paragraph (2)(c) omit the words "or may be";
(d) omit paragraphs (4), (5) and (7)."

pp. 549–550, *Disability Living Allowance Regulations 1991, amendment of reg. 10 to remove disqualification in certain cases where care is paid for from person's own resources*

2.036   With effect from October 6, 2003, reg.10 was amended by reg.3 of the Social Security (Attendance Allowance and Disability Living Allowance) (Amendment) Regulations 2003 (SI 2003/2259) as follows:

"in paragraph (8)
   (i) omit subparagraph (a)
   (ii) in subparagraph (b)(i) omit the words "person's own resources" and substitute "resources of the person for whom it is provided"."

p. 558, *annotation to Disability Living Allowance Regulations 1991 reg. 12: virtually unable to walk*

2.037   In *CSDLA 667/2002*, Commissioner Parker has given further consideration to the relationship between walking ability and severe discomfort. The appellant had appealed against refusal of benefit arguing that his walking ability should be assessed only up to the point when he began to experience severe discomfort. In decision *CSDLA 678/99* a Commissioner had said that severe discomfort—

"may onset and then be relieved by rest so that a further distance can be walked before further onset. In such a case the test stops at the first onset."

Commissioner Parker rejects this view as making an unwarranted gloss upon the statutory definition. "Without severe discomfort" is not the same, she argues, as before the onset of severe discomfort. To apply the test in that way would be to devalue the test of overall walking ability contained in the distance–time–speed formula provided by the regulation. The phrase "without discomfort" means that the claimant is not to be assessed with the inclusion of any progress that he makes only while suffering that discomfort, but so long as the rest time taken to avoid or relieve discomfort is included in the overall time taken for a journey then the consequent calculation of speed will reflect the degree of disablement he suffers. A person who can progress with short, and infrequent periods of rest will probably be able to walk for this purpose; someone who requires frequent or prolonged stops probably will not. The judgement of distance, time and speed is then a matter of fact for the tribunal.

p.653, *Incapacity Benefit Regulations 1994: insertion of a new regulation 7C*

With effect from May 5, 2003, reg.2 of the Social Security (Incapacity Benefit) (Her Majesty's Forces) (Amendment) Regulations 2003 (SI 2003/1068) inserted after reg.7B a new reg.7C reading as follows: 2.038

"Inclusion of days of sickness absence from duty before discharge from Her Majesty's forces in calculating days of entitlement to incapacity benefit

7C.—(1) For the purpose of section 30D(3A) of the Contributions and Benefits Act (days to be included in respect of person discharged from Her Majesty's forces after 3rd May 2003 when calculating the number of days for which the person has been entitled to short-term incapacity benefit) there is prescribed any day which falls within a period—
(a) of 4 or more consecutive days each of which is a day which is recorded by the Secretary of State for Defence as a day on which the person was on sickness absence from duty; and
(b) which ends not more than 8 weeks before the first day of the period to which the claim for incapacity benefit relates.
(2) For the purpose of paragraph (1)(a) any two such periods not separated by a period of more than 8 weeks shall be treated as one period."

The effect of this had already been noted in the annotations to SSCBA 1992, ss.30A(3), 30C(3) and 30D(3A), noting modifications to those sections in respect of a member of Her Majesty's Forces for whom days of sickness absence (recorded by the Secretary of State for Defence) are included in calculating the number of days for which such a person has been entitled to short-term incapacity benefit. Those modifications were effected by the Social Security Contributions and Benefits Act 1992 (Modifications for Her Majesty's Forces and Incapacity Benefit) Regulations 2003 (SI 2003/737) [main volume pp.781–782]. This regulation stipulates the days to be counted as ones of entitlement to short-term incapacity benefit.

p.653, *Incapacity Benefit Regulations 1994, reg. 8: increase in the limit of earnings from councillor's allowance*

2.039   The amount in square brackets was misstated as £66.00 from October 1, 2002. It should have read £67.50, a change effected by reg.3 of SI 2002/2311. With effect from October 1, 2003, it was further increased to £72 by reg.3 of the Social Security (Incapacity) (Miscellaneous Amendments) Regulations 2003 (SI 2003/2262).

pp.687–688, *annotation to Incapacity for Work (General) Regulations 1995, reg. 8: meaning of "sent" and good cause for failure to attend*

2.040   In *CIB 1381/2003*, Deputy Commissioner Wikeley declined, after reviewing a range of authority on analogous provisions in child support and jobseeker's allowance, to determine whether "sent" meant "despatched" or "delivered", since a failure to attend because of not receiving the notice could in any event constitute "good cause" as the tribunal had held.

pp.694–695, *annotation to Incapacity for Work (General) Regulations 1995, reg. 13: deemed incapacity, the personal capability assessment and contributions credits*

2.041   As Commissioner Levenson pointed out in *CIB 2397/2002*, only para. (3) of the regulation deals with the position of those in work on days other than when they receive dialysis. Consequently, whether for benefit purposes or those of contributions credits, regulation 13 treats days of receipt of dialysis as ones of incapacity. But what of the person claiming credits who must establish under the personal capability assessment incapacity throughout the week? Commissioner Levenson applied to the claimant in that case (someone receiving dialysis on three days a week) the broad approach developed in *R(IB) 2/99*, holding her incapable of work throughout the week, the evidence showing that she was more tired on the other days even though on them she was relatively well.

pp.697–698, *annotation to Incapacity for Work (General) Regulations 1995, reg. 13A: welfare to work beneficiary: the notice aspect of reg. 13A(1)(d)(i)*

2.042   In *CIB 1886/2003* and *CIB 1887/2003* (decided together), Commissioner Jacobs drew on *R(U) 3/85*, *R(SB) 8/89* and *CI 337/1992*, to lay down the following principles of law to govern the case before him:

"The circumstances of this case are different from those in all of those decisions I have cited. But they are covered by the principles on which those decisions are based.

What are those principles? The Secretary of State has a legitimate interest in ensuring that action is taken within the time period specified in the legislation. But that interest is less when the information is provided too soon than when it is provided too late. If information is provided too soon and the Secretary of State does not require the claimant to comply with the time limit, the information will be treated as received and held as inchoate until the time begins to run. Certainly, this will be so if the Secretary of State effectively prevents the claimant from complying within the time specified by not giving notice of the need to comply.

In this case, the claimant provided the relevant information to the Secretary of State, but did so too soon. He was prevented from providing it later and in accordance with the legislation, because the Secretary of State did not notify him of the need to do so. In those circumstances, he was not in a position to exercise his right to preserve his position in accordance with the legislation because the Secretary of State had effectively prevented it" (paras 18–20).

He left open the question of how those principles apply where the claimant was never given notice by the Secretary of State and failed to provide the information until it was too late under the legislation (para.22).

p.700, *annotation to Incapacity for Work Regulations 1995, reg.15*

In *CIB/399/2003*, Commissioner Mesher very firmly rejects the approach of Deputy Commissioner Mark in *CIB/243/1998* and prefers the approach of Commissioner Jacobs in *CIB 6244/1997* and Deputy Commissioner Ramsay in *CIB 15482/1996*, thus establishing a strong line of authority against Deputy Commissioner Mark's view of the application of reg.15. Commissioner Mesher thought the rejected approach to be inconsistent with the concept of "reasonable regularity" applicable to the "cannot" descriptors and out of tune with the tenor of *R(IB)2/99(T)*. As he noted, endorsing the reasoning of Commissioner Jacobs,

2.043

"it is not possible to conclude that points are scored for descriptors other than the 'sometimes' descriptors merely because the condition in the descriptor is met for some time during the day. At least in cases where the particular effect of the claimant's physical disablement fluctuate, a longer period must be looked at before it can be said that a person cannot carry out some activity. Only then can the points be scored. Regulation 15 does not bite until it can be said that a person is incapable of work. It does not bite on the individual questions to be answered in reaching an overall conclusion on incapacity for work" (para.13).

pp.701–702, *annotation to Incapacity for Work (General) Regulations 1995, reg.16: ignoring trivial or negligible work as de minimis*

CIB 3507/2003 affords another illustration of work being disregarded as *de minimis*. The work in question was described by the Commissioner as follows:

2.044

"On 28th November 2001, DW Windows wrote a letter in which they said:

51

'In July of this year we approached [the claimant] to see if he would like to do a couple of hours each week at [DW Windows] doing various light duties. ie. Making coffees, emptying bins etc and occasionally driving a vehicle to transport [Mr S. E.] the Manager who holds no driving license.'

There is no dispute about what DW Windows say. Nor is there any dispute about the fact that the claimant was paid £3.85 per hour and that he worked between one and three hours per week. A schedule of his weekly hours and earnings between the beginning of July and the first week of October 2001 has been produced by DW Windows. He never worked for more than three hours and consequently never earned more than £11.55, in any one week. The period covered is one of 14 weeks. During three of those weeks he worked for 1 hour only. He worked for two hours for five of those weeks and for three hours for the remaining six weeks. The average is a little above two hours per week" (paras 6, 7).

p.706, *Incapacity for Work (General) Regulations 1995, reg.17(2)(a): increase in the permitted earnings limit for exempt work*

2.045   With effect from October 1, 2003, this was increased to £72 by reg.4 of the Social Security (Incapacity) (Miscellaneous Amendments) Regulations 2003 (SI 2003/2262).

pp.707–708, *annotation to Incapacity for Work (General) Regulations, reg.17: the current categories of exempt work*

2.046   Note the increase in earnings limit from £67.50 (wrongly noted as £66 on p.708) to £72 with effect from October 1, 2003. See further update to p.706, above.

pp.727–729, *annotation to Incapacity for Work (General) Regulations 1995, reg.25(3)*

2.047   In *CIB 5435/2002*, Commissioner Jacobs considered the meaning of "bodily disablement" in para.(3) in the context of a claimant diagnosed with "chronic pain syndrome". It and "illness behaviour" are recognised by a respectable body of medical opinion as medical conditions. They are

"terms used to describe symptoms that are caused by the influence of psychological makeup and social environment on the perception of the disabling effects of a medical condition. The recognition of this phenomenon is reflected in more modern approaches to treatment, which address the psychosocial as well as the medical factors. The symptoms are subjective in the sense that they depend on an experience of pain or fatigue. This does not, though, mean that they are not genuinely experienced, nor that they do not prevent or restrict function" (para.12).

But where do they fit in para.(3), since classification is crucial in determining which set of activities and descriptors can be applied?

Neither is a disease. Commissioner Jacobs decided that "bodily" refers to the function that is affected rather than to the source of the condition, so that "chronic pain syndrome and related conditions bring the claimant within the scope of the physical disabilities section of the personal capability assessment" (para.16).

In *CIB 4841/2002*, Commissioner Jacobs gave the following description of "illness behaviour": 2.048

"Abnormal illness behaviour is one of a number of terms used to describe symptoms which are caused by the influence of psychological makeup and social environment on the perception of the disabling effects of a medical condition. This phenomenon is reflected by more modern approaches to treatment, which address the psychosocial as well as the medical factors. The symptoms are subjective in the sense that they depend on an experience of pain or fatigue. In order to distinguish between claimants who genuinely experience a particular disability from those who merely claim to do so, it is helpful to consider the history of their daily activity and unobtrusive observations. This can identify consistency or inconsistency" (para.10).

p.733, *annotation to Incapacity for Work (General) Regulations 1995, reg.27: meaning of "substantial risk" where the "old" reg.27(b) is applicable on the basis of the decision in* Howker

In *CIB 3519/2002*, Commissioner Rowland considered that substantial did not only refer to the likelihood of the risk occurring: 2.049

"a risk may be "substantial" if the harm would be serious, even though it was unlikely to occur and, conversely, may not be "substantial" if the harm would be insignificant, even though the likelihood of some such harm is great. Paragraph (b) must be viewed in the light of the other paragraphs of regulation 27 and the general scheme of the Regulations" (para.7).

pp.735–736, *annotation to Incapacity for Work (General) Regulations 1995, reg.28*

Although this regulation is generally forward looking, medical evidence looking to a past period, can be taken into account, provided that it was available at the date of the decision which is under appeal to the appeal tribunal: see Commissioner Mesher in *CIS 2699/2001*. 2.050

pp.752–755, *annotation to Incapacity for Work (General) Regulations 1995, Sch. variable and intermittent conditions: para.15 of R(IB)2/99 applied*

Applying para.15 of *R(IB)2/99* in *CIB 2620/2000*, Commissioner Bano held that the case before him (a sufferer from dysmenorrhoea) was one of the minority of cases in which the broad approach could not be 2.051

applied, one where the claimant could only be considered incapable of work on "bad days".

p.766, annotation to Incapacity for Work (General) Regulations 1995, Sch.: Activity 8: lifting and carrying

2.052   CIB 727/1998 is now reported as R(IB)4/03.

pp.770–772, annotation to Incapacity for Work (General) Regulations 1995, Sch.: Activity 13: continence: descriptor (b): "no voluntary control over bladder"

2.053   In *CIB 3519/2002*, Commissioner Rowland endorsed the views of Commissioner Brown, expressed in the Northern Ireland decision *R2/00(IB)*, on the need to take account of medication. A tribunal must still, however, address the question whether in all the circumstances, including the effect of the medication, the claimant could properly be said to have voluntary control over his bladder.

p.772, annotation to Incapacity for Work (General) Regulations 1995, Sch.: Activity 14: meaning of "epileptic or similar seizures"

2.054   Medically, the cause of an epileptic fit is the abnormal activity of cerebral neurones Its effect is lost or altered consciousness. Migraine does not arise from that abnormal activity, and so, as Commissioner Jacobs recognised in *CIB 4598/2002*, if the medical cause is the relevant one for purposes of Activity 14, the claimant migraine sufferer in that case does not suffer from seizures similar to epileptic ones. He did, however, have sympathy with a different approach suggested in the directions on the appeal given by Commissioner Levenson (who had given leave and transferred the appeal to Commissioner Jacobs). He had suggested that since capacity to work is the central issue, rather than diagnosis, it was arguable that whether a seizure was similar to an epileptic one should be determined by effect rather than cause. Commissioner Jacobs saw this as having two advantages:

> "First, it emphasises the impact of a claimant's symptoms on capacity for work rather than their medical causation. Second, his approach is the easier to apply for decision-makers and appeal tribunals. If the claimant has a firm diagnosis, medical science will probably be able to provide the evidence necessary to apply the medical adviser's approach. But suppose the claimant's condition has not yet been diagnosed. How in those circumstances is it possible for the practical purposes of a decision-maker or an appeal tribunal to prove what is causing the claimant's symptoms?" (para.19).

Since this claimant had not suffered lost or altered consciousness, however, Commissioner Jacobs did not have to decide whether the medical approach, Commissioner Levenson's approach, or some other approach, was the correct one.

p.775, *annotation to Incapacity for Work (General) Regulations 1995, Sch., Pt II: mental disabilities: Activity 15: completion of tasks: descriptor (a) "cannot answer a telephone and reliably take a message"*

In *CIB 5536/2002*, Commissioner Jacobs emphasised that this can be satisfied where the claimant (a) cannot answer the telephone, and (b) where he can answer it, but cannot reliably take a message. If the evidence shows that he can never do either (a) or (b), the descriptor is satisfied. But where he can sometimes do one, or the other, but not always, 2.055

"the tribunal must decide whether on an overall view it is proper to say that the claimant 'cannot' perform the descriptor. In applying the test, it is relevant to consider how often the claimant can and cannot perform the descriptor. However, the test does not depend on a purely arithmetical approach so that the descriptor is only satisfied if (for example) the claimant cannot perform the descriptor more often than not. The issue turns the proper use of the word 'cannot'." (para.9).

Here the evidence showed that difficulties occurred sometimes, but not with a frequency enabling one to say "cannot".

p.777, *new annotation to Incapacity for Work (General) Regulations 1995, Sch., Pt II: mental disabilities: Activity 16: daily living: descriptor (e) "sleeping problems interfere with daytime activities"*

In *CIB 5536/2002*, Commissioner Jacobs held that 2.056

"interference is not limited to preventing the claimant undertaking daytime activities. . . . Daytime activities may be prevented completely, or only be possible at certain times of the day, or be possible but only very intermittently or very slowly. All of these are potentially ways of interfering with the activities. Any of them is sufficient to satisfy the descriptor. This is subject to two qualifications. First, they must result from sleeping problems. Second, as with the word 'cannot' in descriptor 15(a), the issue depends on the proper use of language. When is a change in the activities undertaken or the pattern that would otherwise be followed an interference? A minimal change may not be sufficient to amount to an interference. So, for example, the fact that the claimant cannot start her daytime activities until a little later than normal or needs a rest at some time during the day, is not necessarily sufficient to satisfy the descriptor. Nor would it be necessarily be an interference just because the claimant has to change the time or order in which she performs the activities. This is a question of fact and degree, turning on the proper use of language" (para.14).

p.780, *new annotation to Incapacity for Work (General) Regulations 1995, Sch., Pt II: mental disabilities: Activity 18: interaction with other people: descriptor (a) "cannot look after himself without help from others"*

In *CIB 5536/2002*, Commissioner Jacobs accepted as correct this passage from Commissioner May in *CIB/4916/1997* (para.25): 2.057

"The question as to whether or not a person cannot look after himself without help from others is essentially in my view a question as to whether without such help the claimant would self neglect. It is not in my view meant to encompass asserted assistance with family finance that goes beyond the scope of looking after oneself. It would subvert the whole scheme for incapacity benefit if the meaning of descriptors was to be ingeniously stretched far beyond the scope that the plain English of the descriptors intended."

In Commissioner Jacobs' opinion

"the natural meaning of the language of this descriptor relates to the immediate aspects of self care, like eating and maintaining an appropriate level of personal hygiene. It does not apply to the more remote aspects, like shopping (this case) and handling finances and paying bills (Mr May's case). The language and its context in the personal capability assessment combine to emphasis the claimant rather than the claimant's household, its provisioning or its finances" (para. 19).

p.881, *annotation to the General Benefit Regulations 1982, reg.11(6) and Sch.2*

2.058   In *CI 1293/2003*, Commissioner Jacobs considered entries 26–28 (see main volume, p.884) dealing with amputations in lower limbs and, in particular, the need for a tribunal to specify where the measurement of the stump began and ended. What is assessed is the loss of function consequent upon anatomical loss, rather than the latter itself. The legislation does not specify the start and end points for measurement, but the length of the stump must be related to the likely disablement that will result. Given the possibility of fitting a prosthesis, the length of the stump is likely to relate to the effectiveness of that prosthesis. He concluded that

"In a perfect world, the precise measurement would not matter. The tribunal would take account of the Scheduled assessments as a whole. It would realise that the length of the stump would affect the effectiveness of the prosthesis, which would affect the claimant's disablement. It would take account of the Scheduled assessment only as a starting point. It would adjust this as authorised by regulation 11(6). This process of adjustment, with a focus on disablement, would counteract any variation between adjudicating authorities on the precise way in which the measurement was taken.

But life, in my experience, is not always perfect. This analysis presupposes an impossible degree of precision on a matter that is imprecise and impressionistic. In practice, tribunals begin their assessment of disablement with the Scheduled assessment, if there is one. That is the proper approach under regulation 11(6). Despite the infinite flexibility that regulation 11(6) allows in theory, the reality is that the starting point of the Scheduled assessment will affect the outcome.

Disablement depends on the effectiveness of the prosthesis. That depends on the length of bone rather than soft tissue. So, it is obvious that it is only the supporting bone that should be measured. The key bone is the tibia, not the fibula. As the tibia is the inner of the two bones in the lower limb, the measurement should be made on the inner surface of the remaining stump, not the outer. So far, the Secretary of State's guidance does no more than put those conclusions into medical language. All that remains is the position of the leg when the measurement is taken. The Secretary of State recommends that the knee be flexed, which obviously is the best way to obtain the precise measurement required. In conclusion, therefore, the Secretary of State's guidance agrees with the measurement that can be deduced by normal interpretive principles from the legislation" (paras 23–25).

pp.878–879, *annotation to General Benefit Regulations 1982, reg.11(3): the order of deductions*

In *CI 2746/2002*, Commissioner Bano emphasised the effect of para. (3): 2.059

"Although the tribunal clearly analysed the evidence with care and did consider the interaction between the claimant's pre-existing degenerative lumbar condition and the effects of the relevant accident, they assessed the percentage of disablement due to the relevant accident by subtracting the disablement attributable to the accident from the total disability. In cases where disability results both from a relevant accident and from a pre-accident congenital defect or injury or disease, regulation 11(3) requires the tribunal to take account of "all . . . disablement except to the extent to which the claimant would have been subject thereto during the period taken into account by the assessment if the relevant accident had not occurred." Where disablement results both from a relevant accident and from a pre-accident condition, the regulation is clearly intended to give the claimant the benefit of any overlapping disablement, and that result can only be achieved if a separate assessment is made of the disablement to which the claimant would have been subject as a result of the pre-accident condition alone. I therefore agree with the Secretary of State's representative that regulation 11(3) requires the total disablement to be assessed, and for the percentage disablement resulting from the pre-accident condition to be subtracted from the total percentage disablement in order to arrive at the assessment of the disablement due to the relevant accident" (para.5).

p.881, *annotation to General Benefit Regulations 1982, reg.11(8): a need to make reference to the prescribed degrees of disablement in Sch.2?*

In *CSI 744/2002*, Commissioner May emphasised that para.(8) permits reference to the prescribed degrees of disablement in Sch.2. However, he emphasised that in *R(I)5/95*, Commissioner Rowland had 2.060

stressed that the assessment of disablement was essentially one for the judgment of the tribunal. Accordingly, Commissioner May considered

"that Mr Commissioner Rowland pitches the position too high when he says that a tribunal should indicate to what extent they have had regard to Schedule 2 of the Social Security (General Benefit) Regulations 1982. He himself concedes later in paragraph 16 that consideration of the schedule does not provide assistance in all cases. I do not see how it can be said that in a case such as the present where the issue was not raised before them and where the claimant was represented by an experienced representative that it can be said that they were bound to make such an indication, particularly when the regulations are permissive in their terms. I am also inclined to accept Miss Stirling's submission to me that it is doubtful whether the Schedule would have assisted the tribunal in this case standing the nature of the disablement suffered by the claimant and the terms of the Schedule in which the comparison would require to be made" (para.8).

p.900, annotation to Prescribed Diseases Regulations 1985, reg.6(1), (2)(b): date of onset—application of Whalley

2.061 The decision in *Whalley* that a decision of one tribunal on date of onset for a PD, whether given in respect of disablement benefit or REA, as the case may be, binds a later tribunal considering the issue for either benefit, has been applied in *CI 1605/2002* (Commissioner Rowland) and *CI 226/2001* (Commissioner Howell).

p.916, Prescribed Diseases Regulations 1985: substitution of a new reg.29

2.062 With effect from September 22, 2003, reg.2(2) of the Social Security (Industrial Injuries) (Prescribed Diseases) Amendment (No.2) Regulations 2003 (SI 2003/2190) substituted a new text of reg.29 to read:

"Period to be covered by assessment of disablement in respect of occupational deafness

2.063 [29. Paragraph 6(1) and (2) of Schedule 6 to the Social Security Contributions and Benefits Act 1992 shall be modified so that in respect of occupational deafness, the period to be taken into account by an assessment of the extent of a claimant's disablement shall be the remainder of the claimant's life.]"

pp.916–918, Prescribed Diseases Regulations 1985: revocation of regs 30–33

2.064 With effect from September 22, 2003, reg.2(3) of the Social Security (Industrial Injuries) (Prescribed Diseases) Amendment (No.2) Regulations 2003 (SI 2003/2190) revoked regs 30 to 33.

Non-Means Tested Benefits

pp.925–928, *Prescribed Diseases Regulations 1985: Sch.1: PD A10 (occupational deafness): substitution of occupations (second column entries)*

With effect from September 22, 2003, and subject to a transitional provision (see update to p.981, below), reg.3 of the Social Security (Industrial Injuries) (Prescribed Diseases) Amendment (No.2) Regulations 2003 (SI 2003/2190) substituted for the entries PD A10(a)–(w), a revised and shorter list, to read:

2.065

"*Any occupation involving:*
The use of, or work wholly or mainly in the immediate vicinity of the use of, a—
  (a) band saw, circular saw or cutting disc to cut metal in the metal founding or forging industries, circular saw to cut products in the manufacture of steel, powered (other than hand powered) grinding tool on metal (other than sheet metal or plate metal), pneumatic percussive tool on metal, pressurised air arc tool to gouge metal, burner or torch to cut or dress steel based products, skid transfer bank, knock out and shake out grid in a foundry, machine (other than a power press machine) to forge metal including a machine used to drop stamp metal by means of closed or open dies or drop hammers, machine to cut or shape or clean metal nails, or plasma spray gun to spray molten metal;
  (b) pneumatic percussive tool:—to drill rock in a quarry, on stone in a quarry works, underground, for mining coal, for sinking a shaft, or for tunnelling in civil engineering works;
  (c) vibrating metal moulding box in the concrete products industry, or circular saw to cut concrete masonry blocks;
  (d) machine in the manufacture of textiles for:—weaving man-made or natural fibres (including mineral fibres), high speed false twisting of fibres, or the mechanical cleaning of bobbins;
  (e) multi-cutter moulding machine on wood, planing machine on wood, automatic or semi-automatic lathe on wood, multiple cross-cut machine on wood, automatic shaping machine on wood, double-end tenoning machine on wood, vertical spindle moulding machine (including a high speed routing machine) on wood, edge banding machine on wood, bandsawing machine (with a blade width of not less than 75 millimetres) on wood, circular sawing machine on wood including one operated by moving the blade towards the material being cut, or chain saw on wood;
  (f) jet of water (or a mixture of water and abrasive material) at a pressure above 680 bar, or jet channelling process to burn stone in a quarry;
  (g) machine in a ship's engine room, or gas turbine for:—performance testing on a test bed, installation testing of a replacement engine in an aircraft, or acceptance testing of an Armed Service fixed wing combat aircraft;

2.066

(h) machine in the manufacture of glass containers or hollow ware for:—automatic moulding, automatic blow moulding, or automatic glass pressing and forming;
(i) spinning machine using compressed air to produce glass wool or mineral wool;
(j) continuous glass toughening furnace;
(k) firearm by a police firearms training officer; or
(l) shot-blaster to carry abrasives in air for cleaning."

For commentary to the revised provisions, see update to pp.943–950, below.

pp.943–950, *annotation to Prescribed Diseases Regulations 1985, Sch.1: A10 (occupational deafness)*

2.067   The revision from September 22, 2003 of the occupations in respect of which occupational deafness is prescribed (see update to pp.925–928, above), based largely on the IIAC Report on the prescription of occupational deafness (Cm.5672, November 2002), means that the existing commentary is now relevant only to those whose claim for disablement based on occupational deafness was made, or treated as made, before that date (see update to p.981, below). Specific new case law on the prescription as formulated prior to September 22, 2003, are noted after this update, by reference to the specific page in the existing annotation in the main volume.

For claims made, or treated as made, on or after September 22, 2003, please substitute the following commentary:

A10 (Occupational deafness)

In PD A10 occupational deafness is defined as

"Sensorineural hearing loss amounting to at least 50dB in each ear, being the average of hearing losses at 1, 2 and 3 kHz frequencies, and being due in the case of at least one ear to occupational noise"

CI/4567/1999 (now reported as *R(I)6/02*) contains useful material on a variety of tests measuring hearing loss.

2.068   In *CI/2012/2000*, Commissioner Jacobs said, rightly, that *CI/4567/1999* (now reported as *R(I)6/02*) neither is, nor purports to be, authority that ERA (evoked response audiometry), a form of assessment of hearing loss, is always to be preferred to PTA (pure tone audiometry), another form of assessment of hearing loss)(para.16).

ERA "is a record of a person's brain activity in response to sound" (para.12), which is not dependent on the claimant to acknowledge that sound has been heard (and therefore not contingent on his honesty). However, the claimant's behaviour can affect other brain activity and render it more difficult to interpret the results (para.14). Adults are usually tested by cortical or slow vertex ERA. Young children are usually tested by another type, brainstem ERA so that the results are not affected by the anaesthetic or sedative administered to keep the child quiet and still during the test process (para.15).

PTA is cheap and fairly easy to administer. It is the starting point for all assessments by tribunals and the Secretary of State, but depends upon the claimant acknowledging when a sound (produced at different levels by the PTA equipment) has been heard (para.10).

The Commissioner advances the following approach for tribunals:

> "a tribunal . . . has to weigh the evidence as a whole in order to determine the level of the claimant's sensorineural hearing loss. There is no rule that one type of evidence is always to be preferred to another. The evidence must be considered as a whole. The tribunal may conclude that one type of evidence is preferable to another, but that must be a judgment reached after considering the merits of all the evidence" (para.16).

There was in this case no error of law in the tribunal refusing to order, at public expense, brainstem ERA.

2.069 In *CI 1/2002*, without citing Commissioner Jacobs' decision in *CI/2012/2000*, like him Commissioner Williams also concludes that *CI 4567/1999* (now reported as *R(I) 6/02*) is not authority that CERA (cortical evoked response audiogram) is always to be preferred to PTA (pure tone audiometry). Noting that Prescribed Diseases Regulations, reg.34 gives precise details about testing and assessment but not the method of testing, Commissioner Williams stated that the matter is one for the experts on the tribunal using their expertise to decide. In the decision under appeal before him, the tribunal had relied on that expertise to conclude that in that case CERA would not be more reliable than PTA. However, the Commissioner noted that declining to order a CERA test on the basis of cost might be a denial of a fair hearing under the HRA 1998/ECHR.

Useful information and guidance—which cannot be binding on decision makers, tribunals or Commissioners—on both PTA and CERA can be found in the IIAC Report on the prescription of occupational deafness (Cm 5672, November 2002). See para.117 (audiometric testing) and App.6 (guidance on obtaining cortical evoked response audiometry). The IIAC recommended that Pure tone audiometry (pta) should be retained as the most appropriate routine assessment method for use in the benefit scheme. Where testing is not repeatable, or response to conversational voice seems better or worse than the audiogram would suggest, use of cERA should be considered. In any event, the IIAC recommended that methods of testing should be kept under review.

2.070 The wide range of occupations for which this disease is prescribed led to a significant number of Commissioners' decisions on the interpretation of the various parts of the Schedule relating to the disease. All, however, can only be authoritative today insofar as they deal with equivalent wording.

The expression which prefaces the reformulated occupations in column (2), "*wholly or mainly in the immediate vicinity of,*" was considered in *R(I) 2/85*. That decision held that it was not necessary that the claimant should spend the majority of his time near the specified tools whilst they are in use, and that it was sufficient that the tools were in use more than a negligible amount whilst he was in the vicinity. But the formulation now requires work wholly or mainly in the immediate vicinity *of the use of* a specified tool or piece of equipment, removing the authority of that statement. Note also *CI/226/91* (para.7), citing *Fawcett Properties v Buckinghamshire CC* [1961] A.C. 636 at 669 where Lord Morton said that mainly "probably means more than half". In *R(I) 7/76* it was held that whether the claimant was in the vicinity should be determined by the distance from him to the specified tools, taking into account walls, screens etc., but not measuring the level of residual noise at the claimant's workplace. An employee working in an exceptionally noisy factory may, therefore, be exposed to far greater noise than is acceptable but not entitled to benefit because he is not working near enough to the machines making the noise—

> "Whether an occupation involves work in the immediate vicinity of the designated plant is a question of fact in each case. I think it is to be answered first by ascertaining the locations, that is to say the area within which the designated plants (which from their nature cover considerable areas) are situated, and the area of the claimant's activities. The question whether the area of work is in the immediate vicinity of the plant then depends in my opinion on the weight to be given to the particular circumstances. The distance at which one area lies from the other may itself be decisive of the question. A second factor may be the physical separation of one area from the other because of intervening buildings ... A further factor, as here ... may be the presence of walls and screening, substantially dividing, enclosing or demarking the two areas lying at a distance apart, though under the same factory roof."

2.071　See also *R(I) 8/85* where the distance factor was held to be significant. In *CI/245/1991*, Commissioner Goodman stated that the notion of "working in the immediate vicinity" of percussive tools involved consideration of the physical proximity to the use of such tools and not just the noise level, so that the claimant's non-use of ear muffs or protectors supplied by his employer was legally irrelevant to the issue. The Commissioner concluded that the percussive tools were in constant and daily use and that the claimant worked in the immediate vicinity in his job as storeman, his store being separated from that work area only by a wire mesh (paras 10–13).

The original (see above) specified occupations were, broadly speaking, foundries, shipyards and mines and quarries. Whilst the occupations have been changed and widened, the Schedule still refers in paras. A10(a) and (b) to the use of, or work wholly or mainly in the immediate vicinity of the use of, a pneumatic percussive tool. The nature of such a tool has been considered in *R(I) 5/76* (an "impact wrench" or "screwing up machine"); *R(I) 8/76* (a computer-controlled burning and marking machine); *R(I) 1/80* (a rivet gun); *R(I) 3/80* (upright pedestal grinder); *R(I)/13/80* (machine mounted vertical spindle surface grinder); *R(I)6/83* (press set into the ground and operating on compressed air). Whether a particular tool is pneumatic is a question of fact, and it is necessary to look at the essential nature of the tool and determine its driving force (*R(I)6/83*). But what constitutes a "tool"? The general trend of decisions has been to give the word "tool" a more technical meaning and, as a result, include some machines in the category of tools. A printing press, though pneumatic and percussive was held not to be a "tool" in *CI/17/93*. The test for "tool" was there said to be whether the machine now alleged to be a "tool" is now used to carry out a task traditionally carried out by what everyone would recognise as a hand-held tool. If there is no "recognisable previous identity as a hand-held tool" it is a machine and not a "tool" (*CI/17/93*, para.3. citing *R(I)6/83*, para.6). In *Appleby v CAO* (reported as *R(I)5/99*, judgment of June 29, 1999), the Court of Appeal stated that while the test propounded by Commissioner Sanders in *CI/17/93* was "useful", it was not "an exclusive test", particularly as regards new processes where the existence of a sufficiently manual input may enable the alleged tool to qualify. A useful starting point is whether the implement in question is classified in the trade or industry as a machine tool. In *Appleby*, the Court held the electrodes on the spot welding machine qualified as pneumatic, percussive tools; they banged the metal to be welded to ensure a tight fit before emitting the necessary electrical charge, and were, therefore, the mechanical equivalent of the hand held hammer used in the past when welding was effected by hammering together two pieces of preheated metal. The Court, obiter, was provisionally of the opinion that the spot welding machine had sufficient manual input to qualify as a "tool".

The number of paras has been reduced from 23 to 11, and occupations once in separate paras have been regrouped and reworded to simplify matters to aid understanding and administration (IIAC Report, para.105, and App.4). The revision, however, has added occupations but not removed any previously prescribed, since the IIAC "had no evidence that any of the occupations and processes already prescribed have disappeared, ceased to be a hazard to hearing, or fundamentally altered to the extent that their removal from the list would be appropriate" (para.95). 2.072

Para.(a): "metal founding or forging industries", the IIAC saw no need to clarify "forging", considering it an understandable term with a definite meaning in industry (para.101). The prescription covers the use of powered grinding tools on metal, but not hand-powered ones. On "tool" and "pneumatic percussive tool", see the discussion preceding coverage of this particular para. As regards "metal", note that despite common parlance referring to a metalled road, reg.1(2) provides that "metal" for the purposes of disease A10, does not include stone, concrete, aggregate or similar substances for use in road or railway construction. However in *CI/37/1988* the Commissioner accepted that "on metal" could include the use of pneumatic drills to break up reinforced concrete where the drill would from time to time strike the metal reinforcing rods. But in *CI/540/1994*, where the momentary or occasional contact with a metal reinforcing rod was minimal, the claim was

63

unsuccessful. The ruling in *CI/540/1994* was held in *CI/13238/1996* to apply in respect of noise from drills striking metal reinforcing rods in concrete road structures in a claim by a foreman asphalter.

Note that the terms "foundry", "skid transfer bank" and "knock out and shake out grid" are each specifically defined in reg.1(2), above.

The term "metal nails" has a wider meaning than ordinary nails driven with a hammer; it can include any piece of wire or metal used for holding things together *(R(I) 5/83)*. In *CI/808/95*, Commissioner Mesher agreed

> "with the view expressed by the Commissioner in para. 9 of *R(I) 5/83*, supported by reference in that case to the report of the Industrial Injuries Advisory Council, that the prescription in paragraph A10(f) [the equivalent of A10(a) formulation 'machine to cut or shape or clean metal nails'] relates to the process of making nails. Thus the crucial question is whether what results from the operation of the claimant's machine can be called a nail in the extended sense described by the Commissioner in *R(I) 5/83* [a piece of wire or metal used for holding things together]. One must ask what the product is used for. I conclude that its use in the manufacture of tyres is such that it cannot be called a nail. It does not hold things together in the way in which a nail or rivet holds things together. It does not hold one part of the tyre to another part of the tyre by connecting the two together." (para.9, words in square brackets added.)

2.073 The rubber-coated wire cut by the claimant's machine was used to reinforce the rubber moulding of the tyre.

There was brief consideration in *CI 246/1988* of the features of plasma spray gun to spray molten metal, but unfortunately the matter was not pursued very far since the materials deposited by the gun in the case were silica and quartz, neither of which is a metal.

Para. (b): On "pneumatic percussive tool", see the discussion preceding the commentary on para.(a).

"Underground" means properly underground, with an earth ceiling, and does not include a deep trench which is open to the air, even though the drilling operation is going on below ground level *(R(I) 4/84)*. It means "underneath the natural surface of the earth". It did not therefore embrace the claimant who was not but may have been working on the floor or below floor level in a prepared building, not under a natural roof (*CI/550/89*, para.6). A tunnel like the Mersey Tunnel is properly encompassed by the term "underground", although the inclusion in para.(b) of "for tunnelling in civil engineering works" in any event provides protection (*CI/13238/1996*).

In *CI/550/89*, Commissioner Heald decided, referring indirectly to *CI/308/1989* (now reported as *R(I) 2/92*, noted below) on the meaning of "wood", that "rock" in sub-para.(c) means "rock in its natural state ... and not in the form of a cement aggregate, at which stage the material which was originally rock, no doubt, had changed its nature and formed part of the cement mix." (para.5). Whether the same is true of "stone", so as to not to cover solid products (*e.g.* paving slabs, bricks or blocks) made from reconstituted crushed or powdered stone is unclear. The inclusion of new para.(c) will help some of those who work cutting concrete masonry blocks (*e.g.* builders).

Para.(c): none of the terms in this prescription is defined. Nor does there appear to be any case law on its previous partial manifestation as PD A10(q). Its expansion will help some of those who work cutting concrete masonry blocks (*e.g.* builders).

2.074

Para.(d): This covers the use of machines in the manufacture of textiles. This includes "weaving", but the para is not confined to "weaving".

On "weaving", *CSI/65/94* applying *R(I)13/81* was authority that deafness from working with noisy knitting machines does not come within A10(d) because "knitting" is not "weaving". Commissioner Mitchell reached his decision "with regret" and like the Commissioner in *R(I)13/81* expressed the hope that an anomaly might be rectified by amending the paragraph, since the evidence in the case showed that the knitting machines at the claimant's place of work were just as noisy as weaving machines. This has now been done as regards the process of "high speed false twisting of fibres" after the IIAC recommending it in its 2002 Report which largely formed the basis for these revised prescriptions. The IIAC accepted that there was enough evidence that high speed false twisting is a process that can take place prior to both knitting and weaving, and one which produces yarn for both of these areas of fabric manufacture.

In *CI/2879/1995*, Commissioner Goodman gave some consideration to the phrase "the high speed false twisting of fibres". He set aside the tribunal decision as erroneous in law on the basis that they had failed to consider whether the claimant's occupation from May 6, 1987 to August 12, 1988 (one bringing her within a five-year period prior to the 1994 claim) met the description. But, approving an argument founded on para.12 of *R(I)13/81*, he held that the tribunal was entitled to rely on a definition from a research fellow in a University Department of Textile Industries in conjunction with factual information supplied by the employer on the basis that where words are used in legislation with reference to particular trades or businesses and have a particular meaning within that trade or business, the words in the legislation should be construed in the light of that meaning (para.17). The material before the tribunal and letters before the Commissioner from an officer in the Health and Safety Executive and from another expert in the same University Department all confirmed that "false twisting", a technique rather than a process, involved machines operating at speeds in revolutions per minute varying according to whether dealing with staple yarns (a few tens of thousands per minute) or filament yarns (850,000 per minute in 1968, up to 7 million per minute today). Some suggested "false twisting" was limited to synthetic yarns. But, in setting out that material and in remitting the matter back to the tribunal because factual "loose ends" precluded him giving the decision, Commissioner Goodman stressed that the prescription "high speed" is not expressed as being a minimum of revolutions a minute, nor is the word "fibres" in any way qualified to limit it to "artificial fibres" (para.18). The prescription now explicitly covers man-made and natural fibres, and includes mineral fibres.

2.075 The prescription also covers the "mechanical cleaning of bobbins". It was reworded from the former prescription in the old PD A10(e), "mechanical bobbin cleaning" to clarify that what is prescribed is the mechanical cleaning of bobbins, rather than the cleaning of mechanical bobbins (IIAC, Cm5672, 2002, para.103)

Para. (e): This covers various machines and saws used to work with wood—In *R(I)2/92* Commissioner Rice considered the meaning of "wood" in a previous occupational prescription in respect of occupational deafness. The claimant had worked in the newspaper print industry near machines cutting newsprint. The Commissioner supported the view of the dissenting chairman in the tribunal that this particular prescribed occupation "refers to wood in [the] accepted sense of the word, not to a material of which wood may be a constituent part. The prescribed occupation . . . clearly refers to working of wood or similar material such as chipboard, and not to the newsprint industry." Commissioner Rice stated that although "newsprint is derived from wood, it is not the same as wood. It has undergone a metamorphosis, and in its changed form as newsprint it has become an entirely different material. It follows that the claimant cannot satisfy the relevant statutory requirements," (para.7). *R(I)2/92* (then *CI/309/1989*) was approved and applied in *CI/175/90* (noted below, notes to D7). It was also followed in *CI/43/92*, where Commissioner Rice held that "logs of toilet paper and kitchen paper" had, like newsprint, undergone a metamorphosis and could not be regarded as "wood," (para.6).

2.076 The rewording of the prescription to cover the use of specific machines or saws on wood removes the need to argue over issues such as the meaning of "forestry", which the IIAC Report saw as in need of clarification (paras 99, 100). It recommended that prescription cover the *regular* use of chainsaws. Note that this was not carried into the prescription.

The prescription has been reworded on HSE advice to cover all circular sawing machines, including those operated by moving the blade towards the material to be cut (para.104).

Para. (f): Removal of references to "water-jetting industry" (see *CI 2286/2002* and *CI 5331/2002*) helps clarify the scope of the prescription which is now confined (i) to the use of a jet of water (or a mixture of water and abrasive) above a specified pressure of 680 bar (10,000 psi) (much higher than the "at least 3000 psi" formulation used by the Secretary of State to denote "high pressure" in the previous prescription) (see *CI 5331/2002*, paras 2 and 18), and (ii) to jet channelling process to burn stone in a quarry. The IIAC was concerned in its proposed revision to clarify that it intended to include only those water-jetting processes in which high pressure was used on a commercial basis, and where an employee would be put at regular and frequent risk of exposure to high levels of noise likely to damage hearing (para.97). In setting the 10,000 psi level evidence was taken from HSE experts on the level of pressure likely to be hazardous to hearing and produce disablement (para.98).

Para. (g): this covers a machine in a ship's engine room or gas turbine, provided that it use covers the specified testing. The meaning of "ships engine room" was considered in *R(I)2/97* where the Commissioner saw as "clearly limited to engine rooms on ships, and does not extend to engine rooms on land, regardless of the nature of the engines located there". So, in that case, the fact that the claimant worked in an engine room providing power to a building and the engines in the room were of a type that could be used to power ships, was immaterial. So was the fact that had he been on a ship and rendered deaf by working with the self-same engines, his claim would have succeeded; the occupation has to be a prescribed one (*ibid.* para.11). The Commissioner in so deciding on the appropriate interpretation, made use of a report on Occupational Deafness by the Industrial Injuries Advisory Council. The remainder of the prescription gives aid and comfort to others who work with gas turbines for various specified forms of engine testing.

Para. (h): This applies to machines used for certain specified matters in the manufacture of glass containers and hollow ware. R(I)4/99 remains authority for the proposition that the whole of the prescription is confined to glass manufacture. In that case, considering similar wording in para.(w) of the then prescription, the claimant was a clay worker in the pottery industry. He operated a "forming machine, used in the manufacture of ceramic (pottery) hollow ware, but not glass hollow ware" (para.4). The Commissioner rejected the argument of the claimant's representative that "hollow ware" was not confined to glass, but included metal and ceramics. Taking account of the Industrial Injuries Advisory Council Report [Cm. 817 (1994)], which had led to the introduction of para.(w) in order to interpret ambiguous wording in the legislative prescription, Commissioner Goodman came to the conclusion that the:

2.077

> "prescription is . . . confined to glass manufacture. The words, ' . . . forming machines used in the manufacture of glass containers or hollow ware' do in my view read in such a way that the adjective 'glass' applies not only to 'containers' but also to 'hollow ware'. That is the natural meaning of the sentence and it also coincides with the fact that the rest of sub-paragraphs (i) and (ii) and (iii) of paragraph (w) are all clearly confined to the manufacture of various kinds of glass (save 'mineral wool' in sub-paragraph (ii)). The report of the Advisory Council leads to the same conclusion and I am entitled to look at its contents in view of the ambiguity introduced in [sub–] paragraph (i) of paragraph (w) by the use of the word 'or' between 'glass containers' and 'hollow ware'. Overall, therefore, I am satisfied that the tribunal arrived at the correct decision and that the prescribed occupation in paragraph (w) of Paragraph A10 is not intended to apply to any kind of hollow ware except that made of glass. I must therefore dismiss the claimant's appeal accordingly" (para.13).

2.078   *Para. (k)*: this was recommended for prescription since evidence from the HSE supported the view that the level of exposure to noise in this situation was at least as high as in the occupations already prescribed (IIAC Report, Cm 5672, 2002, para.94)

Note that cases might also fit (as single incidents or small series of incidents producing deafness) as accidents within SSCBA 1992, s.94(1). See further *CI 5029/2002* on assessment of disablement in respect of deafness arising from accident in connection with police firearms' training.

Para. (l): this was recommended for prescription since evidence from the HSE supported the view that the level of exposure to noise in this situation was at least as high as in the occupations already prescribed (IIAC Report, Cm 5672, 2002, para.94)

p.943, *annotation to Prescribed Diseases Regulations 1985, Sch.1: PD A10 (occupational deafness)*

2.079   In *CI 5029/2002*, Commissioner Fellner considered assessment of disablement in respect of deafness arising from accident in connection with police firearms training. She considered that tribunals could have regard to the Department's guidelines and its rather rough and ready conversational voice testing in its *Industrial Injuries Handbook for Adjudicating Medical Authorities*, so long as it was remembered that this was guidance and not statutorily prescribed. The Tables in the Handbook could be taken on board but only as part of a proper accident assessment.

p.949, *annotation to Prescribed Diseases Regulations 1985, Sch.1: PD A10(r) occupational deafness: "the water jetting industry"*

2.080   In *CI 5331/2002*, Commissioner Rowland followed *CI 2668/2002* and the broad approach in *Davis*, to state that the reasoning to the contrary in *CI 11874/1996* should no longer be followed, so that a claimant using jets of water to clean vehicles and also to remove graffiti, could be regarded as using the jets in the water jetting industry, notwithstanding that he was employed by a local authority (para.8). The claimant asserted that the jets used were high pressure. Despite the 10,000 psi recommended by the IIAC in its report on revisions to the prescribed occupations for occupational deafness (now acted on, see update to pp.943–950, above), Commissioner Rowland suggested that the tribunal to which he remitted the case should follow the Secretary of State's 3000 psi threshold (para.18).

p.950, *annotation to Prescribed Diseases Regulations 1985, Sch.1: PD A11 (Vibration white finger): diagnosis and "blanching"*

2.081   In CI 4582/2002, Commissioner Mesher ruled the matter of occupational cause to be irrelevant to the diagnosis question. He accepted that "blanching" means more than the normal paleness in the extremities experienced on exposure to cold, where there is a reduction of the blood supply to the peripheral arteries in order to protect the system as a whole. He was not, however, prepared to limit "blanching" to intense whiteness, the profound deathly white referred to in the medical paper by Dr Reed, *The Blood and Nerve Supply to the Hand*, which the Commissioner embodied in an appendix to his decision. That was characteristic but the meaning of "blanching" was not restricted to that, and was rather a matter to be decided in particular cases by tribunals and medical decision makers. Nor was circumferential blanching a requisite, preferring here Commissioner Rowland in *CI 3596/2001* to Commissioner Henty in *CI/1807/2002*. Indeed Commissioner Mesher rejected Commissioner Henty's view that Commissioner Rowland's decision had been given *per incuriam*. He noted that the matter of the Cold Water Provocation Test in the Department's Notes on the Diagnosis of Prescribed Diseases (NDPD) had successfully been challenged in *R (on the application of the National Association of Colliery Overmen, Deputies and Shotfirers) v Secretary of State for Work and Pensions* [2003] EWHC 607 (Admin). There Pitchford J. found irrational the Secretary of State's refusal to revise the NDPD guidance and required him to amend it to reflect the correct intention behind the words used, namely that a positive result could have diagnostic value but a negative one should be treated as having none (paras 107–109).

In *CI 1720/2001*, Commissioner Rowland gives some guidance to tribunals on the manner of questioning those who claim to suffer from vibration white finger, suggesting that they avoid closed questioning and too technical language (paras 12–14).

p.958, annotation to Prescribed Diseases Regulations 1985, Sch.1: Category D: Miscellaneous Conditions: pneumoconiosis

The Tribunal of Commissioners decisions in *CI 1819, 2314, 2885 and 5130/2001(T)* are now reported together as *R(I)3/03*.   2.082

p.981, *Insertion of a new set of Industrial Injuries (Prescribed Diseases) Amendment Regulations containing a transitional provision affecting claims for occupational deafness (PD A10)*

This transitional provision concerns the amendments to Sch.1 of the Prescribed Diseases Regulations 1985, the text of which is found in the update to pp.925–928, above, and the commentary to which forms the update to pp.944–950, above. Those changes were made with effect from September 22, 2003 by reg.3 of the Social Security (Industrial Injuries) (Prescribed Diseases) Amendment (No.2) Regulations 2003 (SI 2003/2190). Reg.4 of those regulations contains the transitional provision. It provides: 2.083

"**Transitional provision**

4.—(1) Regulation 3 shall not apply to a period of assessment which relates to a claim which is made before the commencement date.   2.084

(2) A provisional assessment of the extent of a claimant's disablement due to occupational deafness, which is in force immediately before the commencement date, shall, from the commencement date, have effect for the remainder of the claimant's life.

(3) For the purposes of this regulation—
(a) "commencement date" means the date on which these Regulations come into force;
(b) the date on which a claim is made is the date on which the claim is made or treated as made in accordance with the Social Security (Claims and Payments) Regulations 1987."

This principally protects those whose claims in respect of hearing loss were made, or treated as made, before the date of the change (para.(1) read with (3)(b)). But note also the provision in para.(2), which turns a provisional assessment of disablement due to occupational deafness, in force on September 21, 2003, into one for life as from September 22, 2003 ("commencement date"—see para.(3)(a)).

PART III

UPDATING MATERIAL
VOL II

INCOME SUPPORT, JOBSEEKER'S ALLOWANCE, STATE PENSION CREDIT AND THE SOCIAL FUND

Income Support, Jobseekers' Allowance, State Pension Credit

p.xiv, Contents

The word "Calculations" has been accidentally omitted after the word "Maintenance" in the title of SI 2001/155.   3.001

p.5, *Social Security Contributions and Benefits Act 1992, s.124*

With effect from October 6, 2003, s.14 of and Sch.2 paras 1 and 2 of the State Pension Credit Act 2002 (c.16), amended s.124 by inserting a new para.(aa) in sub-s.(1) as follows: 3.002

"(aa) he has not attained the qualifying age for state pension credit;"

and a new para.(g) after para.(f) in sub-s.(1) as follows:

"and
(g) if he is a member of a married or unmarried couple, the other member of the couple is not entitled to state pension credit."

With effect from the same date s.21 of and Sch.3 to the 2002 Act repealed the word "and" immediately preceding para. (f) of sub-s.(1).

p.19, *Social Security Contributions and Benefits Act 1992, s.137*

With effect from October 6, 2003, s.14 and Sch.2 paras 1 and 4 of the State Pension Credit Act 2002 (c.16), amended s.137 by inserting the following new definitions in the appropriate alphabetical positions: 3.003

" 'pensionable age' has the meaning given by the rules in paragraph 1 of Sched. 4 to the Pensions Act 1995 (c.26);"
" 'the qualifying age for state pension credit' is (in accordance with section 1(2)(b) and (6) of the State Pension Credit Act 2002)—
(a) in the case of a woman, pensionable age; or
(b) in the case of a man, the age which is pensionable age in the case of a woman born on the same day as the man;"
" 'state pension credit' means state pension credit under the State Pension Credit Act 2002;"

p.51, *Jobseekers Act 1995, s.3, exclusionary effect of State Pension Credit*

With effect from October 6, 2003, the State Pension Credit Act 2002 by s.14 and Sch.2, para.37 amended s.3(1) by inserting in paragraph (b) the words "or state pension credit" after "income support" and inserting after para.(d) a new para.(dd) reading as follows   3.004

"(dd) is not a member of a married or unmarried couple the other member of which is entitled to state pension credit;".

p.52, *annotation to Jobseekers Act 1995, s.3(1)*

The amendments made on October 6, 2003 as a consequence of the introduction of state pension credit exclude entitlement to income-based

JSA if the claimant is entitled to state pension credit (para. (b)) or if he is a member of a couple and his partner is entitled to state pension credit (para.(dd)).

p.52, *Jobseekers Act 1995, s.3A, exclusionary effect of State Pension Credit*

3.005 With effect from October 6, 2003, the State Pension Credit Act 2002 by s.14 and Sch.2, para.38 amended s.3(1) by inserting after para.(c) a new para.(cc) reading as follows

"(cc) that neither member of the couple is entitled to state pension credit;".

p.53, *annotation to Jobseekers Act 1995, s.3A(1)*

3.006 The amendment made on October 6, 2003 as a consequence of the introduction of state pension credit excludes entitlement to income-based JSA in the case of a joint-claim couple if either member of the couple is entitled to state pension credit (para.(cc)).

p.127, *annotation to Jobseekers Act 1995, s.19(9): amounts for minimum wage*

3.007 These were increased to £4.50 and £3.80 respectively with effect from October 1, 2003 by the National Minimum Wage Regulations 1999 (Amendment) Regulations 2003 (SI 2003/1923).

pp.121–123, *annotation to Jobseekers Act 1995, s.19(6)(c): failure to apply*

3.008 A failure properly to complete an application form can amount to a failure to apply (*CJSA 2692/1999*). However, where the applicant disputed the necessity of including a photograph on the employer's application form, contending that it would be accepted without one, the employment officer, without clear information to the contrary from the employer, should have tested the matter by forwarding the form without photograph to see if that indeed was the case. He had not done so and, in *CJSA 2082/2002* and *CJSA/5415/2002*, Commissioner Rowland allowed the appeal against the sanction imposed.

p.157, *Immigration and Asylum Act 1999, s.123(9)*

3.009 With effect from October 6, 2003, s.14 of and Sch.2 para.42 of the State Pension Credit Act 2002 (c.16), amended sub-s.(9)(c) of s.123 to read as follows:

"(c) in relation to a benefit under the Social Security Contributions and Benefits Act 1992 or state pension credit, regulations made by the Secretary of State under that Act, the Social Security Administration Act 1992 (c. 5) or the State Pension Credit Act 2002;"

Income Support, Jobseekers' Allowance, State Pension Credit

p.181, *Income Support Regulations 1987, reg.2(1)—definition of "ERA payment"*

With effect from October 1, 2003, reg.2(2) of the Social Security (Miscellaneous Amendments) (No.2) Regulations 2003 (SI 2003/2279), inserted the following new definition immediately following the definition of "employment zone contractor". 3.010

" 'ERA payment' means a payment made in respect of participation in the Employment Retention and Advancement Scheme for the provision of assistance to individuals to improve their job retention or career advancement (or both) under section 2 of the Employment and Training Act 1973."

p.184, *Income Support Regulations 1987, reg.2(1)—definition of "residential allowance"*

With effect from October 6, 2003, reg.2 of and Sch.1, para.1 to the Social Security (Removal of Residential Allowance and Miscellaneous Amendments) Regulations 2003 (SI 2003/1121), revoked the definition of "residential allowance". 3.011

p.187, *Income Support Regulations 1987, reg.2(1A)*

With effect from May 21, 2003, reg.3 of the Social Security (Hospital In-Patients and Miscellaneous Amendments) Regulations 2003 (SI 2003/1195), substituted the figures "52" for the word "six" reg.2(1A)(i). 3.012

p.192, *annotation to Income Support Regulations 1987, reg.2(1), "dwelling occupied as the home"*

On July 25, 2003 in *Secretary of State for Work and Pensions v Miah* [2003] EWCA Civ 1111; [2003] 4 All E.R. 702, the Court of Appeal dismissed the Secretary of State's appeal against the decision in *CJSA 4620/2000*. In the Court's view the use of the phrase "dwelling occupied as the home" indicated that the focus should be the function served by the concept of a dwelling rather than its constituent elements and that function was a place serving as the home for the claimant. Moreover, commonsense, justice and fairness also supported this approach. If the claimant had been living in one property which was large enough to accommodate him and his family then it would have been disregarded. It could not be fair that he should suffer when the purpose of having two properties was exactly the same. 3.013

p.194, *annotation to Income Support Regulations 1987, reg.2(1), definition of "ERA payment"*

The Employment Retention and Advancement (ERA) scheme set up under s.2 of the Employment and Training Act 1973 started in October 2003 and will operate in certain areas of the country until July 2007. The 3.014

scheme is open to people who are eligible for the New Deal 25 Plus or the New Deal for Lone Parents and certain working tax credit recipients. It includes a number of financial incentives referred to as "ERA payments". Any such ERA payment is ignored as income under para.77 of Sch.9; for the capital disregard see para.69 of Sch.10.

p.234, *annotation to Income Support Regulations 1987, reg.13(2)(b)*

3.015   The reference to the cited paragraphs in the *Decision Makers Guide* is out of date. The relevant paragraphs are now paras 20647–20654.

p.245, *Income Support Regulations 1987, reg.17 (Applicable amounts)*

3.016   With effect from October 6, 2003, reg.2 of and Sch.1 para.2 to the Social Security (Removal of Residential Allowance and Miscellaneous Amendments) Regulations 2003 (SI 2003/1121), revoked sub-para.(bb) of reg.17(1).

p.250, *Income Support Regulations 1987, reg.18 (Polygamous marriages)*

3.017   With effect from October 6, 2003, reg.2 of and Sch.1 para.3 to the Social Security (Removal of Residential Allowance and Miscellaneous Amendments) Regulations 2003 (SI 2003/1121), revoked sub-para.(cc) of reg.18(1).

p.252, *Income Support Regulations 1987, reg.21 (Special cases)*

3.018   With effect from October 6, 2003, reg.2 of and Sch.1 para.4 to the Social Security (Removal of Residential Allowance and Miscellaneous Amendments) Regulations 2003 (SI 2003/1121), substituted the words "paragraph 13(2)" for the words "paragraph 10A, 10B, 10C or 13" in para.(1B) of reg.21.
   Subsequently, with effect from the same day, para.(1B) was revoked by reg.3(a) of the Social Security (Third Party Deductions and Miscellaneous Amendments) Regulations 2003 (SI 2003/2325).
   Also with effect from October 6, 2003, reg.3(b) of SI 2003/2325 substituted the words "paragraph 1, 2 or 3" for the words "paragraph 1, 2, 3 or 18" in para.(2) of reg.21.

p.260, *annotation to Income Support Regulations 1987, reg.21(3): person subject to immigration control; The ECSMA Agreement and the European Social Charter—Meaning of "lawfully present"*

3.019   [*CIS 2091/2001* (which confirmed that the decision of the Court of Appeal in *Kaya v London Borough of Haringey* was applicable in the field of social security) was confirmed by the Court of Appeal in *Szoma v Secretary of State for Work and Pensions* [2003] EWCA Civ 1131 (July 30, 2003) (Pill and Carnwath L.JJ. and Kay J.). The majority of the Court (Pill L.J. and Kay J.) also expressly rejected a submission that *Kaya* was wrongly decided. M. Szoma is petitioning the House of Lords for leave to appeal.

Income Support, Jobseekers' Allowance, State Pension Credit

p.299, *Income Support Regulations 1987, reg.31(3)*

With effect from August 8, 2003, reg.2(2) of the Social Security (Working Tax Credit and Child Tax Credit) (Consequential Amendments) (No. 3) Regulations 2003 (SI 2003/1731) substituted the following paragraph for para.(3):

3.020

"(3) Working tax credit or child tax credit shall be treated as paid—
  (a) where the award of that tax credit begins on the first day of a benefit week, on that day, or
  (b) on the first day of the benefit week that follows the date the award begins, or
  (c) on the first day of the first benefit week that follows the date an award of income support begins, if later,
until the last day of the last benefit week that coincides with or immediately follows the last day for which the award of that tax credit is made."

p.300, *annotation to Income Support Regulations 1987, reg.31(3)*

The new form of para.(3) contains additional rules for attributing an award of working tax credit or child tax credit. At the start of an award it will be treated as paid on the first day of the benefit week after the date of the award unless the award begins on the first day of a benefit week when it is treated as paid on that day (sub-paras (a) and (b)). If an award of working tax credit or child tax credit is already in payment when income support is claimed, it is treated as paid on the first day of the first benefit week that follows the date income support is awarded (sub-para. (c)). At the end of an award it is treated as paid until the last day of the last benefit week that coincides with or immediately follows the end of the award.

3.021

p.329, *annotation to Income Support Regulations 1987, reg.40(1)*

CJSA 1134/2003 confirms that a loan paid to a part-time student counted as Income for the purposes of income-based JSA (this would also apply to income support).

3.022

p.331, *annotation to Income Support Regulations 1987, reg.40(3A)– (3AB)*

The harsh effect of these provisions where a former student voluntarily repays a loan is confirmed in *CJSA 549/2003*.

3.023

p.335, *Income Support Regulations 1987, reg.42(2C)*

With effect from October 6, 2003, reg.29(2) of the State Pension Credit (Consequential, Transitional and Miscellaneous Provisions) Regulations 2002 (SI 2002/3019) substituted the word "person" for the word "claimant".

3.024

p.344, *annotation to Income Support Regulations 1987, reg.42(2A)*

3.025   CIS 4511/2002 rejects the argument that reg.42(2A) contravened ECHR. Even if Art.1 of Protocol 1 or Art.8 was engaged for the purposes of Art.14, the claimant had not shown a sufficient basis of comparison of his position with that of women for Art.14 to be invoked.

p.355, *annotation to Income Support Regulations 1987, reg.46*

3.026   In *CIS 1189/2003* the claimant was the sole residuary beneficiary under her mother's will. Even though the estate had remained unadministered for several years so that her mother's property had not been vested in the claimant, the property counted as the claimant's actual capital for the purposes of income support since her rights in respect of it were closely equivalent to absolute beneficial ownership.

p.376, *annotation to Income Support Regulations 1987, reg.51(1)*

3.027   In *Jones v Secretary of State for Work and Pensions* [2003] EWCA Civ 964 the claimant and her husband sold some land and used the money to pay off a number of their many debts. One of those debts was for £17,000 which was owed to a friend, Mr S. The claimant's husband and Mr S came to an arrangement whereby the claimant purchased a BMW car for £13,500 as security for this debt. The car was to be Mr S's property but he allowed the claimant and her husband full use of it on the basis that they paid all the running costs. The issue was whether the claimant's significant operative purpose in entering into this arrangement was the retention of entitlement to income support.

The Court of Appeal held that since the tribunal had accepted that the car belonged to Mr S, the effect of the transaction had been that the debt to Mr S had been repaid. The fact that Mr S was content for the money to be used to buy him a car was irrelevant, as was the fact that Mr S was content for the claimant and her husband to use the car. On the facts Mr S had been pressing for repayment of the debt and so the claimant had not deprived herself of capital for the purpose of securing entitlement to income support. However, even if the true position was that the claimant had not repaid Mr S and the car was hers, it was subject to a charge by way of security in favour of Mr S for £17,000 and so under reg.49(a)(ii) the charge had to be deducted from the value of the car (with the result that its value was nil). It could not be said that in creating the charge on the car the claimant had deprived herself of capital for the purpose of securing entitlement to income support since clearly this was the only way the claimant could secure use of the car and if the arrangement had not been made the claimant and her husband would have had to repay the £17,000 loan.

The Court further commented that where a debt was not immediately repayable, its repayment would not necessarily be for the purpose of obtaining income support. Whether or not repayment was for such a purpose was a question of fact to be determined according to the circumstances in each case. Conversely (and more rarely) there could be cases where repayment of an immediately repayable debt was for the purpose of securing entitlement to income support—an example might be where the debtor thought the creditor would not call in the debt for some time but still made immediate repayment. It was a question of fact in each case.

p.390, *Income Support Regulations 1987, reg.53(1ZA)*

With effect from October 6, 2003, by reg.29(3) of the State Pension Credit (Consequential, Transitional and Miscellaneous Provisions) Regulations 2002 (SI 2002/3019) the words "is aged 60 or over or" in sub-para.(a) were omitted.

3.028

pp.422–423, *Income Support Regulations 1987, reg.62*

With effect from September 1, 2003 (or if the student's period of study begins between August 1 and 31, 2003, the first day of the period), reg.2(1) and (3)(c) of the Social Security Amendment (Students and Income-related Benefits) Regulations 2003 (SI 2003/1701) substituted the sum "£270" for the sum "£265" in para.(2A)(a).

3.029

Regulation 3(1)(a) and (2)(c) of the same amending regulations substituted the following sub-para. for sub-para.(cc) in para.(2B):

"(cc) any grant paid under the Schedule to the Education (Assembly Learning Grant Scheme) (Wales) Regulations 2002;".

Reg.3(1)(b) and (2)(c) of the same amending regulations substituted the following after sub-para.(d) in para.(2B):

"; and
(e) any grant paid under regulation 15(7) of the Education (Student Support) (No.2) Regulations 2002.".

With effect from September 1, 2003 (or if the student's period of study begins between August 1 and 31, 2003, the first day of the period), reg.2(1) and (2)(c) of the Social Security Amendment (Students and Income-related Benefits) (No.2) Regulations 2003 (SI 2003/1941) substituted the sum "£335" for the sum "£327" in para.(2A)(b).

p.425, *annotation to Income Support Regulations 1987, reg.62*

From September 1, 2003 (or the first day of the student's period of study if that begins between August 1 and 31, 2003), any "Parental Learning Allowance" grant paid under reg.15(7) of the Education (Student Support) (No.2) Regulations 2002 is disregarded (para.(2B)(e)). The Parental Learning Allowance combines some of the additional allowances for students with children that were previously paid separately, including the grant for the eldest or only child and the extra allowance for books, equipment and travel (see the disregards in sub-

3.030

paras (a) and (b) of para.(2B) respectively). In addition the wording of the disregard in sub-para.(cc) of para.(2B) has been clarified to ensure that any grant paid under the National Assembly for Wales Learning Grant Scheme is ignored.

p.431, *Income Support Regulations 1987, reg.66A(5)*

3.031   With effect from September 1, 2003 (or if the student's period of study begins between August 1 and 31, 2003, the first day of the period), reg.2(1) and (3)(c) of the Social Security Amendment (Students and Income-related Benefits) Regulations 2003 (SI 2003/1701) substituted the sum "£270" for the sum "£265" in sub-para.(a).

With effect from September 1, 2003 (or if the student's period of study begins between August 1 and 31, 2003, the first day of the period), reg.2(1) and (2)(c) of the Social Security Amendment (Students and Income-related Benefits) (No.2) Regulations 2003 (SI 2003/1914) substituted the sum "£335" for the sum "£327" in sub-para.(b).

p.432, *annotation to Income Support Regulations 1987, reg.66A*

3.032   The annual increase in the disregards for (i) travel costs, and (ii) books and equipment, mean that these are now £270 and £335 respectively.

p.440, *annotation to Income Support Regulations 1987, reg.70: pre-April 3, 2000 asylum seekers; meaning of "on arrival"*

3.033   In *Shire v Secretary of State for Work and Pensions* [2003] EWCA Civ 1465 (October 13, 2003) (Lord Woolf L.C.J. Chadwick and Buxton L.JJ.) held that the words "on his arrival" in reg.70(3A) did not extend to cover the circumstances of the claimant who had arrived at Gatwick from the Yemen at 10.30 pm on August 29, 1999 and did not apply for asylum until August 31, 1999 because she was under the control of the agent who had arranged the documents on which she was admitted to the country. The court said that a person who uses an agent must be regarded as putting themselves under the control of that agent so that they are responsible for his or her actions unless there is clear evidence of some form of physical duress. The Court did not find it necessary to decide between the "clearing immigration control" and "leaving the port of entry" tests.

p.447, *Income Support Regulations 1987, reg.71 (Applicable amounts in urgent cases)*

3.034   With effect from October 6, 2003, reg.2 of and Sch.1 para.5 to the Social Security (Removal of Residential Allowance and Miscellaneous Amendments) Regulations 2003 (SI 2003/1121), revoked para.(1)(a)(iv), para.(1)(c) and para.(1A) of reg.71.

Income Support, Jobseekers' Allowance, State Pension Credit

p.459, *Income Support Regulations 1987, Sch.1B, para.14A*

With effect from August 8, 2003, by reg.2(3)(a) of the Social Security (Working Tax Credit and Child Tax Credit) (Consequential Amendments) (No.3) Regulations 2003 (SI 2003/1731) the words "working families' tax credit, disabled person's tax credit" in para.(1)(c) were omitted.

By reg.2(3)(b) of the same amending regulations the words "but subject in any case to calculations of those amounts made in accordance with the Tax Credits (Income Thresholds and Determination of Rates) Regulations 2002." were added at the end of para.(2).

3.035

p.459, *Income Support Regulations 1987, Sch.1B, para.14B*

With effect from August 8, 2003, by reg.2(3)(a) of the Social Security (Working Tax Credit and Child Tax Credit) (Consequential Amendments) (No. 3) Regulations 2003 (SI 2003/1731) the words "working families' tax credit, disabled person's tax credit" in para.(2)(b) were omitted.

By reg.2(3)(b) of the same amending regulations the words "but subject in any case to calculations of those amounts made in accordance with the Tax Credits (Income Thresholds and Determination of Rates) Regulations 2002." were added at the end of para.(3).

3.036

p.460, *Income Support Regulations 1987, Sch.1B, para.17*

With effect from October 6, 2003, by reg. 29(4) of the State Pension Credit (Consequential, Transitional and Miscellaneous Provisions) Regulations 2002 (SI 2002/3019) para.17 was omitted.

3.037

pp.466–467, *annotations to Income Support Regulations 1987, Sch.1B, paras 14A and 14B*

The references to "working families' tax credit" and "disabled person's tax credit" in paras 14A(1)(c) and 14B(2)(b) have been deleted as they are now obsolete.

3.038

p.472, *Income Support Regulations 1987, Sch.2, para.2A*

With effect from October 6, 2003, reg.2 of and Sch.1, para.6 to the Social Security (Removal of Residential Allowance and Miscellaneous Amendments) Regulations 2003 (SI 2003/1121), revoked para.2A of Sched.2.

3.039

p.475, *Income Support (General) Regulations 1987, Sch.2, para.9 (Pensioner premium for persons under 75)*

With effect from October 6, 2003, reg.29(5)(a) of the State Pension Credit (Consequential, Transitional and Miscellaneous Provisions) Regulations 2002 (SI 2002/3019) substituted a new para.9 (Pensioner premium for persons under 75) as follows:

3.040

Income Support, Jobseekers' Allowance, State Pension Credit

"9. The condition is that the claimant has a partner aged not less than 60 but less than 75."

p.475, *Income Support (General) Regulations 1987, Sch.2, para.9A (Pensioner premium for persons 75 and over)*

3.041   With effect from October 6, 2003, reg.29(5)(b) of the State Pension Credit (Consequential, Transitional and Miscellaneous Provisions) Regulations 2002 (SI 2002/3019) substituted a new para.9A (Pensioner premium for persons 75 and over) as follows:

"9A.—The condition is that the claimant has a partner aged not less than 75 but less than 80."

p.475, *Income Support (General) Regulations 1987, Sch.2, para.10 (Higher Pensioner Premium)*

3.042   With effect from October 6, 2003, reg.29(5)(c) of the State Pension Credit (Consequential, Transitional and Miscellaneous Provisions) Regulations 2002 (SI 2002/3019) substituted the following paragraph for sub-paras (1) and (2) of para. 10 (Higher Pensioner Premium):

"(1) The condition is that—
 (a) the claimant's partner is aged not less than 80; or
 (b) the claimant's partner is aged less than 80 but not less than 60 and either—
  (i) the additional condition specified in paragraph 12(1)(a) or (c) is satisfied; or
  (ii) the claimant was entitled to, or was treated as being in receipt of, income support and—
   (aa) the disability premium was or, as the case may be, would have been, applicable to him in respect of a benefit week within eight weeks of his partner's 60th birthday; and
   (bb) he has, subject to sub-paragraph (3), remained continuously entitled to income support since his partner attained the age of 60."

and amended head (b) of sub-para. (3) to read:

"(b) in so far as sub-paragraph (1)(b)(ii) is concerned, if a claimant ceases to be entitled to or treated as entitled to income support for a period not exceeding eight weeks which includes his partner's 60th birthday, he shall, on becoming re-entitled to income support, thereafter be treated as having been continuously entitled thereto."

Subsequently, also with effect from October 6, 2003, reg.2(1) and (2) of the Income Support (General) Amendment Regulations 2003 (SI 2003/2379), further amended para.10(1)(b)(i) to read as follows:

Income Support, Jobseekers' Allowance, State Pension Credit

"(i) the additional condition specified in paragraph 12(1)(a), (c) or (d) is satisfied; or"

pp.476–477, *Income Support (General) Regulations 1987, Sch.2, para.12 (Additional condition for the Higher Pensioner and Disability Premiums)*

With effect from October 6, 2003, reg.29(5)(e) of the State Pension Credit (Consequential, Transitional and Miscellaneous Provisions) Regulations 2002 (SI 2002/3019) substituted the following heads for head (c) of sub-para.(1) of para.12: 3.043

> "(c) the claimant's partner was in receipt of long-term incapacity benefit under Part II of the Contributions and Benefits Act when entitlement to that benefit ceased on account of the payment of a retirement pension under that Act and—
> (i) the claimant has since remained continuously entitled to income support;
> (ii) the higher pensioner premium or disability premium has been applicable to the claimant; and
> (iii) the partner is still alive;
> (d) except where paragraph (1)(a), (b), (c)(ii) or (d)(ii) of Schedule 7 (patients) applies, the claimant or, as the case may be, his partner was in receipt of attendance allowance or disability living allowance—
> (i) but payment of that benefit has been suspended under the Social Security (Hospital In-Patients) Regulations 1975 or otherwise abated as a consequence of the claimant or his partner becoming a patient within the meaning of regulation 21(3); and
> (ii) a higher pensioner premium or disability premium has been applicable to the claimant."

Subsequently, also with effect from October 6, 2003, reg.2(1) and (4) of the Income Support (General) Amendment Regulations 2003 (SI 2003/2379), further amended the references to "sub-paragraph (1)(c)" in sub-para.12(4) to read "sub-paragraph (1)(c) and (d)" and the reference to "sub-paragraph (1)(a)(i) and (c)(i)" in sub-para.12(6) to read "sub-paragraph (1)(a)(i) and (c)".

p.476, *Income Support (General) Regulations 1987, Sch.2, para.11 (Disability Premium)*

With effect from October 6, 2003, reg.29(5)(d) of the State Pension Credit (Consequential, Transitional and Miscellaneous Provisions) Regulations 2002 (SI 2002/3019) amended para.11 (Disability Premium) to read as follows: 3.044

> "11. The condition is that—
> (a) where the claimant is a single parent or a lone parent, the additional condition in paragraph 12 is satisfied; or
> (b) where the claimant has a partner, either—

Income Support, Jobseekers' Allowance, State Pension Credit

(i) the claimant satisfies the additional condition specified in paragraph 12(1)(a), (b) or (c); or
(ii) his partner is aged less than 60 and the additional condition specified in paragraph 12(1)(a) or (c) is satisfied by his partner"

Subsequently, also with effect from October 6, 2003, reg.2(1) and (3) of the Income Support (General) Amendment Regulations 2003 (SI 2003/2379), further amended para.11(b) to read as follows:

"(b) where the claimant has a partner, either—
(i) the claimant satisfies the additional condition specified in paragraph 12(1)(a), (b), (c) or (d); or
(ii) his partner is aged less than 60 and the additional condition specified in paragraph 12(1)(a), (c) or (d) is satisfied by his partner".

p.478, *Income Support (General) Regulations 1987, Sch.2, para.13A (Enhanced disability premium)*

3.045   With effect from May 21, 2003, reg.3 of the Social Security (Hospital In-Patients and Miscellaneous Amendments) Regulations 2003 (SI 2003/1195), substituted the figures "52" for the word "six" para.13A(2) in both cases where that word occurs.

With effect from October 6, 2003, reg.29(5)(f) of the State Pension Credit (Consequential, Transitional and Miscellaneous Provisions) Regulations 2002 (SI 2002/3019) amended the concluding words of sub-para.(1) of para.13A. (Enhanced disability premium) to read as follows:

" . . . in respect of—
(a) the claimant, or
(b) a member of the claimant's family who is aged less than 60."

p.479, *Income Support Regulations 1987, Sch.2, para.14ZA (Carer premium)*

3.046   With effect from October 1, 2003, reg.2(3) of the Social Security (Miscellaneous Amendments) (No.2) Regulations 2003 (SI 2003/2279), revoked the following parts of para.14ZA:
— sub-para.(2);
— the words "or ceases to be treated as entitled" in head (b) of sub-para.(3);
— head (b) of sub-para.(3A);
— head (b) of sub-para.(4);
inserted the words "where sub-paragraph (3)(a) applies," immediately before the words "the Sunday" in head (a) of sub-para.(3A) and substituted the following for head (c) of sub-para.(4):

Income Support, Jobseekers' Allowance, State Pension Credit

"(c) in any other case, the person who has been entitled to a carer's allowance ceased to be entitled to that allowance."

p.480, *Income Support Regulations 1987, Sch.2, para.15 (Weekly Amounts of Premiums)*

With effect from October 6, 2003, reg.29(5)(g) of the State Pension Credit (Consequential, Transitional and Miscellaneous Provisions) Regulations 2002 (SI 2002/3019) amended sub-paras (2)–(3) of para.15 to read as follows:

3.047

Column (1)	Column (2)
Premium	*Amount*
15 (2) Pensioner premium for persons to whom paragraph 9 applies.	(2) £70.05
(2A) Pensioner premium for persons to whom paragraph 9A applies.	(2A) £70.05
(3) Higher pensioner premium for persons to whom paragraph 10 applies.]	(3) £70.05

p.492, *annotation to Income Support Regulations 1987, Sch.2, para.12(1)(b): Additional condition for the Higher Pensioner and Disability Premiums*

In *CIS/2699/2001* Mr Commissioner Mesher considered whether the requirement that a claimant should have been incapable of work for a continuous period of 364 days (or 196 days if terminally ill) could be satisfied on the basis of retrospective medical evidence. He concluded that this was permitted by regulation 28(2)(a) of the Social Security (Incapacity for Work) (General) Regulations 1995 and regulation 2(1)(d) of the Social Security (Medical Evidence) Regulations 1976. However, by virtue of section 12(8)(b) of the Social Security Act 1998 (which prohibits a tribunal from considering circumstances arising after the date of the decision under appeal), such medical evidence had to be provided *before* the date of the Secretary of State's decision. This was because under reg.28(2)(a), the production of medical evidence was *itself* a circumstance relevant to the claimant's entitlement and not merely evidence related to some relevant circumstance. In so holding, Mr Commissioner Mesher differed from the decision of Mr Commissioner

3.048

Rowland in *CIS/4772/2000* in which the point about section 12(8)(b) had not been raised.

p.496, *Income Support Regulations 1987, Sch.3, para.14ZA*

At the end of the first paragraph of the commentary, delete the final sentence and insert "For the legal basis for the advice given in the Memo see *CIS/367/2003*".

p.503, *Income Support Regulations 1987, Sch.3, para.6*

3.049   With effect from October 6, 2003, reg.29(6)(a) of the State Pension Credit (Consequential, Transitional and Miscellaneous Provisions) Regulations 2002 (SI 2002/3019) inserted the words "or state pension credit" after the words "jobseeker's allowance" in sub-para.(1B).

p.505, *Income Support Regulations 1987, Sch.3, para.8*

3.050   With effect from October 6, 2003, reg.29(6)(b) of the State Pension Credit (Consequential, Transitional and Miscellaneous Provisions) Regulations 2002 (SI 2002/3019) inserted the words "or state pension credit" after the words "jobseeker's allowance" in sub-para.(1B).

p.505, *Income Support Regulations 1987, Sch.3, para.9(1)*

3.051   With effect from October 6, 2003, reg.29(6)(c) of the State Pension Credit (Consequential, Transitional and Miscellaneous Provisions) Regulations 2002 (SI 2002/3019) substituted the following head for head (a):

"(a) the claimant's partner has attained the qualifying age for state pension credit;".

p.507, *Income Support Regulations 1987, Sch.3, para.12*

3.052   With effect from November 16, 2003, reg.2 of the Income Support (General) (Standard Interest Rate Amendment) Regulations 2003 (SI 2003/2693) substituted the words "5.07 per cent" for the words "5.34 per cent" in para.12(1)(a).

p.511, *Income Support Regulations 1987, Sch.3, para.14*

3.053   With effect from October 6, 2003, reg.29(6)(d) of the State Pension Credit (Consequential, Transitional and Miscellaneous Provisions) Regulations 2002 (SI 2002/3019) added at the end a new sub-para.(14):

"(14) For the purpose of determining whether the linking rules set out in this paragraph apply in a case where a claimant's former partner was entitled to state pension credit, any reference to income support in

Income Support, Jobseekers' Allowance, State Pension Credit

this Schedule shall be taken to include also a reference to state pension credit.".

p.513, *Income Support Regulations 1987, Sch.3, para.18(1)*

With effect from October 6, 2003, reg.29(6)(e) of the State Pension Credit (Consequential, Transitional and Miscellaneous Provisions) Regulations 2002 (SI 2002/3019) substituted the following heads (a) to (c) for heads (a) and (b): 3.054

"(a) in respect of a non-dependant aged 18 or over who is engaged in any remunerative work but is not in receipt of state pension credit, £47.75;
(b) in respect of a non-dependant who is engaged in remunerative work and in receipt of state pension credit, £7.40;
(c) in respect of a non-dependant aged 18 or over to whom neither head (a) nor head (b) applies, £7.40.".

p.514, *Income Support Regulations 1987, Sch.3, para.18(7)(g)*

With effect from May 21, 2003, reg.3(4) of the Social Security (Hospital In-Patients and Miscellaneous Amendments) Regulations 2003 (SI 2003/1195) substituted "52" for the word "six" in both places that it occurred in para.18(7)(g). 3.055

p.528, *annotation to Income Support Regulations 1987, Sch.3, para.4(8)*

CIS 4712/2002 holds that "payable in . . ." in para.4(8)(b)(i) refers to entitlement for the week in issue rather than to actual payment in that week. 3.056

p.537, *annotation to Income Support Regulations 1987, Sch.3, para.9*

From October 6, 2003 sub-para.(1)(a) has been amended so that it now only applies to claimants whose partner has attained the qualifying age for state pension credit (this is currently 60 but between 2010 and 2020 will gradually rise until it reaches 65). This is because a person who has reached the qualifying age for state pension credit or whose partner is entitled to state pension credit is not entitled to income support (SSCBA, s.124(1)(aa) and (g)). 3.057

p.538, *annotation to Income Support Regulations 1987, Sch.3, para.11(4)–(11)*

CIS 4320/2002 holds that the £100,000 ceiling on loans is not *ultra vires* and not contrary to Art.8, or Art.8 in conjunction with Art.14, of ECHR. 3.058

pp.538–539, *annotation to Income Support Regulations 1987, Sch.3, para.12*

3.059   The standard rate at which interest on eligible loans is paid is decreased to 5.07 per cent with effect from November 23, 2003.

p.546, *annotation to Income Support Regulations 1987, Sch.3, para.14(14)*

3.060   This provides that for the purposes of the linking rules in para.14, if a claimant's former partner was entitled to state pension credit, any reference to income support in Sch.3 also includes a reference to state pension credit.

p.555, *annotation to Income Support Regulations 1987, Sch.3, para.18(1)*

3.061   If a non-dependant who is in remunerative work is getting state pension credit the deduction is the same as for a non-dependant who is not in remunerative work.

p.556, *annotation to Income Support Regulations 1987, Sch.3, para.18(7)(g)*

3.062   A deduction for a non-dependant in hospital will now continue to be made until the person has been an in-patient for more than 52 weeks; under the previous form of para.18(7)(g) the deduction ceased after the non-dependant had been in hospital for more than six weeks. This change takes effect from the first day of the first benefit week beginning on or after May 21, 2003 if income support is paid in advance or the first day of the benefit week which includes May 21, 2003 if income support is paid in arrears.

p.569, *Income Support Regulations 1987, Sch.3C*

3.063   With effect from October 6, 2003, by reg.2 of and para.7 of Sch.1 to the Social Security (Removal of Residential Allowance and Miscellaneous Amendments) Regulations 2003 (SI 2003/1121) Sch.3C was omitted.

p.570, *Income Support Regulations 1987, Sch.7, para.1*

3.064   With effect from May 21, 2003, reg.3 of the Social Security (Hospital In-Patients and Miscellaneous Amendments) Regulations 2003 (SI 2003/1195), substituted the figure "3" for the figures "3 and 18", the figure "52" for the word "six", and revoked sub-para.(a) (in both columns).

p.570, *Income Support Regulations 1987, Sch.7, para.13*

3.065   With effect from May 21, 2003, reg.3 of the Social Security (Hospital In-Patients and Miscellaneous Amendments) Regulations 2003 (SI

2003/1195), revoked sub-para.(2) and the words "Subject to sub-paragraph (2)" in sub-para.(1) of para.13.

pp.573–574, *Income Support Regulations 1987, Sch.7, paras 10A–10C*

With effect from October 6, 2003, reg.2 of and Sch.1, para.8 to the Social Security (Removal of Residential Allowance and Miscellaneous Amendments) Regulations 2003 (SI 2003/1121), revoked paras 10A—10C of Sch.7. **3.066**

pp.575–578, *Income Support Regulations 1987, Sch.7, paras 13–13B*

With effect from October 6, 2003, reg.2 of and Sch.1, para.8 to the Social Security (Removal of Residential Allowance and Miscellaneous Amendments) Regulations 2003 (SI 2003/1121), revoked paras 13(1), 13A and 13B of Sch.7. **3.067**

p.577, *Income Support Regulations 1987, Sch.7, para.13B*

With effect from May 21, 2003, reg.3 of the Social Security (Hospital In-Patients and Miscellaneous Amendments) Regulations 2003 (SI 2003/1195), substituted the figure "52" for the figure "6" in, and revoked head (ii) of, column (2) of sub-para.(a) of para.13B. **3.068**

pp.583–584, *Income Support Regulations 1987, Sch.8*

With effect from October 6, 2003, by reg.29(7)(a) of the State Pension Credit (Consequential, Transitional and Miscellaneous Provisions) Regulations 2002 (SI 2002/3019) head (i) in para.1(a) was omitted. **3.069**

Reg.29(7)(b) of the same amending regulations inserted the following new para.1A after para.1:

> "1A. If the claimant's partner has been engaged in remunerative work as an employed earner or, had the employment been in Great Britain, would have been so engaged, any earnings paid or due to be paid on termination of that employment by way of retirement but only if the partner has attained the qualifying age for state pension credit on retirement."

Reg.29(7)(c) of the same amending regulations amended para.4 to read as follows:

> "4.—(1) In a case to which this paragraph applies, £20: but notwithstanding regulation 23 (calculation of income and capital of members of claimant's family and of a polygamous marriage), if this paragraph applies to a claimant it shall not apply to his partner except where, and to the extent that, the earnings of the claimant which are to be disregarded under this paragraph are less than £20. **3.070**

(2) This paragraph applies where the claimant's applicable amount includes, or but for his being an in-patient or in residential accommodation would include, an amount by way of a disability premium under Schedule 2 (applicable amounts).

(3) This paragraph applies where—

(a) the claimant is a member of a couple, and—
   (i) his applicable amount would include an amount by way of the disability premium under Schedule 2 but for the higher pensioner premium under that Schedule being applicable; or
   (ii) had he not been an in-patient or in residential accommodation his applicable amount would include the higher pensioner premium under that Schedule and had that been the case he would also satisfy the condition in (i) above; and

(b) [. . .]

(4) This paragraph applies where—

(a) the claimant's applicable amount includes, or but for his being an in-patient or in residential accommodation would include, an amount by way of the higher pensioner premium under Schedule 2; and

[(b) the claimant's partner has attained the qualifying age for state pension credit;]

(c) immediately before attaining that age [. . .] his partner was engaged in part-time employment and the claimant was entitled by virtue of sub-paragraph (2) [. . .] to a disregard of £20; and

(d) he or, as the case may be, he or his partner has continued in part-time employment.

3.071

(7) For the purposes of this paragraph—

(a) except where head (b) or (c) applies, no account shall be taken of any period not exceeding eight consecutive weeks occurring—
   [(i) on or after the date on which the claimant's partner attained the qualifying age for state pension credit during which the partner was not engaged in part-time employment or the claimant was not entitled to income support; or]
   (ii) immediately after the date on which the claimant or his partner ceased to participate in arrangements for training made under section 2 of the Employment and Training Act 1973 or section 2 of the Enterprise and New Towns (Scotland) Act 1990 or to attend a course at an employment rehabilitation centre established under that section of the 1973 Act;

(b) in a case where the claimant has ceased to be entitled to income support because he, or if he is a member of a couple, he or his partner becomes engaged in remunerative work, no account shall be taken of any period, during which he was not entitled to income support, not exceeding the permitted period determined in accordance with regulation 3A (permitted period)

Income Support, Jobseekers' Allowance, State Pension Credit

occurring on or after the date on which [the claimant's partner attains the qualifying age for state pension credit];

(c) no account shall be taken of any period occurring on or after the date on which [the claimant's partner, if he is a member of a couple, attained the qualifying age for state pension credit] during which the claimant was not entitled to income support because he or his partner was participating in arrangements for training made under section 2 of the Employment and Training Act 1973 or section 2 of the Enterprise and New Towns (Scotland) Act 1990 or attending a course at an employment rehabilitation centre established under that section of the 1973 Act."

p.587, *annotation to Income Support Regulations 1987, Sch.8, paras 1 and 1A*

Claimants who have reached the qualifying age for state pension credit (this is currently 60 but between 2010 and 2020 will gradually rise until it reaches 65) or whose partner is entitled to state pension credit are not entitled to income support (SSCBA, s.124(1)(aa) and (g)). Head (ii) of para.1(a) has therefore been omitted because there is no longer any need for a disregard of a claimant's earnings paid on termination of employment due to retirement. The new para.1A provides for a disregard of a partner's earnings paid in these circumstances provided that the partner has reached the qualifying age for state pension credit.

3.072

p.587, *annotation to Income Support Regulations 1987, Sch.8, para.4*

The amendments that have been made to para. 4 with effect from October 6, 2003 reflect the fact that claimants who have attained the qualifying age for state pension credit or whose partner is entitled to state pension credit are not entitled to income support (SSCBA, s.124(1)(aa) and (g)).

3.073

p.590, *Income Support Regulations 1987, Sch.9, para.9*

With effect from October 6, 2003, by reg.2 of and para.9(a) of Sch.1 to the Social Security (Removal of Residential Allowance and Miscellaneous Amendments) Regulations 2003 (SI 2003/1121) para.9 was amended to read as follows:

3.074

"**9.** Any attendance allowance or the care component of disability living allowance."

p.592, *Income Support Regulations 1987, Sch.9, para.15B*

With effect from October 6, 2003, by reg.2 of and para.9(b) of Sch.1 to the Social Security (Removal of Residential Allowance and Miscellaneous Amendments) Regulations 2003 (SI 2003/1121) para.15B was omitted.

3.075

Income Support, Jobseekers' Allowance, State Pension Credit

p.594, *Income Support Regulations 1987, Sch.9, para.25*

3.076 With effect from October 1, 2003, reg.2(4)(a)(i) of the Social Security (Miscellaneous Amendments) (No.2) Regulations 2003 (SI 2003/2279) amended head (a) of sub-para.(1) to read as follows:

"(a) in accordance with regulations made pursuant to section 57A of the Adoption Act 1976 (permitted allowances) [or paragraph 3 of Schedule 4 to the Adoption and Children Act 2002] or with a scheme approved by the Secretary of State under section 51 of the Adoption (Scotland) Act 1978 (schemes for payment of allowances to adopters);".

Reg.2(4)(a)(ii) of the same amending regulations inserted the following sub-para. after sub-para.(1):

"(1A) Any payment, other than a payment to which sub-paragraph (1)(a) applies, made to the claimant in accordance with regulations made under paragraph 3 of Schedule 4 to the Adoption and Children Act 2002.".

p.600, *Income Support Regulations 1987, Sch.9, paras 76–78*

3.077 With effect from October 1, 2003, reg.2(4)(b) of the Social Security (Miscellaneous Amendments) (No.2) Regulations 2003 (SI 2003/2279) substituted the following sub-para. for sub-para.(1) of para.76:

"**76.**—(1) Any payment made by a local authority, or by the National Assembly for Wales, to or on behalf of the claimant or his partner relating to a service which is provided to develop or sustain the capacity of the claimant or his partner to live independently in his accommodation.".

Reg.2(4)(c) of the same amending regulations inserted the following new paragraph after para.76:

"**77.** Any ERA payment".

With effect from October 27, 2003, reg.13(a) of the Social Security (Incapacity Benefit Work-focused Interviews) Regulations 2003 (SI 2003/2439) added the following new para. after para.77:

"**78.** Any payment made to a claimant's partner in respect of the partner's participation in the Return to Work Credit Scheme pursuant to section 2 of the Employment and Training Act 1973 (functions of the Secretary of State).".

p.606, *annotation to Income Support Regulations 1987, Sch.9, para.9*

3.078 From October 6, 2003 there is no longer any special provision under para.9 for claimants living in Polish resettlement homes.

Income Support, Jobseekers' Allowance, State Pension Credit

p.608, *annotation to Income Support Regulations 1987, Sch.9, para.15B*

From October 6, 2003 there is no longer any special disregard of occupational or personal pensions for claimants living in Polish resettlement homes. Such income will now be taken into account in full in the normal way.

3.079

p.617, *annotation to Income Support Regulations 1987, Sch.9, paras 76–78*

Paragraph 76

The disregard in para.76(1) has been reworded to remove the existing legislative references in order to ensure that it covers all payments made under the Supporting People programme.

3.080

Paragraph 77

The Employment Retention and Advancement (ERA) scheme set up under s.2 of the Employment and Training Act 1973 started in October 2003 and will operate in certain areas of the country until July 2007. The scheme is open to people who are eligible for the New Deal 25 Plus or the New Deal for Lone Parents and certain working tax credit recipients. It includes a number of financial incentives referred to as "ERA payments" (see the definition in reg.2(1)). Any such ERA payment is ignored as income; for the capital disregard see para.69 of Sch.10.

Paragraph 78

The Return to Work Credit Scheme is intended to encourage people who have been receiving benefit on the ground of incapacity for work to return to or take up employment. It is paid at £40 per week for 52 weeks to a person who ceases to receive incapacity benefit, income support on the ground of incapacity for work (including income support that was payable because s/he was appealing against a decision that s/he was capable of work) or severe disablement allowance because s/he starts work of at least 16 hours per week and whose earnings will be less than £15,000 a year. Under the new para.78 any payments under the Return to Work Credit Scheme to a claimant's partner are ignored. For the indefinite capital disregard of such payments see the new para.70 of Sch.10.

p.622, *Income Support Regulations 1987, Sch.10, paras 44 and 45*

With effect from October 1, 2003, reg.2(5)(a) of the Social Security (Miscellaneous Amendments) (No.2) Regulations 2003 (SI 2003/2279) substituted the words "or the County Court under Rule 21.11(1) of the Civil Procedure Rules 1998" for the words "under the provisions of Order 80 of the Rules of the Supreme Court, the County Court under Order 10 of the County Court Rules 1981" in para.44.

Regulation 2(5)(b) of the same amending regulations substituted the words "section 13 of the Children (Scotland) Act 1995" for the words

3.081

Income Support, Jobseekers' Allowance, State Pension Credit

"Rule 43.15 of the Act of Sederunt (Rules of the Court of Session 1994) 1994 or under Rule 131 of the Act of Sederunt (Rules of the Court, consolidation and amendment) 1965" in para.45.

p.625, *Income Support Regulations 1987, Sch.10, paras 66–70*

3.082   With effect from October 1, 2003, reg.2(5)(c) of the Social Security (Miscellaneous Amendments) (No.2) Regulations 2003 (SI 2003/2279) substituted the following sub-para. for sub-para.(1) of para.66:

"**66.**—(1) Any payment made by a local authority, or by the National Assembly for Wales, to or on behalf of the claimant or his partner relating to a service which is provided to develop or sustain the capacity of the claimant or his partner to live independently in his accommodation.".

Reg.2(5)(d) of the same amending regulations added the following new paras after para.66:

"**67.** Any payment made under the Community Care (Direct Payments) Act 1996, regulations made under section 57 of the Health and Social Care Act 2001 or under section 12B of the Social Work (Scotland) Act 1968.

68. Any payment made to the claimant in accordance with regulations made under paragraph 3 of Schedule 4 to the Adoption and Children Act 2002.

69. Any ERA payment but only for a period of 52 weeks from the date of receipt of that payment.".

With effect from October 27, 2003, reg.13(b) of the Social Security (Incapacity Benefit Work-focused Interviews) Regulations 2003 (SI 2003/2439) added the following new para. after para.69:

"**70.** Any payment made to a claimant's partner in respect of the partner's participation in the Return to Work Credit Scheme pursuant to section 2 of the Employment and Training Act 1973.".

pp.634–635, *annotation to Income Support Regulations 1987, Sch.10, para.10*

3.083   Note *CIS 2208/2003* which considers the actual and notional capital issues that arise when personal possessions have been acquired for the purpose of securing entitlement to income support.

p.642, *annotation to Income Support Regulations 1987, Sch.10, paras 66, 69 and 70*

Paragraph 66

3.084   See the note to para.76(1) of Sch.9 above.

Income Support, Jobseekers' Allowance, State Pension Credit

Paragraph 69

See the note to the new para.77 of Sch.9 above. Note that if such a payment counts as capital it is only disregarded for 52 weeks from the date of receipt.

Paragraph 70

See the note to the new para.78 of Sch.9 above.

p.660, *Social Security (Immigration and Asylum) Consequential Amendments Regulations 2000, reg.2(1)*

With effect from October 6, 2003, reg.6 of the State Pension Credit (Transitional and Miscellaneous Provisions) Amendment Regulations 2003 (SI 2003/2274), amended reg.2 to read as follows:

3.085

"**2.**—(1) For the purposes of entitlement to income-based jobseeker's allowance, income support, a social fund payment, housing benefit or council tax benefit under the Contributions and Benefits Act, or state pension credit under the State Pension Credit Act 2002, as the case may be, a person falling within a category or description of persons specified in Part I of the Sched. is a person to whom section 115 of the Act does not apply."

p.661, *Social Security (Immigration and Asylum) Consequential Amendments Regulations 2000, reg.2(4)(c)*

With effect from October 6, 2003, reg.6 of the State Pension Credit (Transitional and Miscellaneous Provisions) Amendment Regulations 2003 (SI 2003/2274), inserted a new sub-para.(c) in para.(4) of reg.2 as follows:

3.086

"(c) state pension credit under the State Pension Credit Act 2002, a person to whom sub-paragraph (a) would have applied but for the fact that they have attained the qualifying age for the purposes of state pension credit, is a person to whom section 115 of the Act does not apply."

p.661, *Social Security (Immigration and Asylum) Consequential Amendments Regulations 2000, regs 2(7) and (8)*

With effect from October 6, 2003, reg.6 of the State Pension Credit (Transitional and Miscellaneous Provisions) Amendment Regulations 2003 (SI 2003/2274), inserted new paras (7) and (8) in reg.2 as follows:

3.087

"(7) For the purposes of entitlement to state pension credit under the State Pension Credit Act 2002, a person to whom paragraph (5) would have applied but for the fact that they have attained the qualifying age for the purposes of state pension credit, is a person to whom section 115 of the Act does not apply.

(8) Where paragraph 1 of Part I of the Schedule to these Regulations applies in respect of entitlement to state pension credit, the period for which a claimant's state pension credit is to be calculated shall be any period, or the aggregate of any periods, not exceeding 42 days during any one period of leave to which paragraph 1 of Part I of the Schedule to these Regulations applies."

p.667, *State Pension Credit (Consequential, Transitional and Miscellaneous Provisions) Regulations 2002, reg.36(7)*

3.088   With effect from October 6, 2003, reg.3(a) of the State Pension Credit (Transitional and Miscellaneous Provisions) Amendment Regulations 2003 (SI 2003/2274) inserted the words "Notwithstanding the provisions of Schedule 3B of the Decisions and Appeals Regulations," at the beginning of para.(7).

Reg.3(b) of the same amending regulations inserted the following para. after para.(7):

"(7A) Notwithstanding the provisions of paragraph (7), where the relevant change of circumstances is that the transferee becomes a patient again within the same benefit week in which he ceased to be a patient, the superseding decision in respect of becoming a patient again shall take effect from the first day of the benefit week following the benefit week in which the change occurs.".

p.668, *State Pension Credit (Consequential, Transitional and Miscellaneous Provisions) Regulations 2002, reg.36(15)–(19)*

3.089   With effect from May 21, 2003, by reg.9 of the Social Security (Hospital In-Patients and Miscellaneous Amendments) Regulations 2003 paras (15) to (19) of reg.36 were omitted.

pp.672–673, *Social Security (Working Tax Credit and Child Tax Credit) (Consequential Amendments) Regulations 2003, reg.7*

3.090   With effect from August 8, 2003, reg.6 of the Social Security (Working Tax Credit and Child Tax Credit) (Consequential Amendments) (No. 3) Regulations 2003 (SI 2003/1731), amended paras (1)–(3) and (7) of reg.7 to read as follows:

"Income Support—transitional arrangements

7.—(1) [¹ Subject to paragraph (2) and regulation 31(3) of the Income Support Regulations 1987,] in the case of a claimant for income support who makes a claim, or whose partner makes a claim, for a child tax credit, the Secretary of State shall treat that claimant's income as including an amount equivalent to the amount of child tax credit to which he, or his partner, is entitled for the period specified in paragraph (3).

(2) In a case where a claimant for income support—
  (a) has a child or young person who is a member of his family for the purposes of his claim for income support; and

Income Support, Jobseekers' Allowance, State Pension Credit

(b) is, or has a partner who is, aged not less than 60,
the Secretary of State shall, [¹ in the benefit week which begins on or includes 5th October 2003, disregard from his income an amount equivalent to the amount of child tax credit to which he is entitled.]

(3) For the purposes of paragraphs [¹ paragraph (1)], the specified period begins on the first day of the first benefit week to commence for that claimant on or after 7th April 2003, or the date the award of child tax credit begins if later, and ends on the day before the first day of the first benefit week to commence for that claimant on or after 6th April 2004.

[(4)–(6) As Main Volume]

(7) For the purposes of paragraph (6), the specified period begins on the first day of the first benefit week to commence for that claimant on or after 7th April 2003 and ends on—
   (a) [¹ subject to sub-paragraph (d)] in a case where the claimant, or his partner, is awarded child tax credit for a period beginning before 6th April 2004, the first day of the first benefit week to commence for that claimant on or after 6th April 2004;
   (b) [¹ subject to sub-paragraph (d)] in a case where the claimant, or his partner, is awarded child tax credit for a period beginning on or after 6th April 2004 the first day of the first benefit week to commence for that claimant on or after the day that award of child tax credit begins;
   (c) [¹ subject to sub-paragraph (d)] the first day of the first benefit week in which the award of child benefit in respect of that child ends, if earlier.
   (d) the first day of the benefit week in which the child's first birthday occurs, if earlier."

pp.673–674, *Social Security (Working Tax Credit and Child Tax Credit) (Consequential Amendments) Regulations 2003, reg.8*

With effect from August 8, 2003, reg.6(3) of the Social Security (Working Tax Credit and Child Tax Credit) (Consequential Amendments) (No.3) Regulations 2003 (SI 2003/1731), amended paras (1) and (6) of reg.8 to read as follows:

3.091

3.092

"**8.**—(1) Subject to regulation 96(3) of the Jobseeker's Allowance Regulations, in the case of a claimant for jobseeker's allowance who makes a claim, or whose partner makes a claim, for a child tax credit, the Secretary of State shall treat that claimant's income as including an amount equivalent to the amount of child tax credit to which he, or his partner, is entitled for the period specified in paragraph (2).

[(2)–(5) As Main Volume]

(6) For the purposes of paragraph (5), the specified period begins on the first day of the first benefit week to commence for that claimant on or after 7th April 2003 and ends on—

(a) subject to paragraph (d) in a case where the claimant, or his partner, is awarded child tax credit for a period beginning before 6th April 2004, the first day of the first benefit week to commence for that claimant on or after 6th April 2004;
(b) subject to paragraph (d) in a case where the claimant, or his partner, is awarded child tax credit for a period beginning on or after 6th April 2004 the first day of the first benefit week to commence for that claimant on or after the day on which that award of child tax credit begins; or
(c) subject to paragraph (d) the first day of the first benefit week in which the award of child benefit in respect of that child ends, if earlier or
(d) the first day of the benefit week in which the child's first birthday occurs, if earlier."

p.676, *Community Charges (Deductions from Income Support) (No.2) Regulations 1990, reg.1(2)*

3.093   With effect from October 6, 2003, reg.35 of the State Pension Credit (Consequential, Transitional and Miscellaneous Provisions) Regulations 2002 (SI 2002/3019) amended reg.1(2) by inserting the following definition after the definition of "single debtor":

" 'state pension credit' means the benefit of that name payable under the State Pension Credit Act 2002;"

p.677, *Community Charges (Deductions from Income Support) (No.2) Regulations 1990, reg.2*

3.094   With effect from October 6, 2003, reg.35 of the State Pension Credit (Consequential, Transitional and Miscellaneous Provisions) Regulations 2002 (SI 2002/3019) amended the heading of reg.2 and the text of paras (1) and (2)(e) by adding the words ", state pension credit" after the words "income support".

pp.678–679, *Community Charges (Deductions from Income Support) (No.2) Regulations 1990, reg.3*

3.095   With effect from October 6, 2003, reg.35 of the State Pension Credit (Consequential, Transitional and Miscellaneous Provisions) Regulations 2002 (SI 2002/3019) amended the heading and text of reg.3 by adding the words ", state pension credit" after the words "income support" wherever the latter words occur.

p.680, *Community Charges (Deductions from Income Support) (No.2) Regulations 1990, reg.4*

3.096   With effect from October 6, 2003, reg.35 of the State Pension Credit (Consequential, Transitional and Miscellaneous Provisions) Regulations 2002 (SI 2002/3019) amended reg.4 by adding the words ", state pension credit" after the words "income support" wherever the latter words occur.

Income Support, Jobseekers' Allowance, State Pension Credit

p.683, *Fines (Deductions from Income Support) Regulations 1992, reg. 1(2)—definition of "application"*

With effect from June 20, 2003, reg.2(a) of the Fines (Deductions from Income Support) (Amendment) Regulations 2003 (SI 2003/1360), revoked the words "in the form and" in regulation 1(2).

3.097

p.683, *Fines (Deductions from Income Support) Regulations 1992, reg.1(2)*

With effect from October 6, 2003, reg.32 of the State Pension Credit (Consequential, Transitional and Miscellaneous Provisions) Regulations 2002 (SI 2002/3019) amended reg.1(2) by adding the words "regulation 1(2) of the State Pension Credit Regulations 2002 or" after the words "as the case may be" in the definition of "benefit week".

3.098

p.684, *Fines (Deductions from Income Support) Regulations 1992, reg.1(2)*

With effect from October 6, 2003, reg.32 of the State Pension Credit (Consequential, Transitional and Miscellaneous Provisions) Regulations 2002 (SI 2002/3019) amended reg.1(2) by:

3.099

— substituting the following for the definition of "personal allowance for a single claimant aged not less than 25"
  " 'personal allowance for a single claimant aged not less than 25' " means—
  (a) in the case of a person who is entitled to either income support or state pension credit, the amount for the time being specified in paragraph 1(1)(e) of column (2) of Schedule 2 to the Income Support Regulations 1987; or
  (b) in the case of a person who is entitled to an income-based jobseeker's allowance, the amount for the time being specified in paragraph 1(1)(e) of column (2) of Schedule 1 to the Jobseeker's Allowance Regulations 1996;"
— adding the following definition after the definition of "social security office":
  " 'state pension credit' means the benefit of that name payable under the State Pension Credit Act 2002;"

p.685, *Fines (Deductions from Income Support) Regulations 1992, reg.2*

With effect from October 6, 2003, reg.32 of the State Pension Credit (Consequential, Transitional and Miscellaneous Provisions) Regulations 2002 (SI 2002/3019) amended reg.2 by adding the words ", state pension credit" after the words "income support" on both the occasions where they occur.

3.100

p.685, *Fines (Deductions from Income Support) Regulations 1992, reg.3*

With effect from June 20, 2003, reg.2(b) of the Fines (Deductions from Income Support) (Amendment) Regulations 2003 (SI 2003/1360),

3.101

Income Support, Jobseekers' Allowance, State Pension Credit

revoked the words "shall be made in the form set out in Schedule 3, or a form to like effect, and" in reg.3.

p.686, *Fines (Deductions from Income Support) Regulations 1992, reg.4(1)(a)*

3.102   With effect from October 6, 2003, reg.32 of the State Pension Credit (Consequential, Transitional and Miscellaneous Provisions) Regulations 2002 (SI 2002/3019) amended the heading of reg.4 and the text of para.(1)(a) by adding the words ", state pension credit" after the words "income support".

pp.687–688, *Fines (Deductions from Income Support) Regulations 1992, reg.7*

3.103   With effect from October 6, 2003, reg.32 of the State Pension Credit (Consequential, Transitional and Miscellaneous Provisions) Regulations 2002 (SI 2002/3019) amended reg.7 by adding the words ", state pension credit" after the words "income support" wherever the latter words occur.

p.691, *Fines (Deductions from Income Support) Regulations 1992, Sch.3*

3.104   With effect from June 20, 2003, reg.2(c) of the Fines (Deductions from Income Support) (Amendment) Regulations 2003 (SI 2003/1360), revoked Sch.3.

p.691, *Council Tax (Deductions from Income Support) Regulations 1992, reg.1(2)*

3.105   With effect from October 6, 2003, reg.33 of the State Pension Credit (Consequential, Transitional and Miscellaneous Provisions) Regulations 2002 (SI 2002/3019) amended reg.1(2) by adding the words "regulation 1(2) of the State Pension Credit Regulations 2002 or" after the words "as the case may be" in the definition of "benefit week".

p.692, *Council Tax (Deductions from Income Support) Regulations 1992, reg.1(2)*

3.106   With effect from October 6, 2003, reg.33 of the State Pension Credit (Consequential, Transitional and Miscellaneous Provisions) Regulations 2002 (SI 2002/3019) amended reg.1(2) by:

— substituting the following for the definition of "personal allowance for a single claimant aged not less than 25"
  " 'personal allowance for a single claimant aged not less than 25' " means—
  (a) in the case of a person who is entitled to either income support or state pension credit, the amount for the time being specified in paragraph 1(1)(e) of column (2) of Schedule 2 to the Income Support Regulations 1987; or

Income Support, Jobseekers' Allowance, State Pension Credit

(b) in the case of a person who is entitled to an income-based jobseeker's allowance, the amount for the time being specified in paragraph 1(1)(e) of column (2) of Schedule 1 to the Jobseeker's Allowance Regulations 1996;"

— adding the following definition after the definition of "social security office":

" 'state pension credit' means the benefit of that name payable under the State Pension Credit Act 2002;"

p.693, *Council Tax (Deductions from Income Support) Regulations 1992, reg.2*

With effect from October 6, 2003, reg.33 of the State Pension Credit (Consequential, Transitional and Miscellaneous Provisions) Regulations 2002 (SI 2002/3019) amended reg.2 by adding the words ", state pension credit" after the words "income support" wherever the latter words occur. 3.107

p.693, *Council Tax (Deductions from Income Support) Regulations 1992, reg.3*

With effect from October 6, 2003, reg.33 of the State Pension Credit (Consequential, Transitional and Miscellaneous Provisions) Regulations 2002 (SI 2002/3019) amended reg.3 by adding the words ", state pension credit" after the words "income support" wherever the latter words occur. 3.108

p.694, *Council Tax (Deductions from Income Support) Regulations 1992, reg.4(1)(f)*

With effect from October 6, 2003, reg.33 of the State Pension Credit (Consequential, Transitional and Miscellaneous Provisions) Regulations 2002 (SI 2002/3019) amended reg.4(1)(f) by adding the words ", state pension credit" after the words "income support". 3.109

p.694, *Council Tax (Deductions from Income Support) Regulations 1992, reg.5*

With effect from October 6, 2003, reg.33 of the State Pension Credit (Consequential, Transitional and Miscellaneous Provisions) Regulations 2002 (SI 2002/3019) amended the heading of reg.5 and the text of para.(1)(a) by adding the words ", state pension credit" after the words "income support". 3.110

pp.696–697, *Council Tax (Deductions from Income Support) Regulations 1992, reg.8*

With effect from October 6, 2003, reg.33 of the State Pension Credit (Consequential, Transitional and Miscellaneous Provisions) Regulations 2002 (SI 2002/3019) amended reg.8(1)–(3) and (5) by adding the words 3.111

pp.722–723, *Social Security (Back to Work Bonus) (No.2) Regulations 1996, reg.17*

3.112   With effect from October 6, 2003, reg.7(2) of the State Pension Credit (Consequential, Transitional and Miscellaneous Provisions) (No.2) Regulations 2002 (SI 2002/3197) substituted the words "state pension credit" for the words "income support" in all the places that they occur in paras (4) and (6) and added at the end a new para.(8):

"(8) In this regulation, ", state pension credit" means the benefit of that name payable under the State Pension Credit Act 2002."

pp.739–740, *Social Security (Child Maintenance Bonus) Regulations 1996, reg.8*

3.113   With effect from October 6, 2003, reg.7(1) of the State Pension Credit (Consequential, Transitional and Miscellaneous Provisions) (No.2) Regulations 2002 (SI 2002/3197) substituted the words "state pension credit" for the words "income support" in both places that they occur in para.(2) and inserted the following para. after para.(2):

"(2A) In paragraph (2), ", state pension credit" means the benefit of that name payable under the State Pension Credit Act 2002."

p.755, *Child Support (Maintenance Calculation Procedure) Regulations 2000, reg.8(2)(b)*

3.114   With effect from November 4, 2003, reg.5(2)(a) of the Child Support (Miscellaneous Amendments) (No.2) Regulations 2003 (SI 2003/2779) substituted the words "the circumstances in regulation 14(4) or 15(4), as the case may be, apply;" for the words "becomes payable at one of the rates indicated in regulation 14(4) or, as the case may be, regulation 15(4);".

Reg.5(2)(b) of the same amending regulations substituted the words "the circumstances in regulation 14(4) or 15(4), as the case may be, apply," for the words "relevant benefit is payable at one of the rates indicated in regulation 15(4) or, as the case may be, regulation 16(4),".

p.758, *Child Support (Maintenance Calculation Procedure) Regulations 2000, reg.14*

3.115   With effect from November 4, 2003, by reg.5(3)(a) of the Child Support (Miscellaneous Amendments) (No.2) Regulations 2003 (SI 2003/2779) the words "when a modified applicable amount is payable" in the heading were omitted.

By reg.5(3)(b) of the same amending regulations, in para.(1), the words "but the circumstances in paragraph (4) apply to her" were substituted for the words "but her applicable amount falls to be calculated under the provisions mentioned in paragraph (4)" and the words "those circumstances apply" were substituted for the words "her applicable amount falls to be calculated under the provisions mentioned in that paragraph".

By reg.5(3)(c) of the same amending regulations para.(2) was omitted.

By reg.5(3)(d) of the same amending regulations the words "or 2" in para.(3) were omitted.

By reg.5(3)(e) of the same amending regulations the following paras were substituted for para.(4):

"(4) The circumstances referred to in paragraph (1) are that—
   (a) she is resident in a care home or an independent hospital;
   (b) she is being provided with a care home service or an independent health care service; or
   (c) her applicable amount falls to be calculated under regulation 21 of and any of paragraphs 1 to 3 of Schedule 7 to the Income Support Regulations (patients).
(5) In paragraph (4)—
"care home" has the meaning assigned to it by section 3 of the Care Standards Act 2000;
"care home service" has the meaning assigned to it by section 2(3) of the Regulation of Care (Scotland) Act 2001;
"independent health care service" has the meaning assigned to it by section 2(5)(a) and (b) of the Regulation of Care (Scotland) Act 2001; and "independent hospital" has the meaning assigned to it by section 2 of the Care Standards Act 2000."

p.759, *Child Support (Maintenance Calculation Procedure) Regulations 2000, reg.15*

With effect from November 4, 2003, by reg.5(4)(a) of the Child Support (Miscellaneous Amendments) (No.2) Regulations 2003 (SI 2003/2779) the words "when a modified applicable amount is payable" in the heading were omitted. 3.116

By reg.5(4)(b) of the same amending regulations, in para.(1), the words "but the circumstances in paragraph (4) apply to her" were substituted for the words "but her applicable amount falls to be calculated under the provisions mentioned in paragraph (4)" and the words "those circumstances apply" were substituted for the words "the applicable amount falls to be calculated under those provisions".

By reg.5(4)(c) of the same amending regulations para.(2) was omitted.

By reg.5(4)(d) of the same amending regulations the words "or 2" in para.(3) were omitted.

By reg.5(4)(e) of the same amending regulations the following paras were substituted for para.(4): 3.117

"(4) The circumstances referred to in paragraph (1) are that—
   (a) she is resident in a care home or an independent hospital;

Income Support, Jobseekers' Allowance, State Pension Credit

  (b) she is being provided with a care home service or an independent health care service; or
  (c) her applicable amount falls to be calculated under regulation 85 of and paragraph 1 or 2 of Schedule 5 to the Jobseeker's Allowance Regulations (patients).
 (5) In paragraph (4)—
"care home" has the meaning assigned to it by section 3 of the Care Standards Act 2000;
"care home service" has the meaning assigned to it by section 2(3) of the Regulation of Care (Scotland) Act 2001;
"independent health care service" has the meaning assigned to it by section 2(5)(a) and (b) of the Regulation of Care (Scotland) Act 2001; and
"independent hospital" has the meaning assigned to it by section 2 of the Care Standards Act 2000."

p.764, *Child Support (Maintenance Calculations and Special Cases) Regulations 2000, reg.4*

3.118 With effect from October 6, 2003, reg.27(3) of the State Pension Credit (Consequential, Transitional and Miscellaneous Provisions) Regulations 2002 (SI 2002/3019) added at the end of reg.4(2):

"and
 (c) state pension credit".

With effect from November 4, 2003, reg.6(3) of the Child Support (Miscellaneous Amendments) (No.2) Regulations 2003 (SI 2003/2779) omitted the words "or war widow's pension" in para.(1)(e) and added the following after para.(1)(e):

"and
 (f) a war widow's pension or a war widower's pension.".

p.778, *Jobseeker's Allowance Regulations, reg.1(3)—definition of "ERA payment"*

3.119 With effect from October 1, 2003, reg.3(2) of the Social Security (Miscellaneous Amendments) (No.2) Regulations 2003 (SI 2003/2279), inserted the following new definition immediately following the definition of "employment zone contractor":

" "ERA payment" means a payment made in respect of participation in the Employment Retention and Advancement Scheme for the provision of assistance to individuals to improve their job retention or career advancement (or both) under section 2 of the Employment and Training Act 1973."

p.783, *Jobseeker's Allowance Regulations, reg.1(3)—definition of "residential allowance"*

3.120 With effect from October 6, 2003, reg.4 of and Sch.2 para.1 to the Social Security (Removal of Residential Allowance and Miscellaneous

Amendments) Regulations 2003 (SI 2003/1121), revoked the definition of "residential allowance".

p.787, *Jobseeker's Allowance Regulations, reg.1(3F)*

3.121 With effect from May 21, 2003, reg.6 of the Social Security (Hospital In-Patients and Miscellaneous Amendments) Regulations 2003 (SI 2003/1195), substituted the figures "52" for the word "six" in reg.1(3F)(a).

p.854, *annotation to Jobseeker's Allowance Regulations 1996, reg.26*

3.122 *Ferguson v Secretary of State for Work and Pensions* is now reported as *R(JSA)6/03*

pp.943–945, *annotation to Jobseeker's Allowance Regulations 1996, reg.81: "lump sum" redundancy payment ranking as "pension payment"*

3.123 In *CJSA 1542/2000*, Commissioner Rowland followed *CJSA 1501/2000* (now reported as *R(JSA)6/02*) to hold that a lump sum payment amounting to three month's redundancy payment was a pension payment for the purposes of this regulation.

p.946, *Jobseeker's Allowance Regulations 1996, reg.83 (Applicable amounts)*

3.124 With effect from October 6, 2003, reg.4 of and Sch.2 para.2 to the Social Security (Removal of Residential Allowance and Miscellaneous Amendments) Regulations 2003 (SI 2003/1121), revoked sub-para.(c) of reg.83.

p.947, *Jobseeker's Allowance Regulations 1996, reg.84 (Polygamous marriages)*

3.125 With effect from October 6, 2003, reg.4 of and Sch.2 para.3 to the Social Security (Removal of Residential Allowance and Miscellaneous Amendments) Regulations 2003 (SI 2003/1121), revoked sub-para.(d) of reg.84(1).

p.948, *Jobseeker's Allowance Regulations 1996, reg.85 (Special cases)*

3.126 With effect from October 6, 2003, reg.4 of and Sch.2 para.4 to the Social Security (Removal of Residential Allowance and Miscellaneous Amendments) Regulations 2003 (SI 2003/1121), revoked para.(2A) of reg.85.

p.951, *Jobseeker's Allowance Regulations 1996, reg.86A (Applicable amounts for joint-claim couples)*

3.127 With effect from October 6, 2003, reg.4 of and Sch.2 para.5 to the Social Security (Removal of Residential Allowance and Miscellaneous

Income Support, Jobseekers' Allowance, State Pension Credit

Amendments) Regulations 2003 (SI 2003/1121), revoked sub-para.(b) of reg.86A.

p.952, *Jobseeker's Allowance Regulations 1996, reg.86B (Applicable amounts for joint-claim couples): polygamous marriages*

3.128   With effect from October 6, 2003, reg.4 of and Sch.2 para.6 to the Social Security (Removal of Residential Allowance and Miscellaneous Amendments) Regulations 2003 (SI 2003/1121), revoked sub-para.(c) of reg.86B.

p.965, *Jobseeker's Allowance Regulations 1996, reg.96(3)*

3.129   With effect from August 8, 2003, reg.4 of the Social Security (Working Tax Credit and Child Tax Credit) (Consequential Amendments) (No. 3) Regulations 2003 (SI 2003/1731) substituted the following para. for para.(3):

"(3) Working tax credit or child tax credit shall be treated as paid—
  (a) where the award of that tax credit begins on the first day of a benefit week, on that day, or
  (b) on the first day of the benefit week that follows the date the award begins, or
  (c) on the first day of the first benefit week that follows the date an award of income support begins, if later,
until the last day of the last benefit week that coincides with or immediately follows the last day for which the award of that tax credit is made."

p.1017, *Jobseeker's Allowance Regulations 1996, reg.131*

3.130   With effect from September 1, 2003 (or if the student's period of study begins between August 1 and 31, 2003, the first day of the period), reg.2(1) and (3)(d) of the Social Security Amendment (Students and Income-related Benefits) Regulations 2003 (SI 2003/1701) substituted the sum "£270" for the sum "£265" in para.(3)(a).

Reg.3(1)(a) and (2)(d) of the same amending regulations substituted the following sub-para. for sub-para.(cc) in para.(3A):

"(cc) any grant paid under the Schedule to the Education (Assembly Learning Grant Scheme) (Wales) Regulations 2002;".

Reg.3(1)(b) and (2)(d) of the same amending regulations substituted the following after sub-para. (d) in para. (3A):

"; and
  (f) any grant paid under regulation 15(7) of the Education (Student Support) (No.2) Regulations 2002.".

With effect from September 1, 2003 (or if the student's period of study begins between August 1 and 31, 2003, the first day of the period), reg.2(1) and (2)(d) of the Social Security Amendment (Students and

Income-related Benefits) (No.2) Regulations 2003 (SI 2003/1914) substituted the sum "£335" for the sum "£327" in para.(3)(b).

p.1019, *annotation to Jobseeker's Allowance Regulations 1996, reg.131*

See the note to reg.62 of the Income Support Regulations 1987 above for the effect of these amendments.   3.131

p.1023, *Jobseeker's Allowance Regulations 1996, reg.136(5)*

With effect from September 1, 2003 (or if the student's period of study begins between August 1 and 31, 2003, the first day of the period), reg.2(1) and (3)(d) of the Social Security Amendment (Students and Income-related Benefits) Regulations 2003 (SI 2003/1701) substituted the sum "£270" for the sum "£265" in sub-para.(a).   3.132

With effect from September 1, 2003 (or if the student's period of study begins between August 1 and 31, 2003, the first day of the period), reg.2(1) and (2)(d) of the Social Security Amendment (Students and Income-related Benefits) (No.2) Regulations 2003 (SI 2003/1914) substituted the sum "£335" for the sum "£327" in sub-para.(b).

p.1050, *Jobseeker's Allowance Regulations 1996, reg.148 (Applicable amount in urgent cases)*

With effect from October 6, 2003, reg.4 of and Sch.2, para.7 to the Social Security (Removal of Residential Allowance and Miscellaneous Amendments) Regulations 2003 (SI 2003/1121), revoked para. (1)(a)(v), para.(1)(c) and para.(1A) of reg.148.   3.133

p.1052, *Jobseeker's Allowance Regulations 1996, reg.148A (Applicable amount in urgent cases: joint-claim couples)*

With effect from October 6, 2003, reg.4 of and Sch.2, para.8 to the Social Security (Removal of Residential Allowance and Miscellaneous Amendments) Regulations 2003 (SI 2003/1121), revoked para. (1)(a)(iv), para.(1)(c) and para.(1A) of reg.148A.   3.134

p.1066, *Jobseeker's Allowance Regulations 1996, Sch.1 (Applicable amounts)*

With effect from October 6, 2003, reg.4 of and Sch.2, para.11 to the Social Security (Removal of Residential Allowance and Miscellaneous Amendments) Regulations 2003 (SI 2003/1121), substituted the words "and 15" for the words "15 and 17" in column (1) of para.1.   3.135

p.1071, *Jobseeker's Allowance Regulations 1996, Sch.1, para.15A(2) (Enhanced disability premium)*

With effect from May 21, 2003, reg.6 of the Social Security (Hospital In-Patients and Miscellaneous Amendments) Regulations 2003 (SI   3.136

2003/1195), substituted the figures "52" for the word "six" para.15A(2) in both cases where that word occurs.

p.1072, *Jobseeker's Allowance Regulations 1996, Sch.1, para.17 (Carer premium)*

3.137   With effect from October 1, 2003, reg.3(3) of the Social Security (Miscellaneous Amendments) (No.2) Regulations 2003 (SI 2003/2279), revoked the following parts of para.17:

— sub-para.(2);
— the words "or ceases to be treated as entitled" in head (b) of sub-para.(3);
— head (b) of sub-para.(3A);
— head (b) of sub-para.(4);

inserted the words "where sub-paragraph (3)(a) applies," immediately before the words "the Sunday" in head (a) of sub-para.(3A) and substituted the following for head (c) of sub-para.(4):

"(c) in any other case, the person who has been entitled to a carer's allowance ceased to be entitled to that allowance."

p.1078, *Jobseeker's Allowance Regulations 1996, Sch.1, para.20IA(2) (Enhanced disability premium)*

3.138   With effect from May 21, 2003, reg.6 of the Social Security (Hospital In-Patients and Miscellaneous Amendments) Regulations 2003 (SI 2003/1195), substituted the figures "52" for the word "six" in para. 20IA(2).

p.1078, *Jobseeker's Allowance Regulations 1996, Sch.1, para.20J (Carer premium)*

3.139   With effect from October 1, 2003, reg.3(3) of the Social Security (Miscellaneous Amendments) (No.2) Regulations 2003 (SI 2003/2279), revoked the following parts of para.20J:

— the words "and in receipt of" in sub-para.(1);
— sub-para.(2);
— the words "or ceases to be treated as entitled" in head (b) of sub-para.(3);
— head (b) of sub-para.(3A);
— head (b) of sub-para.(4);

inserted the words "where sub-paragraph (3)(a) applies," immediately before the words "the Sunday" in head (a) of sub-para.(3A) and substituted the following for head (c) of sub-para.(4):

"(c) in any other case, the person who has been entitled to a carer's allowance ceased to be entitled to that allowance."

Income Support, Jobseekers' Allowance, State Pension Credit

p.1089, *Jobseeker's Allowance Regulations 1996, Sch.2, para.6(3)*

3.140 With effect from October 6, 2003, reg.30(a) of the State Pension Credit (Consequential, Transitional and Miscellaneous Provisions) Regulations 2002 (SI 2002/3019) inserted the words "or state pension credit" after the words "income support".

p.1097, *Jobseeker's Allowance Regulations 1996, Sch.2, para.13*

3.141 With effect from October 6, 2003, reg.30(b) of the State Pension Credit (Consequential, Transitional and Miscellaneous Provisions) Regulations 2002 (SI 2002/3019) added at the end a new sub-para.(16):

"(16) For the purpose of determining whether the linking rules set out in this paragraph apply in a case where a claimant's former partner was entitled to state pension credit, any reference to income-based jobseeker's allowance in this Schedule shall be taken to include also a reference to state pension credit.".

pp.1098–1099, *Jobseeker's Allowance Regulations 1996, Sch.2, para.17*

3.142 With effect from October 6, 2003, reg.30(c) of the State Pension Credit (Consequential, Transitional and Miscellaneous Provisions) Regulations 2002 (SI 2002/3019) substituted the following heads (a) to (c) for heads (a) and (b) in sub-para.(1):

"(a) in respect of a non-dependant aged 18 or over who is engaged in any remunerative work but is not in receipt of state pension credit, £47.75;
(b) in respect of a non-dependant who is engaged in remunerative work and in receipt of state pension credit, £7.40;
(c) in respect of a non-dependant aged 18 or over to whom neither head (a) nor head (b) applies, £7.40.".

With effect from May 21, 2003, reg.6(4) of the Social Security (Hospital In-Patients and Miscellaneous Amendments) Regulations 2003 (SI 2003/1195) substituted "52" for the word "six" in both places that it occurred in sub-para.(7)(g).

p.1102, *annotation to Jobseeker's Allowance Regulations 1996, Sch.2*

3.143 The amendments to paras 6(3), 13 and 17 have been made as a consequence of the introduction of state pension credit. See the notes to Sch.3 of the Income Support Regulations above for the effect of these amendments.

p.1103, *Jobseeker's Allowance Regulations 1996, Sch.3*

3.144 With effect from October 6, 2003, by reg.4 of and para.10 of Sch.2 to the Social Security (Removal of Residential Allowance and Miscellaneous Amendments) Regulations 2003 (SI 2003/1121) Sch.3 was omitted.

Income Support, Jobseekers' Allowance, State Pension Credit

p.1104, *Jobseeker's Allowance Regulations 1996, Sch.5, para.1*

3.145   With effect from May 21, 2003, reg.6 of the Social Security (Hospital In-Patients and Miscellaneous Amendments) Regulations 2003 (SI 2003/1195), substituted the figure "52" for the word "six" in para.1.

p.1106, *Jobseeker's Allowance Regulations 1996, Sch.5, paras 7–9*

3.146   With effect from October 6, 2003, reg.4 of and Sch.2, para.11 to the Social Security (Removal of Residential Allowance and Miscellaneous Amendments) Regulations 2003 (SI 2003/1121), revoked paras 7–9 of Sch.5.

p.1109, *Jobseeker's Allowance Regulations 1996, Sch.5, para.15*

3.147   With effect from May 21, 2003, reg.6 of the Social Security (Hospital In-Patients and Miscellaneous Amendments) Regulations 2003 (SI 2003/1195), revoked sub-para.(2) and the words "Subject to sub-paragraph (2)" in sub-para.(1) of para.15.

With effect from October 6, 2003, reg.4 of and Sch.2, para.11 to the Social Security (Removal of Residential Allowance and Miscellaneous Amendments) Regulations 2003 (SI 2003/1121), revoked para.15(1) of Sch.5.

p.1110, *Jobseeker's Allowance Regulations 1996, Sch.5, para.17A*

3.148   With effect from October 6, 2003, reg.4 of and Sch.2, para.11 to the Social Security (Removal of Residential Allowance and Miscellaneous Amendments) Regulations 2003 (SI 2003/1121), revoked the words "or 86" in column 2 of para.17A of Sch.5 in both the places in which they occur.

p.1111, *Jobseeker's Allowance Regulations 1996, Sch.5A, para.1*

3.149   With effect from May 21, 2003, reg.6 of the Social Security (Hospital In-Patients and Miscellaneous Amendments) Regulations 2003 (SI 2003/1195), substituted the figures "52" for the word "six" para.1 in both cases where that word occurs.

With effect from October 6, 2003, reg.4 of and Sch.2, para.12 to the Social Security (Removal of Residential Allowance and Miscellaneous Amendments) Regulations 2003 (SI 2003/1121), substituted the word "A" for the words "Subject to paragraphs 9 and 11, a" in column (1) of para.1.

p.1114, *Jobseeker's Allowance Regulations 1996, Sch.5A, para.9*

3.150   With effect from October 6, 2003, reg.4 of and Sch.2, para.12 to the Social Security (Removal of Residential Allowance and Miscellaneous Amendments) Regulations 2003 (SI 2003/1121), revoked para.9 of Sch.5A.

Income Support, Jobseekers' Allowance, State Pension Credit

p.1126, *Jobseeker's Allowance Regulations 1996, Sch.7, para.26*

With effect from October 1, 2003, reg.3(4)(a)(i) of the Social Security (Miscellaneous Amendments) (No.2) Regulations 2003 (SI 2003/2279) amended head (a) of sub-para.(1) to read as follows: 3.151

"(a) in accordance with regulations made pursuant to section 57A of the Adoption Act 1976 (permitted allowances) [or paragraph 3 of Schedule 4 to the Adoption and Children Act 2002] or with a scheme approved by the Secretary of State under section 51 of the Adoption (Scotland) Act 1978 (schemes for payment of allowances to adopters);".

Reg.3(4)(a)(ii) of the same amending regulations inserted the following sub-para. after sub-para.(1):

"(1A) Any payment, other than a payment to which sub-paragraph (1)(a) applies, made to the claimant in accordance with regulations made under paragraph 3 of Schedule 4 to the Adoption and Children Act 2002.".

p.1132, *Jobseeker's Allowance Regulations 1996, Sch.7, paras 72–74*

With effect from October 1, 2003, reg.3(4)(b) of the Social Security (Miscellaneous Amendments) (No.2) Regulations 2003 (SI 2003/2279) substituted the following sub-para. for sub-para.(1) of para.72: 3.152

"72.—(1) Any payment made by a local authority, or by the National Assembly for Wales, to or on behalf of the claimant or his partner relating to a service which is provided to develop or sustain the capacity of the claimant or his partner to live independently in his accommodation.".

Reg.3(4)(c) of the same amending regulations inserted the following new para. after para.72:

"73. Any ERA payment".

With effect from October 27, 2003, reg.16(a) of the Social Security (Incapacity Benefit Work-focused Interviews) Regulations 2003 (SI 2003/2439) added the following new para. after para.73:

"74. Any payment made to a claimant's partner in respect of the partner's participation in the Return to Work Credit Scheme pursuant to section 2 of the Employment and Training Act 1973."

p.1135, *annotation to Jobseeker's Allowance Regulations 1996, Sch.7*

On the substituted para.72(1), see the note to para.76 of Sch.9 to the Income Support Regulations 1987 above; and on the new paras 73 and 74, see the notes to the new paras 77 and 78 respectively of Sch.9 above. 3.153

pp.1139–1140, *Jobseeker's Allowance Regulations 1996, Sch.8, paras 42 and 43*

3.154　With effect from October 1, 2003, reg.3(5)(a) of the Social Security (Miscellaneous Amendments) (No.2) Regulations 2003 (SI 2003/2279) substituted the words "or the County Court under Rule 21.11(1) of the Civil Procedure Rules 1998" for the words "under the provisions of Order 80 of the Rules of the Supreme Court, the County Court under Order 10 of the County Court Rules 1981" in para.42.

Reg.3(5)(b) of the same amending regulations substituted the words "section 13 of the Children (Scotland) Act 1995" for the words "Rule 43.15 of the Act of Sederunt (Rules of the Court of Session 1994) 1994 or under Rule 131 of the Act of Sederunt (Rules of the Court, consolidation and amendment) 1965" in para.43.

p.1142, *Jobseeker's Allowance Regulations 1996, Sch.8, paras 59–63*

3.155　With effect from October 1, 2003, reg.3(5)(c) of the Social Security (Miscellaneous Amendments) (No.2) Regulations 2003 (SI 2003/2279) substituted the following sub-para. for sub-para.(1) of para.59:

"**59.**—(1) Any payment made by a local authority, or by the National Assembly for Wales, to or on behalf of the claimant or his partner relating to a service which is provided to develop or sustain the capacity of the claimant or his partner to live independently in his accommodation.".

Reg.3(5)(d) of the same amending regulations added the following new paras after para.59:

"**60.** Any payment made under the Community Care (Direct Payments) Act 1996, regulations made under section 57 of the Health and Social Care Act 2001 or under section 12B of the Social Work (Scotland) Act 1968.

Any payment made to the claimant in accordance with regulations made under paragraph 3 of Schedule 4 to the Adoption and Children Act 2002.

61. Any ERA payment but only for a period of 52 weeks from the date of receipt of that payment.".

With effect from October 27, 2003, reg.16(b) of the Social Security (Incapacity Benefit Work-focused Interviews) Regulations 2003 (SI 2003/2439) added the following new para. after para.62:

"**63.** Any payment made to a claimant's partner in respect of the partner's participation in the Return to Work Credit Scheme pursuant to section 2 of the Employment and Training Act 1973.".

p.1144, *annotation to Jobseeker's Allowance Regulations 1996, Sch.8*

3.156　On the substituted para.59(1), see the note to para.66 of Sch.10 to the Income Support Regulations 1987 above; and on the new paras 62 and 63, see the note to paras 69 and 70 of Sch.10 above.

Income Support, Jobseekers' Allowance, State Pension Credit

p.1153, *Commencement of State Pension Credit Act 2002*

The final Commencement Order for the State Pension Credit Act 2002 was the State Pension Credit Act 2002 (Commencement No. 5) and Appointed Day Order 2003 (SI 2003/1766 (C. 75)). This brought into force on October 6, 2003 all those provisions of the Act which were not already in force and appointed that day as the "appointed day" for the purposes of s.13 of the Act (transitional provisions).

3.157

p.1171, *State Pension Credit Act 2002, s.13(3)*

The "appointed day" has been confirmed as October 6, 2003: see State Pension Credit Act 2002 (Commencement No. 5) and Appointed Day Order 2003 (SI 2003/1766 (C. 75)). See also note to p.1153, above.

3.158

p.1180, *State Pension Credit Regulations 2002: amendment of reg.1(2) (definitions)*

With effect from October 6, 2003, reg.2(2) of the State Pension Credit (Transitional and Miscellaneous Provisions) Amendment Regulations 2003 (SI 2003/2274) inserted after the definition of "the 1992 Act" the following definition:

3.159

" "adoption leave" means a period of absence from work on ordinary or additional adoption leave in accordance with section 75A or 75B of the Employment Rights Act 1996;"

p.1182, *State Pension Credit Regulations 2002: amendment of reg.1(2) (definitions)*

With effect from October 6, 2003, reg.2(2) of the State Pension Credit (Transitional and Miscellaneous Provisions) Amendment Regulations 2003 (SI 2003/2274) inserted after the definition of "patient" the following definition:

3.160

" "paternity leave" means a period of absence from work on leave in accordance with section 80A or 80B of the Employment Rights Act 1996;"

p.1185, *State Pension Credit Regulations 2002: amendment of reg.2 (persons not in Great Britain)*

With effect from October 6, 2003, reg.2(3) of the State Pension Credit (Transitional and Miscellaneous Provisions) Amendment Regulations 2003 (SI 2003/2274) inserted after reg.2(d) the following further exception:

3.161

"(e) a person in Great Britain who left the territory of Montserrat after 1st November 1995 because of the effect on that territory of a volcanic eruption."

p.1185, *State Pension Credit Regulations 2002: amendment of reg.3 (persons temporarily absent from Great Britain)*

3.162   With effect from October 6, 2003, reg.2(4) of the State Pension Credit (Transitional and Miscellaneous Provisions) Amendment Regulations 2003 (SI 2003/2274) substituted the word "claimant's" for "person's" in reg.3(1).

p.1187, *State Pension Credit Regulations 2002: amendment of reg.5 (persons treated as being or not being members of the same household)*

3.163   With effect from October 6, 2003, reg.2(5) of the State Pension Credit (Transitional and Miscellaneous Provisions) Amendment Regulations 2003 (SI 2003/2274) amended reg.5 to read as follows:

"**Persons treated as being or not being members of the same household**

5.—(1) A person is to be treated as not being a member of the same household as the claimant if—
   (a) he is living away from the claimant and—
       (i) he does not intend to resume living with the claimant; or
       (ii) his absence is likely to exceed 52 weeks except where there are exceptional circumstances (for example the person is in hospital or otherwise has no control over the length of his absence), and the absence is unlikely to be substantially more than 52 weeks;
   (b) he or the claimant is permanently in a care home;
   (c) he or the claimant is, or both are—
       (i) detained in a hospital provided under [the provisions of the Mental Health Act 1983, the Mental Health (Scotland) Act 1984, or the Criminal Procedure (Scotland) Act 1995; or]
       (ii) detained in custody pending trial or sentence upon conviction or under a sentence imposed by a court; or
       (iii) on temporary release in accordance with the provisions of the Prison Act 1952 or the Prison (Scotland) Act 1989;
   (d) the claimant is abroad and does not satisfy [. . .] regulation 3 (persons temporary absent from Great Britain);
   (e) either he or the claimant is not in Great Britain and is not treated as being in Great Britain in accordance with regulation 4;
   [(f) he is absent from Great Britain—
       (i) for more than 8 weeks where he is accompanying a young person solely in connection with arrangements made for the treatment of that person for a disease or bodily or mental disablement, and those arrangements relate to treatment outside Great Britain by, or under the supervision of, a person appropriately qualified to carry out the treatment, during the period whilst he is temporarily absent from Great Britain; or

(ii) for more than 4 weeks in all other cases;]

[(g) ... ;

(h) he is a person subject to immigration control within the meaning of section 115(9) of the Immigration and Asylum Act 1999.]

(2) Subject to paragraph (1), partners shall be treated as members of the same household notwithstanding that they are temporarily living apart.

[(3) in paragraph (1)(f) "young person" and "appropriately qualified" shall have the meaning given to them in regulation 3(4).]"

3.164

p.1192, *State Pension Credit Regulations 2002: amendment of reg.10 (assessed income period)*

With effect from October 6, 2003, reg.2(6) of the State Pension Credit (Transitional and Miscellaneous Provisions) Amendment Regulations 2003 (SI 2003/2274) inserted after para.10(1)(b) the following.

3.165

"(c) that—
  (i) the Secretary of State has sent the claimant the notification required by regulation 32(6)(a) of the Claims and Payments Regulations; and
  (ii) the claimant has not provided sufficient information to enable the Secretary of State to determine whether there will be any variation in the claimant's retirement provision throughout the period of 12 months beginning with the day following the day on which the previous assessed income period ends."

Presumably this amendment must be read as preceded by an "or" at the end of para.10(1)(b).

p.1198, *State Pension Credit Regulations 2002: amendment of reg.15 (income for the purposes of the Act)*

With effect from October 6, 2003, reg.2(7) of the State Pension Credit (Transitional and Miscellaneous Provisions) Amendment Regulations 2003 (SI 2003/2274) omitted the word "and" at the end of reg.15(5)(f) and inserted after reg.15(5)(g) the following:

3.166

"(h) any income in lieu of that specified in—
  (i) paragraphs (a) to (i) of section 15(1) of the Act, or
  (ii) in this regulation;
(i) any payment of rent made to a claimant who—
  (i) owns the freehold or leasehold interest in any property or is a tenant of any property;
  (ii) occupies part of that property; and
  (iii) has an agreement with another person allowing that person to occupy that property on payment of rent."

pp.1218–1219, State Pension Credit Regulations 2002: amendment of Sch.I

3.167   With effect from October 6, 2003, reg.2(8) of the State Pension Credit (Transitional and Miscellaneous Provisions) Amendment Regulations 2003 (SI 2003/2274) substituted "carer's allowance" for "invalid care allowance" in paras 1(1)(a)(iii) and 4(2).

p.1223, State Pension Credit Regulations 2002: amendment of Sch.II (housing costs)

3.168   With effect from October 6, 2003, reg.2(9) of the State Pension Credit (Transitional and Miscellaneous Provisions) Amendment Regulations 2003 (SI 2003/2274) inserted ", paternity leave or adoption leave," after "maternity leave" in para.2(7).

p.1234, State Pension Credit Regulations 2002: amendment of Sch.II (housing costs)

3.169   With effect from October 6, 2003, reg.2(9) of the State Pension Credit (Transitional and Miscellaneous Provisions) Amendment Regulations 2003 (SI 2003/2274) amended para.14(2) (non-dependant deductions) to read:

"(2) In the case of a non-dependant aged 18 or over to whom sub-paragraph (1)(a) applies because he is in remunerative work, where the claimant satisfies the Secretary of State that the non-dependant's gross weekly income is—
(a) less than [£92.00], the deduction to be made under this paragraph shall be the deduction specified in sub-paragraph (1)(c);
(b) not less than [£92.00] but less than [£137.00], the deduction to be made under this paragraph shall be £17.00;
(c) not less than [£137.00] but less than [£177.00], the deduction to be made under this paragraph shall be £23.35;
(d) not less than [£177.00] but less than [£235.00], the deduction to be made under this paragraph shall be £38.20;
(e) not less than [£235.00] but less than [£293.00], the deduction to be made under this paragraph shall be £43.50."

p.1236, State Pension Credit Regulations 2002: amendment of Sch.III (special groups)

3.170   With effect from October 6, 2003, reg.2(10) of the State Pension Credit (Transitional and Miscellaneous Provisions) Amendment Regulations 2003 (SI 2003/2274) amended para.1(8) to read:

"(8) In regulations 3,5, 6(8), 10,12 and 14 and in paragraph [6(5)(b)(v)] of Schedule 1 and in Schedule 2, any reference to a partner includes also a reference to any additional spouse to whom this paragraph applies."

Income Support, Jobseekers' Allowance, State Pension Credit

pp.1237–1238, *State Pension Credit Regulations 2002: amendment of Sch.IV (income disregards)*

With effect from October 6, 2003, reg.2(11)(a)–(e) of the State Pension Credit (Transitional and Miscellaneous Provisions) Amendment Regulations 2003 (SI 2003/2274) inserted "or widower" after "widow" in paras 1(c) and 6(1)(a), "or widowers" after "widows" in paras 4 and 5 and "and widowers" after "widows" in para.6(1)(b).

3.171

p.1240, *State Pension Credit Regulations 2002: amendment of Sch.IV (income disregards)*

With effect from October 6, 2003, reg.2(11)(f) of the State Pension Credit (Transitional and Miscellaneous Provisions) Amendment Regulations 2003 (SI 2003/2274) inserted after para.16 the following further disregards:

3.172

"17. Any special war widows payment made under—
 (a) the Naval and Marine Pay and Pensions (Special War Widows Payment) Order 1990 made under section 3 of the Naval and Marine Pay and Pensions Act 1865;
 (b) the Royal Warrant dated 19th February 1990 amending the Sched. to the Army Pensions Warrant 1977;
 (c) the Queen's Order dated 26th February 1990 made under section 2 of the Air Force (Constitution) Act 1917;
 (d) the Home Guard War Widows Special Payments Regulations 1990 made under section 151 of the Reserve Forces Act 1980;
 (e) the Orders dated 19th February 1990 amending Orders made on 12th December 1980 concerning the Ulster Defence Regiment made in each case under section 140 of the Reserve Forces Act 1980,
and any analogous payment made by the Secretary of State for Defence to any person who is not a person entitled under the provisions mentioned in sub-paragraphs (a) to (e) of this paragraph.
 18. Except in the case of income from capital specified in Part II of Schedule V, any actual income from capital."

p.1241, *State Pension Credit Regulations 2002: amendment of Sch.V (income from capital: disregards), new para.1A*

With effect from October 6, 2003, reg.2(12)(a) of the State Pension Credit (Transitional and Miscellaneous Provisions) Amendment Regulations 2003 (SI 2003/2274) inserted after para.1 the following further disregard:

3.173

"1A. The dwelling occupied by the claimant as his home but only one home shall be disregarded under this paragraph."

This amendment ensures that the claimant's home is disregarded for all purposes in calculating income (the limited disregard for the purposes solely of determining deemed income by Sch.V, para.27 has been repealed).

p.1242, State Pension Credit Regulations 2002: amendment of Sch. V (income from capital: disregards), para. 9A

3.174   With effect from October 6, 2003, reg.2(12)(b) of the State Pension Credit (Transitional and Miscellaneous Provisions) Amendment Regulations 2003 (SI 2003/2274) amended para.9A to read:

> "**9A.** The assets of any business owned in whole or in part by the claimant if—
> (a) he is not engaged as a self-employed earner in that business by reason of some disease or bodily or mental disablement; but
> (b) he intends to become engaged (or, as the case may be, re-- engaged) as a self-employed earner in that business as soon as he recovers or is able to become engaged, or re-engaged, in that business [. . .]."

The effect of the amendment is to abolish the limitation that this disregard applies only for 26 weeks or such longer period as is reasonable, so making the disregard potentially open-ended.

p.1243, State Pension Credit Regulations 2002: amendment of Sch. V (income from capital: disregards), para.13

3.175   With effect from October 6, 2003, reg.2(12)(c) of the State Pension Credit (Transitional and Miscellaneous Provisions) Amendment Regulations 2003 (SI 2003/2274) amended para.13 to read:

> "**13.**—(1) Subject to sub-paragraph (2), the amount of any trust payment made to a claimant or a claimant's partner [who is]—
> (a) [. . .] a diagnosed person;
> (b) [a diagnosed person's partner or] was a diagnosed person's partner at the time of the diagnosed person's death;
> (c) [. . .] a parent of a diagnosed person, a person acting in place of the diagnosed person's parents or a person who was so acting at the date of the diagnosed person's death.
> (2) Where [a trust payment is made to]—
> (a) [a person referred to in sub-paragraph (1)(a) or (b), that sub-paragraph] shall apply for the period beginning on the date on which the trust is made and ending on the date on which [that person] dies;
> (b) [a person referred to in sub-paragraph (1)(c), that sub-paragraph] shall apply for the period beginning on the date on which the trust payment is made and ending two years after that date.

3.176
> (3) Subject to sub-paragraph (4), the amount of any payment by a person to whom a trust payment has been made or of any payment out of the estate of a person to whom a trust payment has been made, which is made to a claimant or a claimant's partner [who is]—
> (a) [. . .] the diagnosed person;

Income Support, Jobseekers' Allowance, State Pension Credit

(b) [a diagnosed person's partner or] was a diagnosed person's partner at the date of the diagnosed person's death; or

(c) [. . .] a parent of a diagnosed person, a person acting in place of the diagnosed person's parents or a person who was so acting at the date of the diagnosed person's death.

(4) Where [a payment referred to in sub-paragraph (3) is made to]—

(a) [a person referred to in sub-paragraph (3)(a) or (b), that sub-paragraph] shall apply for the period beginning on the date on which the payment is made and ending on the date on which [that person] dies;

(b) [a person referred to in sub-paragraph (3)(c), that sub-paragraph] shall apply for the period beginning on the date on which the payment is made and ending two years after that date.

(5) In this paragraph, a reference to a person—

(a) being the diagnosed person's partner;

(b) acting in place of the diagnosed person's parents,

at the date of the diagnosed person's death shall include a person who would have been such a person or a person who would have been so acting, but for the diagnosed person being in a care home.

(6) In this paragraph—

"diagnosed person" means a person who has been diagnosed as suffering from, or who, after his death, has been diagnosed as having suffered from, variant [Creutzfeldt]–Jakob disease;

"relevant trust" means a trust established out of funds provided by the Secretary of State in respect of persons who suffered, or who are suffering, from variant [Creutzfeldt]–Jakob disease for the benefit of persons eligible for payments in accordance with its provisions;

"trust payment" means a payment under a relevant trust."

p.1245, *State Pension Credit Regulations 2002: amendment of Sch. V (income from capital: disregards), para. 20(1)*

With effect from October 6, 2003, reg.2(12)(d) of the State Pension Credit (Transitional and Miscellaneous Provisions) Amendment Regulations 2003 (SI 2003/2274) substituted a new para.20(1)(d): 3.177

"(d) any payment made by a local authority (including in England a county council), or by the National Assembly for Wales, to or on behalf of the claimant or his partner relating to a service which is provided to develop or sustain the capacity of the claimant or his partner to live independently in his accommodation."

pp.1245–1246, *State Pension Credit Regulations 2002: amendment of Sch. V (income from capital: disregards), para. 20(2)*

With effect from October 6, 2003, reg.2(12)(e) of the State Pension Credit (Transitional and Miscellaneous Provisions) Amendment Regulations 2003 (SI 2003/2274) amended para.20(2) to read: 3.178

"(2) In paragraph (1), "benefit" means—

Income Support, Jobseekers' Allowance, State Pension Credit

(a) attendance allowance under section 64 of the Contributions and Benefits Act;
(b) disability living allowance;
(c) income support;
(d) income-based jobseeker's allowance;
(e) housing benefit;
(f) state pension credit;
(g) [. . .];
(h) [an increase of a disablement pension under section 104 of the Contributions and Benefits Act (increase where constant attendance needed), and any further increase of such a pension under section 105 of that Act (increase for exceptionally severe disablement)];
(i) any amount included on account of the claimant's exceptionally severe disablement [or need for constant attendance] in a war disablement pension or a war widow's or widower's pension;
(j) council tax benefit;
(k) social fund payments;
(l) child benefit;
(m) [. . .];
(n) child tax credit under the Tax Credits Act 2002."

p.1246, *State Pension Credit Regulations 2002: amendment of Sch.V (income from capital: disregards), para.20A*

3.179   With effect from October 6, 2003, reg.2(12)(f) of the State Pension Credit (Transitional and Miscellaneous Provisions) Amendment Regulations 2003 (SI 2003/2274) substituted a new para.20A:

"**20A.**—(1) Subject to sub-paragraph (3), any payment of £5,000 or more to which paragraph 20(1)(a), (b) or (c) applies, which has been made to rectify, or to compensate for, an official error relating to a relevant benefit and has been received by the claimant in full on or after the day on which he became entitled to benefit under these Regulations.

(2) Subject to sub-paragraph (3), the total amount of any payment disregarded under—

(a) paragraph 7(2) of Schedule 10 to the Income Support (General) Regulations 1987;
(b) paragraph 12(2) of Schedule 8 to the Jobseeker's Allowance Regulations 1996;
(c) paragraph 8(2) of Schedule 5 or paragraph 21A of Schedule 5ZA to the Housing Benefit (General) Regulations 1987; or
(d) paragraph 8(2) of Schedule 5 or paragraph 21A of Schedule 5ZA to the Council Tax Benefit (General) Regulations 1992,

where the award during which the disregard last applied in respect of the relevant sum either terminated immediately before the relevant date or is still in existence at that date.

(3) Any disregard which applies under sub-paragraph (1) or (2) shall have effect until the award comes to an end.

Income Support, Jobseekers' Allowance, State Pension Credit

(4) In this paragraph—

"the award", except in sub-paragraph (2), means—

(a) the award of State Pension Credit under these Regulations during which the relevant sum or, where it is received in more than one instalment, the first instalment of that sum is received; or

(b) where that award is followed immediately by one or more further awards which begins immediately after the previous award ends, such further awards until the end of the last award, provided that, for such further awards, the claimant—

(i) is the person who received the relevant sum;

(ii) is the partner of that person; or

(iii) was the partner of that person at the date of his death;

"official error"—

(a) where the error relates to housing benefit or council tax benefit, has the meaning given by regulation 1(2) of the Housing Benefit and Council Tax Benefit (Decisions and Appeals) Regulations 2001; and

(b) where the error relates to any other relevant benefit, has the meaning given by regulation 1(3) of the Social Security and Child Support (Decisions and Appeals) Regulations 1999;

"the relevant date" means the date on which the claimant became entitled to benefit under the Act;

"relevant benefit" means any benefit specified in paragraph 20(2); and

"the relevant sum" means the total payment referred to in sub-paragraph (1) or, as the case may be, the total amount referred to in sub-paragraph (2)."

p.1246, *State Pension Credit Regulations 2002: amendment of Sch. V (income from capital: disregards), para. 27*

With effect from October 6, 2003, reg.2(12)(g) of the State Pension Credit (Transitional and Miscellaneous Provisions) Amendment Regulations 2003 (SI 2003/2274) repealed para.27 (but see the insertion of a new para.1A above).

3.180

p.1249, *State Pension Credit Regulations 2002: amendment of Sch. VI (sums disregarded from claimant's earnings), new para. 2B*

With effect from October 6, 2003, reg.2(12)(g) of the State Pension Credit (Transitional and Miscellaneous Provisions) Amendment Regulations 2003 (SI 2003/2274) inserted a new para.2B:

3.181

"**2B.** Where only one member of a couple is in employment specified in paragraph 2(2), so much of the earnings of the other member of the couple as would not, in aggregate with the earnings disregarded under paragraph 2, exceed £20."

Income Support, Jobseekers' Allowance, State Pension Credit

p.1258, *Social Fund Cold Weather Payments (General) Regulations 1988, reg.1A*

3.182   With effect from October 6, 2003, reg.31(3)–(6) of the State Pension Credit (Consequential, Transitional and Miscellaneous Provisions) Regulations 2002 (SI 2002/3019) and reg.3 of the Social Security (Removal of Residential Allowance and Miscellaneous Amendments) Regulations 2003 (SI 2003/1121), taken together amended reg.1A to read as follows:

"**Prescribed description of persons**

1A.—(1) Subject to paragraph (3), the description of persons prescribed as persons to whom a payment may be made out of the Social Fund to meet expenses for heating under section 32(2A) of the Act is claimants who have been awarded income support state pension credit or income-based jobseeker's allowance in respect of at least one day during the recorded or the forecasted period of cold weather specified in regulation 2(1)(a) and either—
  (i)   whose applicable amount includes one or more of the premiums specified in paragraphs 9 to 14 of Part III of Schedule 2 to the General Regulations; or
  [(ia) whose applicable amount includes one or more of the premiums specified in paragraphs 10 to 16 of Part III of Schedule 1 to the Jobseeker's Allowance Regulations 1996; or
  (ii) whose family includes a member aged less than 5.
  (ib) the person is entitled to state pension credit and is not resident in a care home;
  (2) In paragraph (1)(ib), the expression "care home" means an establishment which is a care home for the purposes of the Care Standards Act 2000.
  (3) Paragraph (1) does not apply to a person who resides in—
  (a) a nursing home within the meaning given by regulation 2(1) of the Income Support (General) Regulations 1987;
  (b) a residential care home within the meaning given by regulation 2(1) of the Income Support (General) Regulations 1987;
  (c) residential accommodation within the meaning given by regulation 21(3) of the Income Support (General) Regulations 1987; or
  (d) accommodation provided under section 3(1) of, and Part II of the Sched. to, the Polish Resettlement Act 1947 (provision by the Secretary of State of accommodation in camps)."

p.1262, *Social Fund Cold Weather Payments (General) Regulations 1988, Sch.1*

3.183   With effect from November 1, 2003, reg.2 of and Sch.1 to the Social Fund Cold Weather Payments (General) Amendment Regulations 2003 (SI 2003/2605), substituted the following for Sch.1.

Income Support, Jobseekers' Allowance, State Pension Credit

SCHEDULE

Regulation 2(1)(a) and (2)

IDENTIFICATION OF STATIONS AND POSTCODE DISTRICTS 3.184

Column (1)	Column (2)
Meteorological Office Station	**Postcode districts**
1. Aberporth	SA35–48, SA64–65. SY20, SY23–25.
2. Andrewsfield	AL1–10. CB10–11. CM1–9, CM11–24, CM77. CO9. RM14–20. SG1–2, SG9–14.
3. Aultbea	IV21–22, IV26, IV40, IV52–54
4. Aviemore	AB31, AB33–34, AB36–37. PH18–26.
5. Bedford	LU1–7. MK1–19, MK40–46. NN1–16, NN29. PE19. SG3–7, SG15–19.
6. Bingley	BB4, BB8–12, BB18. BD1–24. DE4, DE45. HD1–9. HX1–7. LS21, LS29. OL3, OL12–15. S32–33, S35–36. SK12, SK17, SK22–23. ST13.
7. Bishopton	G1–5, G11–15, G20–23, G31–34, G40–46, G51–53, G60–62, G64–69, G71–78, G81–84. KA1–26, KA28–30. ML1–5. PA1–27, PA30, PA32.
8. Boltshope Park	DH8–9. DL8, DL11–17. NE19, NE44, NE47–48.
9. Boscombe Down	BA12. RG28. SP1–5, SP7, SP9–11.
10. Boulmer	NE22, NE24, NE61–71. TD12, TD15.
11. Braemar	AB35.
12. Brize Norton	CV36. GL54–56. OX1–8, OX10–18, OX20, OX25–29, OX33, OX39, OX44, OX49. SN7.
13. Capel Curig	LL24–25, LL41.
14. Cardinham (Bodmin)	PL13–17, PL22–35. TR2, TR9.
15. Carlisle	CA1–11, CA16–17. LA6–10, LA22–23. NE49.
16. Cassley	IV27–28. KW11, KW13.
17. Charlwood	BN5–6, BN44. GU5–8, GU26–33, GU35. ME14–20. RH1–20. TN1–20, TN22, TN27.
18. Chivenor	EX22–23, EX31–34, EX39.
19. Coleshill	B1–21, B23–38, B40, B42–50, B60–80, B90–98. CV1–12, CV21–23, CV31–35, CV37, CV47. DY1–14. LE10. WS1–15. WV1–16.
20. Coltishall	NR1–35.

Income Support, Jobseekers' Allowance, State Pension Credit

Column (1)	Column (2)
Meteorological Office Station	**Postcode districts**
21. Craibstone	AB10–16, AB21–25, AB30, AB32, AB39, AB41–43, AB51–54. DD8–11.
22. Crosby	BB1–3, BB5–7. CH1–8, CH41–49, CH60–66. FY1–8. L1–40. LL11–14. PR1–9, PR25–26. SY14. WA1–2, WA4–12. WN1–6, WN8.
23. Culdrose	TR1, TR3–6, TR10–20, TR26–27.
24. Dundrennan	DG1–2, DG5–7, DG11–12, DG16.
25. Dunkeswell Aerodrome	DT6–8. EX1–15, EX24. TA21. TQ1–6, TQ9–14.
26. Edinburgh Gogarbank	EH1–42, EH47–49, EH51–55. FK1–21. G63. KY3, KY11–13. PH3–6. TD5, TD11, TD13–14.
27. Eskdalemuir	DG3–4, DG10, DG13–14. ML12. TD1–4, TD6–10.
28. Fylingdales	TS13. YO11–18, YO21–22, YO25.
29. Great Malvern	GL1–6, GL10–20, GL50–53. HR1–9. NP15, NP25. SY8. WR1–15.
30. Heathrow	BR1–8. CR0, CR2–8. DA1–2, DA4–8, DA14–18. E1–18. E1W. EC1–4. EN1–11. HA0–9. IG1–11. KT1–24. N1–22. NW1–11. RM1–13. SE1–28. SL0, SL3. SM1–7. SW1–20. TW1–20. UB1–10. W1–14. WC1–2. WD1–7, WD17–19, WD23–25.
31. Herstmonceux, West End	BN7–8, BN20–24, BN26–27. TN21, TN31–40.
32. High Wycombe	HP1–23, HP27. OX9. RG9. SL7–9.
33. Hurn (Bournemouth Airport)	BH1–25, BH31. DT1–2, DT11. SP6.
34. Isle of Portland	DT3–5.
35. Kinloss	AB38, AB44–45, AB55–56. IV1–3, IV5, IV7–20, IV30–32, IV36.
36. Kirkwall	KW15–17.
37. Lake Vyrnwy	LL20–21, LL23. SY10.
38. Lerwick	ZE1–3.
39. Leuchars	DD1–7. KY1–2, KY4–10, KY14–16. PH1–2, PH7, PH12–14.
40. Linton on Ouse	DL1–7, DL9–10. HG1–5. LS1–20, LS22–28. S21, S62–64, S70–75.TS1–12, TS14–26. WF1–17. YO1, YO7–8, YO10, YO19, YO23–24, YO26, YO30–32, YO41–43, YO51, YO60–62.

Income Support, Jobseekers' Allowance, State Pension Credit

Column (1)	Column (2)
Meteorological Office Station	**Postcode districts**
41. Liscombe	EX16–21, EX35–38. PL19–20. TA22, TA24.
42. Loch Glascarnoch	IV4, IV6, IV23–24, IV63.
43. Lusa	IV47–49, IV51, IV55–56.
44. Lyneham	BA1–3, BA11, BA13–15. GL7–9. RG17. SN1–6, SN8–16, SN25–26.
45. Machrihanish	KA27. PA28–29, PA31, PA34, PA37, PA41–49, PA60–76. PH36, PH38–41.
46. Manston	CM0. CT1–21. DA3, DA9–13. ME1–13. SS0–17. TN23–26, TN28–30.
47. Marham	IP24–28. PE12–14, PE30–38.
48. Newcastle	DH1–7. NE1–13, NE15–18, NE20–21, NE23, NE25–43, NE45–46. SR1–8. TS27–29.
49. Nottingham	CV13. DE1–3, DE5–7, DE11–15, DE21–24, DE55–56, DE65, DE72–75. LE1–9, LE11–14, LE16–19, LE65, LE67. NG1–22, NG25, NG31–34. S1–14, S17–18, S20, S25–26, S40–45, S60–61, S65–66, S80–81. ST10, ST14.
50. Pembrey Sands	SA1–8, SA10–18, SA31–34, SA61–63, SA66–73.
51. Plymouth	PL1–12, PL18, PL21. TQ7–8.
52. Rhyl	LL15–19, LL22, LL26–32.
53. St. Athan	BS1–11, BS13–16, BS20–24, BS29–32, BS34–37, BS39–41, BS48–49. CF3, CF5, CF10–11, CF14–15, CF23–24, CF31–36, CF61–64, CF71–72. NP10, NP16, NP18–20, NP26.
54. St. Catherine's Point	PO30, PO38–41.
55. St. Mawgan	TR7–8.
56. Salsburgh	EH43–46. ML6–11.
57. Scilly, St. Mary's	TR21–25.
58. Sennybridge	CF37–48, CF81–83. LD1–8. NP4, NP7–8, NP11–13, NP22–24, NP44. SA9, SA19–20. SY7, SY9, SY15–19, SY21–22.
59. Shawbury	ST1–9, ST11–12, ST15–21. SY1–6, SY11–13. TF1–13.
60. South Farnborough	GU1–4, GU9–25, GU46–47, GU52. RG1–2, RG4–8, RG10, RG12, RG14, RG18–27, RG29–31, RG40–42, RG45. SL1–2, SL4–6.

Income Support, Jobseekers' Allowance, State Pension Credit

Column (1)	Column (2)
Meteorological Office Station	**Postcode districts**
61. Stornoway Airport	HS1–9.
62. Thorney Island	BN1–3, BN9–18, BN25, BN41–43, BN45. GU34. PO1–22, PO31–37. SO14–24, SO30–32, SO40–43, SO45, SO50–53.
63. Tiree	IV41–46. PA77–78. PH42–44.
64. Tulloch Bridge	PA33, PA35–36, PS38, PA40. PH8–11, PH15–17, PH30–35, PH37, PH49–50.
65. Valley	LL33–40, LL42–49, LL51–78.
66. Waddington	DN1–22, DN31–41. HU1–20. LN1–13. NG23–24. PE10–11, PE20–25.
67. Walney Island	CA12–15, CA18–28. LA1–5, LA11–21.
68. Wattisham	CB9. CO1–8, CO10–16. IP1–23, IP29–33.
69. West Freugh	DG8–9.
70. Wick Airpot	IV25. KW1–3, KW5–10, KW12, KW14.
71. Wittering	CB1–8. LE15. NN17–18. PE1–9, PE15–17, PE26–29. SG8.
72. Woodford	BL0–9. CW1–12. M1–9, M11–35, M38, M40–41, M43–46, M50, M90. OL1–2, OL4–11, OL16. SK1–11, SK13–16. WA3, WA13–16. WN7.
73. Yeovilton	BA4–10, BA16, BA20–22. BS25–28. DT9–10. SP8. TA1–20, TA23."

p.1265, *Social Fund Cold Weather Payments (General) Regulations 1988, Sch.2*

3.185   With effect from November 1, 2003, reg.3 of and Sch.2 to the Social Fund Cold Weather Payments (General) Amendment Regulations 2003 (SI 2003/2605), substituted the following for Sch.2.

"SCHEDULE 2

Regulation 2(1A)(a) and 2(1B)(a).

SPECIFIED ALTERNATIVE STATIONS

Column (1)	Column (2)
Meteorological Office Station	Specified Alternative Station
Charlwood	Kenley Airfield
Coleshill	Church Lawford

Income Support, Jobseekers' Allowance, State Pension Credit

Column (1)	Column (2)
Meteorological Office Station	*Specified Alternative Station*
Kinloss	Lossiemouth
Linton on Ouse	Church Fenton
St Athan	Cardiff Weather Centre."

p.1266, *Social Fund Winter Fuel Payments Regulations 2000, reg.1(2)—definition of "nursing home"*

With effect from October 6, 2003, reg.5 of the Social Security (Removal of Residential Allowance and Miscellaneous Amendments) Regulations 2003 (SI 2003/1121), amended the definition of "nursing home" in reg.1(2) to read as follows:

3.186

" "nursing home" has the meaning it bears in regulation 2(1) of the Income Support Regulations 1987 (interpretation);"

pp.1266–1267, *Social Fund Winter Fuel Payments Regulations 2000, reg.1(3A)*

With effect from October 6, 2003, reg.5 of the Social Security (Removal of Residential Allowance and Miscellaneous Amendments) Regulations 2003 (SI 2003/1121), substituted the following for sub-para.(3A) of reg.1:

3.187

"(3A) For the purposes of paragraph (3)(a)(i) "residential care home" has the meaning given to that expression by virtue of sub-paragraphs (a), (c) and (d) of that definition in regulation 2(1) of the Income Support Regulations 1987."

p.1267, *Social Fund Winter Fuel Payments Regulations 2000, reg. 2*

With effect from September 1, 2003, reg.2 of the Social Fund Winter Fuel Payment (Amendment) Regulations 2003 (SI 2003/1737), substituted the following for reg.2:

3.188

"**2.**—(1) Subject to paragraphs (2) and (3) and regulation 3 of these Regulations, and regulation 36(2) of the Social Security (Claims and Payments) Regulations 1987, the Secretary of State shall pay to a person who—
  (a) in respect of any day falling within the qualifying week is ordinarily resident in Great Britain; and
  (b) has attained the age of 60 in or before the qualifying week,
a winter fuel payment of—
   (i) £200 unless he is in residential care or head (ii)(aa) applies; or
   (ii) £100 if income support or an income-based jobseeker's allowance has not been, nor falls to be, paid to him in respect of the qualifying week and he is—

(aa) in that week living with a person to whom a payment under these Regulations has been, or falls to be, made in respect of the winter following the qualifying week; or

(bb) in residential care.

(2) Where such a person has attained the age of 80 in or before the qualifying week—

(a) in paragraph (1)(i), for the sum of £200 there shall be substituted the sum of £300; and

(b) in paragraph (1)(ii), for the sum of £100 there shall be substituted the sum of £200, except that where he is in that week living with a person to whom a payment under these Regulations has been, or falls to be, made in respect of the winter following that week who has also attained the age of 80 in or before that week, there shall be substituted the sum of £150.

(3) Where such a person has not attained the age of 80 in or before the qualifying week but he is a partner of and living with a person who has done so, in paragraph (1)(i) for the sum of £200 there shall be substituted the sum of £300."

With effect from September 3, 2003, reg.2 was further amended by reg.2 of the Social Fund Winter Fuel Payment (Amendment) (No.2) Regulations 2003 (SI 2003/2192). Sub-para.(b) of paragraph (2) (which had only come into force two days previously) was replaced by the following sub-paragraph:

"(b) in paragraph (1)(ii), for the sum of £100 there shall be substituted the sum of £200, except that—

(i) where he is in that week living with a person to whom a payment under these Regulations has been, or falls to be, made in respect of the winter following that week who has also attained the age of 80 in or before that week, or

(ii) where he is in residential care,

there shall be substituted the sum of £150."

p.1270, *annotation to Social Fund Winter Fuel Payments Regulations 2000, reg.4*

3.189   In *CIS 2497/2002* an argument was raised that the operation of reg.4 discriminated indirectly against men on the grounds of their sex contrary to Directive 79/7/EEC. The evidence was that those selected by the Secretary of State to receive a winter fuel payment without a claim had been identified from official records of those receiving social security benefits (including retirement pension) in the qualifying week. As the pensionable age for women is lower than that for men, it was argued that there would be significantly more men than women in that category. However, Mr Commissioner Mesher rejected that argument on the basis that, even if the operation of the rules allowing the Secretary of State to make payments without a claim was discriminatory, the claimant had not been disadvantaged by reg.4 but by "the overall and identical time-limit [i.e., March 31, after the winter in question] set for claims and for the making of payments without a claim".

Income Support, Jobseekers' Allowance, State Pension Credit

p.1278, *Social Fund Maternity and Funeral Expenses (General) Regulations 1987, reg.5(1)(a)*

With effect from October 6, 2003, reg.31(1) and (2) of the State Pension Credit (Consequential, Transitional and Miscellaneous Provisions) Regulations 2002 (SI 2002/3019) amended reg.5(1)(a) by adding the words "state pension credit" after the words "income support". 3.190

p.1282, *Social Fund Maternity and Funeral Expenses (General) Regulations 1987, reg.7(1)(a)(i)*

With effect from October 6, 2003, reg.31(1) and (2) of the State Pension Credit (Consequential, Transitional and Miscellaneous Provisions) Regulations 2002 (SI 2002/3019) amended reg.7(1)(a)(i) by adding the words "state pension credit" after the words "income support". 3.191

p.1289, *annotations to Social Fund Maternity and Funeral Expenses (General) Regulations 1987, reg.7(1)(e)*

In *CIS 788/2003* the deceased was a boy who had died at the age of three months. The child's mother was herself a minor and the funeral directors refused to enter into a contract with her for that reason. The child's grandmother therefore undertook responsibility for the expenses and claimed a payment from the Social Fund. In these circumstances, Mr Commissioner Turnbull held that the grandmother could be treated as a "close friend" of the deceased under reg.7(1)(e)(iv). The Secretary of State had argued that as child benefit had been paid to the child's mother, she would have satisfied reg.7(1)(e)(ii)(aa) if she had accepted responsibility for the funeral expenses and therefore that the words "(ii) and (iii) above do not apply" in reg.7(1)(e)(iv) were not satisfied. The Commissioner rejected that argument. Reg.7(1)(e)(ii) "did not apply" because there was no real possibility of the mother's taking responsibility for the funeral expenses. Neither the existence of a family relationship between the grandmother and the child nor the child's very young age prevented her from being treated as his "close friend" for the purposes of the regulation. 3.192

p.1293, *Social Fund Maternity and Funeral Expenses (General) Regulations 1987, reg.7A*

In respect of deaths occurring on or after October 6, 2003, reg.2 of the Social Fund Maternity and Funeral Expenses (General) Regulations 1987 (SI 2003/1570), substituted the figure "£120" for the figure "£100" in reg.7A. 3.193

PART IV

UPDATING MATERIAL
VOLUME III

ADMINISTRATION, ADJUDICATION AND THE EUROPEAN DIMENSION

p.23, *Social Security Administration Act 1992, s.1(4)(ab)*

4.001 The entry into force of the amendment which inserted this provision is July 2, 2002 for the purpose of making regulations and April 7, 2003 for all other purposes.

p.29, *Social Security Administration Act, insertion of new s.2AA*

4.002 With effect from July 5, 2003, the Employment Act 2002, s.49 inserted as new s.2AA as follows:

"2AA Full entitlement to certain benefits conditional on work-focused interview for partner

(1) Regulations may make provision for or in connection with imposing, at a time when—
   (f) a person ("the claimant") who—
      (i) is under the age of 60, and
      (ii) has a partner who is also under that age,
is entitled to a benefit to which this section applies at a higher rate referable to his partner, and
   (g) prescribed circumstances exist,
a requirement for the partner to take part in a work-focused interview as a condition of the benefit continuing to be payable to the claimant at that rate.

(2) The benefits to which this section applies are—
   (a) income support;
   (b) an income-based jobseeker's allowance other than a joint-claim jobseeker's allowance;
   (c) incapacity benefit;
   (d) severe disablement allowance; and
   (e) invalid care allowance.

(3) For the purposes of this section a benefit is payable to a person at a higher rate referable to his partner if the amount that is payable in his case—
   (a) is more than it would be if the person concerned was not a member of a couple; or
   (b) includes an increase of benefit for his partner as an adult dependant of his.

(4) Regulations under this section may, in particular, make provision— 4.003
   (a) for securing, where the partner of the claimant would otherwise be required to take part in work-focused interviews relating to two or more benefits—
      (i) that the partner is required instead to take part in only one such interview; and
      (ii) that the interview is capable of counting for the purposes of all those benefits;
   (b) in a case where the claimant has more than one partner, for determining which of those partners is required to take part in

the work-focused interview or requiring each of them to take part in such an interview;
(c) for determining the persons by whom work-focused interviews are to be conducted;
(d) conferring power on such persons or the designated authority to determine when and where work-focused interviews are to take place (including power in prescribed circumstances to determine that they are to take place in the homes of those being interviewed);
(e) prescribing the circumstances in which partners attending work-focused interviews are to be regarded as having or not having taken part in them;
(f) for securing that if—
(i) a partner who has been notified of a requirement to take part in a work-focused interview fails to take part in it, and
(ii) it is not shown (by him or by the claimant), within the prescribed period, that he had good cause for that failure,
the amount payable to the claimant in respect of the benefit in relation to which the requirement applied is to be reduced by the specified amount until the specified time;
(g) prescribing—
(i) matters which are or are not to be taken into account in determining whether a partner does or does not have good cause for any failure to comply with the regulations; or
(ii) circumstances in which a partner is or is not to be regarded as having or not having good cause for any such failure.

4.004
(5) Regulations under this section may, in relation to a reduction under subsection (4)(f), provide—
(a) for the amount of the reduction to be calculated in the first instance by reference to such amount as may be prescribed;
(b) for the amount as so calculated to be restricted, in prescribed circumstances, to the prescribed extent;
(c) where the claimant is entitled to two or more benefits in relation to each of which a requirement to take part in a work-focused interview applied, for determining the extent to, and the order in, which those benefits are to be reduced in order to give effect to the reduction required in his case.

(6) Regulations under this section may provide that any requirement to take part in a work-focused interview that would otherwise apply to a partner by virtue of the regulations—
(a) is, in any prescribed circumstances, either not to apply or not to apply until the specified time;
(b) is not to apply if the designated authority determines that such an interview would not be of assistance to him or appropriate in the circumstances;
(c) is not to apply until such time as the designated authority determines (if that authority determines that such an interview

Administration, Adjudication and the European Dimension

would not be of assistance to him or appropriate in the circumstances until that time);
and the regulations may make provision for treating a partner to whom any such requirement does not apply, or does not apply until a particular time, as having complied with that requirement to such extent and for such purposes as are specified.

(7) In this section—

"couple" means a married or unmarried couple (within the meaning of Part 7 of the Contributions and Benefits Act);

"designated authority" means such of the following as may be specified, namely—

(a) the Secretary of State,
(b) a person providing services to the Secretary of State,
(c) a local authority, and
(d) a person providing services to, or authorised to exercise any function of, a local authority;

"partner" means a person who is a member of the same couple as the claimant;

"specified" means prescribed by or determined in accordance with regulations;

and

"work-focused interview" has the same meaning as in section 2A above.

4.005

pp.29–30, *Social Security Administration Act 1992, s.2B*

A number of amendments to this section have been made. For ease of reference the whole section together with the list of amending provisions is reproduced here.

4.006

Supplementary provisions relating to work-focused interviews

"**2B.**—(1) Chapter II of Part I of the Social Security Act 1998 (social security decisions and appeals) shall have effect in relation to relevant decisions subject to and in accordance with subsections (3) to (8) below (and in those subsections "the 1998 Act" means that Act).

(2) For the purposes of this section a "relevant decision" is a decision made under regulations under section 2A above that a person—

(a) has failed to comply with a requirement to take part in an interview which applied to him by virtue of the regulations, or
(b) has not shown, within the prescribed period mentioned in section 2A(3)(e)(ii) above, that he had good cause for such a failure.

[³(2A) For the purposes of this section a "relevant decision", in relation to regulations under section 2AA above, is a decision that—

(a) the partner of a person entitled to a benefit has failed to comply with a requirement to take part in an interview which applied to the partner by virtue of the regulations, or

(b) it has not been shown within the prescribed period mentioned in section 2AA(4)(f)(ii) above that the partner had good cause for such a failure.]

(3) Section 8(1)(c) of the 1998 Act (decisions falling to be made under or by virtue of certain enactments are to be made by the Secretary of State) shall have effect subject to any provisions of regulations under section 2A [⁴ or 2AA] above by virtue of which relevant decisions fall to be made otherwise than by the Secretary of State.

(4) For the purposes of each of sections 9 and 10 of the 1998 Act (revision and supersession of decisions of Secretary of State) any relevant decision made otherwise than by the Secretary of State shall be treated as if it were such a decision made by the Secretary of State (and accordingly may be revised by him under section 9 or superseded by a decision made by him under section 10).

(5) Subject to any provisions of regulations under either section 9 or 10 of the 1998 Act, any relevant decision made, or (by virtue of subsection (4) above) treated as made, by the Secretary of State may be—
  (a) revised under section 9 by a person or authority exercising functions under regulations under section 2A [⁴ or 2AA] above other than the Secretary of State, or
  (b) superseded under section 10 by a decision made by such a person or authority,
as if that person or authority were the Secretary of State.

(6) Regulations shall make provision for conferring (except in any prescribed circumstances) a right of appeal under section 12 of the 1998 Act (appeal to appeal tribunal) against—
  (a) any relevant decision, and
  (b) any decision under section 10 of that Act superseding any such decision, whether made by the Secretary of State or otherwise,

(7) Subsections (4) to (6) above apply whether—
  (a) the relevant decision, or
  (b) (in the case of subsection (6)(b)) the decision under section 10 of the 1998 Act,
    is as originally made or has been revised (by the Secretary of State or otherwise) under section 9 of that Act; and regulations under subsection (6) above may make provision for treating, for the purposes of section 12 of that Act, any decision made or revised otherwise than by the Secretary of State as if it were a decision made or revised by him.

(8) Section 12 of the 1998 Act shall not apply to any decision falling within subsection (6) above except in accordance with regulations under that subsection.

(9) In [³ . . .]
  (b) section 72(6) of the Welfare Reform and Pensions Act 1999 (supply of information),
any reference to information relating to social security includes any information supplied by a person for the purposes of an interview which he is required to take part in by virtue of section 2A [⁴ or 2AA] above.

(10) In this section "interview" means a work-focused interview within the meaning of section 2A above.]

AMENDMENTS

1. Welfare Reform and Pensions Act, 1999 s.57 (November 11, 1999)
2. Employment Act 2002 (2002 c.22) s.54 and Sch.8 (November 24, 2002).
3. Employment Act 2002 (2002 c.22) s.54 and Sch.7 (July 5, 2003)
4. Employment Act 2002 (2002 c.22) s.53 and Sch.7 (July 5, 2003)

p.31, *Social Security Administration Act 1992, amendment of s.2C*

With effect from July 5, 2003, subs.(2) is amended by the Employment Act 2002, s.53 and Sch.7 to read as follows, 4.008

"(2) This section applies to[. . .] [—
(a) persons making claims for or entitled to any of the benefits listed in section 2A(2) above or any prescribed benefit; and
(b) partners of persons entitled to any of the benefits listed in section 2AA(2) above or any prescribed benefit;]
and it so applies regardless of whether such persons have, in accordance with regulations under section 2A [or 2AA] above, already taken part in interviews conducted under such regulations."

pp.34–6, *Social Security Administration Act 1992, s.5 repealed in part*

With effect from April 8, 2003, subs.(2)(c) and (d) are repealed by the Tax Credits Act 2002, s.60 and Sch.6.

p.41, *Social Security Administration Act 1992, s.11 repealed*

With effect from April 8, 2003, this section is repealed by the Tax Credits Act 2002, s.60 and Sch.6. 4.009

pp.45–49, *Social Security Administration Act 1992, s.15A date of entry into force of amendments*

Those amendments referred to in note 4 are brought fully into effect from October 6, 2003 by SI 2003/1766, art.2. 4.010

pp.52–53, *Social Security Administration Act 1992, s.71*

With effect from April 8, 2003, subs.(11)(c) and (d) are repealed by the Tax Credits Act 2002, s.60 and Sch.6. 4.011

pp.111–112, *Social Security Administration Act 1992, s.124*

With effect from April 8, 2003, subs.(2)(b) the words "and working families' tax credit" are repealed by the Tax Credits Act 2002, s.60 and Sch.6. 4.012

pp.134–136, *Social Security Administration Act 1992, s.179*

4.013   With effect from April 8, 2003, subs. (5)(b) and (c) are repealed by the Tax Credits Act 2002, s.60 and Sch.6.

p.141, *Social Security Administration Act 1992, s.190 insertion of new paragraph*

4.014   With effect from July 5, 2003, a new subsection (1)(ab) is inserted after subs.(1)(aa) by the Employment Act 2002, s.53 and Sch.7 as follows,

"(ab) the first regulations to be made under section 2AA;"

pp.155–158, *Recovery of Benefits Act 1997, annotation to s.1*

4.015   Where a person suffers personal injury due to two accidents, benefit paid in consequence of the injury cannot be attributed to both accidents. It is paid "in respect of" only one or the other. Benefit that would have been paid as a result of the first accident even if the second accident had not occurred is attributable to the first accident, whereas benefit that would not have been paid but for the second accident is attributable to the second accident (*CCR/427/03*).

pp.165–166, *Recovery of Benefits Act 1997, annotation to s.8*

4.016   In *Williams v Devon County Council* [2003] EWCA Civ 365 (mentioned in the main work), the Court of Appeal did not go so far as to say that benefits should be deducted under s.8 only in so far as they were payable in respect of the period for which compensation in respect of the relevant head of damages has been paid. However, in *CCR/427/03*, the Commissioner suggested that that is what the legislation required. He also suggested that the calculation under s.8 should be made *before* the amount of compensation is reduced to take account of contributory negligence. However, as he also held that the proper operation of s.8 was a matter for the courts and not for tribunals or Commissioners, those suggestions are *obiter dicta*. The Commissioner further suggested that, if a trial judge has not considered the operation of s.8, that issue can be brought before the court in proceedings to enforce the judgment of the court because the effect of too great a deduction is that the judgment has not been fully satisfied.

p.170, *Recovery of Benefits Act 1997, annotation to s.11*

4.017   *R(CR) 2/02* (mentioned in the main work) was distinguished in *R(CR) 1/04*. In the latter case, incapacity benefit had been awarded pending the carrying out of a personal capability assessment on the basis of medical certificates supplied by the claimant's doctor, which referred to an eye injury sustained when a fire extinguisher had gone off accidentally. The Commissioner found that the eye injury caused by the fire extinguisher had in fact had no disabling effect on the claimant after a week and that the disablement was the result of a pre-existing condition in the claimant's eye and, later, from both that cause and a depressive illness. In those circumstances, he held that the incapacity benefit had not been paid "in respect of" the relevant accident, notwithstanding that the claimant had been deemed to be incapable of work on the strength of the medical certificates.

p.175, *Recovery of Benefits Act 1997, annotation to s.15*

See the supplementary annotation to s.8, above. 4.018

pp.186–187, *Recovery of Benefits Act 1997, annotation to Sch.1*

In *Lowther v Chatwin* [2003] EWCA Civ 729, the claimant had to close her business due to injuries sustained in an accident. She had been trading at a loss but had been able to pay 5/7ths of her business rent from the income of the business. She claimed damages in respect of her continuing liability to her landlord and the judge awarded her 5/7ths of the rent settlement. However, he held that the compensation was not for loss of earnings but for the destruction of the business. The Court of Appeal held that it was "compensation for earnings lost" within Sch.1 and that the compensator was therefore entitled to deduct from that compensation the amount of relevant benefits paid to the claimant. 4.019

p.195, *Social Security Act 1998, annotation to s.6*

In *Secretary of State for Work and Pensions v Gillies* [2004] S.L.T. 14, the Court of Session has reversed *CSDLA/1019/99* (mentioned in the main work) and held that the fact that a medically qualified member of an appeal tribunal carries out examinations and provides reports for the Benefits Agency as an examining medical practitioner "would not be sufficient to raise in the mind of the reasonable and well-informed observer an apprehension as to her impartiality as a member of a disability appeal tribunal. The mere fact that the tribunal would require to consider and assess reports by other doctors who acted as EMPs would not be such as to raise such an apprehension." 4.019a

pp.198–199, *Social Security Act 1998, annotation to s.8(2)*

In *CDLA/4331/02*, it was held that, when making an advance award on a renewal claim, the Secretary of State is entitled to anticipate changes of circumstances that are almost certain to occur before the date from which the decision will be effective. This may be limited to events that are bound to occur through the mere passage of time which, although changes of circumstances for the purposes of supersession, are plainly not changes of circumstances for the purpose of making advance awards of benefit. In that particular case, the renewal claim was to take effect from the claimant's 16th birthday so that s.72(6) of the Social Security Contributions and Benefits Act 1992 would no longer apply in respect of her claim for the care component of disability living allowance. 4.020

p.201, Social Security Act 1998, annotation to s.9(1)

4.020a   The question whether a tribunal may give a supersession decision on an appeal following a decision given in terms of revision or *vice versa* has been considered by a Tribunal of Commissioners in *CIB/4751/02* (see the supplemental annotation to s.12(1) below).

p.204, Social Security Act 1998, annotation to s.10(5)

4.021   *Secretary of State for Work and Pensions v Adams* [2003] EWCA Civ 769 has been reported as *R(G) 1/03*.

In *CIB/4751/02*, the Tribunal of Commissioners took much the same approach as was taken in *CDLA/4217/01* (mentioned in the main work) and decided that where a claimant has applied for supersession in order to obtain an increase of benefit but the Secretary of State supersedes the award so as to reduce entitlement, the supersession is made on the Secretary of State's own initiative and not on the claimant's application. Therefore, it is effective from the date of the decision and not the date of the claimant's application. Similarly, where the Secretary of State's supersession decision is not less favourable than the original decision but the claimant appeals and the tribunal not only does not allow the appeal but also makes a decision even less favourable than the original decision, the tribunal's decision is effective from the date of the Secretary of State's supersession decision. See paras 95 to 97 of the Tribunal's decision.

p.207, Social Security Act 1998, annotation to s.12

4.022   Reg.12 of the Social Security (Incapacity Benefit Work-focused Interviews) Regulations 2003 (SI 2003/2439) provides for a right of appeal under s.12 against decisions made under those Regulations.

p.210, Social Security Act 1998, annotation to s.12(1)

4.023   The hearing before the Tribunal of Commissioners to which reference is made at the end of page 210 was postponed and did not take place until the end of November 2003. The 198-paragraph decision (*CIB/4751/02*), surely the longest decision ever delivered by a Commissioner or Tribunal of Commissioners, was signed on January 21, 2004. In it, the Tribunal considered in depth the jurisdiction of tribunals and the extent to which tribunals are limited, or not limited, by the terms of the decision against which an appeal has been brought. The Tribunal did not try to analyse the many decisions of Commissioners on the question of the scope of appeals under s.12 of the 1998 Act but it is clear that most of the decisions mentioned in the annotation to s.12(1) in the main work are no longer to be followed or, at least, are no longer to be followed in full. In particular, the Tribunal's reasoning is inconsistent with the reasoning in *CSIB/1268/00* (which was expressly disapproved), *CDLA/2733/02*, *CDLA/4977/01*, *CSIS/1298/01*, *CDLA/2033/01*, *CDLA/5196/01* and *CIS/4935/01*.

Nonetheless, the decision is rooted firmly in Commissioners' jurisprudence. The Tribunal noted that s.12 makes no positive provision at all as to a tribunal's powers so that those powers must be found by a process of implication. They therefore considered the case law on adjudication before the 1998 Act came into force (in particular, *R(F) 1/72, R(P) 1/55, R(SB) 1/82* and *R(SB) 42/83*). That led to the conclusion that an appeal to an appeal tribunal under s.12 is by way of rehearing. At para.24, the Tribunal said:

> "As a matter of principle, on such an appeal the tribunal may make any decision which the officer below could have made on the legal questions before that officer. That principle encompasses dealing with new questions so as to reach the right result on an appeal, within the limit that the appeal tribunal has no jurisdiction (in the absence of express legislation to that effect) to determine questions which fall outside the scope of that which the officer below could have done on the proper legal view of the issues before him, by way of a claim or an application or otherwise."

They pointed out, at para.31, that s.12(8)(a) of the 1998 Act reinforces that approach because it is implicit in that provision that an appeal tribunal is not limited to considering issues actually raised by the parties.

4.023a

Against that background, the Tribunal considered three issues concerning the powers of tribunals: whether supersession decisions can be substituted for revision decisions and *vice versa*, whether defects in supersession decisions can be remedied, and whether a tribunal can make a decision less favourable to a claimant than the decision under appeal. (Other issues considered by the Tribunal are noted in the supplemental annotations to regs 3 and 6 of the Social Security and Child Support (Decisions and Appeals) Regulations 1999, below.)

Can supersession decisions be substituted for revision decisions and vice versa

The Tribunal's decision on this issue is based on their view of the nature of appeals following supersession decisions under s.10 and revision decisions under s.9. In the former case, the appeal is, both in form and in substance, an appeal against the decision to supersede or not to supersede. Where there has been a revision or a refusal to revise, any appeal is, in form, against the original decision because s.12(1) does not provide for an appeal against the decision under s.9 but reg.31(2) of the Social Security and Child Support (Decisions and Appeals) Regulations 1999 extends the time for appealing against the earlier decision as revised or, where the revision or non-revision was under regs 3(1) or (3), not revised. If there is a refusal to revise under, say, reg.3(5)(a) on the ground of "official error", there is a question whether there is any right of appeal at all. That question is to be considered by the Tribunal in *CIS/ 4/03*. However, it was common ground before the Tribunal in *CIB/ 4751/02* that, if a claimant is entitled to appeal against a refusal to revise a decision on the ground of "official error", he or she must show that the original decision did arise from an official error if the appeal is to be

4.023b

allowed. Therefore, the Tribunal held at para.40, an appeal following a revision or refusal to revise is, in substance, an appeal against the decision under s.9, even if in form it is an appeal against the original decision.

4.023c The parties nonetheless argued that the legislation did not allow a tribunal to give a supersession decision on appeal from a revision decision and *vice versa*, although counsel for the claimants submitted that it should readily be implied that a revision decision included a refusal to supersede and that a supersession decision included a refusal to revise. However, the Tribunal considered that the result of taking the approach advocated by the parties had too often been absurd. At para.50, they said:

> "The meaning of a statutory provision which is so clear that it admits only one possible construction cannot be altered or departed from by reference to the consequences, however inconvenient or anomalous. However, in our judgement the statutory provisions relevant to this issue fail by some margin to reach the degree of clarity which would bring that principle into play. In these circumstances, in ascertaining the legislature's intention, it is quite proper to have regard to the potential consequences of possible alternative constructions, in the context of the statutory scheme as a whole. In the field of benefit decisions and appeals procedure, we consider it proper, in construing the relevant provisions, to assume that the legislature did not intend to create a scheme which would be likely to lead to impracticable or indeed absurd results in a significant number of cases. On the contrary, we proceed on the basis that the legislature intended the provisions relating to decisions and appeals (and in particular those relating to provisions changing the effect of a previous decision) to form at least a reasonably workable scheme."

4.023d Having given examples of some of the more absurd consequences of the parties' submissions, the Tribunal held, at paragraph 55:

> "In our judgment, if an appeal tribunal decides that the Secretary of State's decision under Section 9 or Section 10 changing or refusing to change a previous decision was wrong then, subject to the restriction in Section 12(8)(b), if relevant) it has jurisdiction to make the revision or supersession decision which it considers the Secretary of State ought to have made, even if that means making a decision under Section 9 when the Secretary of State acted only under Section 10, and vice versa."

They rejected the need to resort to the theory of implied decisions on the ground that "the 1998 legislation could not have been intended to involve consideration of such arid technicalities and complications" (para.59).

Can defects in supersession decisions be remedied?

4.023e The Tribunal held that an appeal tribunal can remedy defects in a decision such as failing to acknowledge that an existing decision needed superseding, failing to state the grounds of supersession or relying on the wrong grounds of supersession.

"72.... there may be some decisions made by the Secretary of State which have so little coherence or connection to legal powers that they do not amount to decisions under Section 10 at all....

73. If, however, the Secretary of State's decision was made under Section 10 (as to which, see Paragraph 76 below), ... the appeal tribunal has jurisdiction, on appeal, to decide whether the outcome arrived at by that decision (i.e. either to change or not to change the original decision) was correct....

76. In our judgment a decision should generally be regarded as having been made under Section 10, regardless of the form in which it may be expressed, if it has the effect of terminating an existing entitlement from the date of the decision (or from some later date than the effective date of the original decision).... Similarly, a decision should generally be regarded as having been made under Section 9 if it changes the original decision with effect from the effective date of that decision."

However, although the Tribunal therefore agreed with the result reached in *CSIB/1266/00* (mentioned in the main work) they rejected, at paras 77 to 80, the distinction drawn in that case and earlier cases between defects of form and defects of substance, pointing out that reliance on a factual basis that the tribunal considered wrong would generally be regarded as a defect of substance and that decisions of the Secretary of State are not required to be in any particular form. The implication of the Tribunal's decision appears to be that an appeal tribunal should limit its decision to holding that the Secretary of State's decision was invalid only in cases where the Secretary of State's decision is completely incoherent and the nature of the decision cannot be implied or where the Secretary of State had no power to make any decision at all.

The Tribunal went on to say, at para.82, that it is necessary for an appeal tribunal chairman to "perfect" or "recast" a defective decision in the tribunal's decision notice only "if either (i) the decision as expressed is wrong in some material respect (*e.g.* states an incorrect ground of appeal) or (ii) there is likely to be some particular practical benefit to the claimant or to the adjudication process in future in reformulating the decision". However, if a statement of reasons is requested, giving reasons for the tribunal's decision is likely to involve explaining how any defects in the Secretary of State's decision were approached.

Can a tribunal make a decision less favourable to a claimant than a supersession decision under appeal?

The Tribunal held that a tribunal could make a decision less favourable to a claimant than a supersession decision under appeal. This followed both from the Tribunal's view as to the nature of an appeal to an appeal tribunal and from the terms of s.12(8)(a), implicitly providing that a tribunal may consider issues not raised by the parties. However,

4.023f

the Tribunal made two important comments at paragraphs 94 and 97 of their decision.

First, a tribunal must consciously exercise the discretion in s.12(8)(a) to consider a point not raised by the parties and, if a statement of reasons is requested, must explain in that statement why the discretion was exercised in the manner it was. For the points to be taken into account when exercising the discretion, see the supplemental annotation to s.12(8)(a) below.

Secondly, where the tribunal's decision is even less favourable to the claimant than the original decision that was the subject of the supersession decision under appeal, the tribunal's decision is "effectively the exercise by the tribunal of the Secretary of State's power to supersede 'on his own initiative'" and so, by virtue of s.10(5), the decision is effective from the date of the Secretary of State's decision under appeal rather than from the date of the claimant's application for supersession.

pp.211 to 213, *Social Security Act 1998, annotation to s.12(8)(a)*

4.023g   In *CIB/4751/02* at paras 93 and 94, the Tribunal of Commissioners held that, where an appeal tribunal is minded to make a decision less favourable to the claimant than the one under appeal and the respondent has not invited them to make such a decision, the appeal tribunal must address their minds to the power conferred by s.12(8)(a) not to consider the issue. The discretion is one to be exercised judicially, taking into account all the circumstances of the particular case. Furthermore, the tribunal's decision is likely to be held to be erroneous in point of law if the statement of reasons does not show that there has been a conscious exercise of the discretion.

> "In exercising the discretion, the appeal tribunal must of course have in mind, in particular, two factors. First, it must bear in mind the need to comply with Article 6 of the Convention and the rules of natural justice. This will involve, at the very least, ensuring that the claimant has had sufficient notice of the tribunal's intention to consider superseding adversely to him to enable him properly to prepare his case. The fact that the claimant is entitled to withdraw his appeal any time before the appeal tribunal's decision may also be material to what Article 6 and the rules of natural justice demand. Second, the appeal tribunal may consider it more appropriate to leave the question whether the original decision should be superseded adversely to the claimant to be decided subsequently by the Secretary of State. This might be so if, for example, deciding that question would involve factual issues which do not overlap those raised by the appeal, or if it would necessitate an adjournment of the hearing."

p.216, *Social Security Act 1998, annotation to s.12(8)(b)*

4.024   In *CDLA/4331/02*, it was held that, when hearing an appeal from a decision on a renewal claim effective from the claimant's 16th birthday, a tribunal is required to determine the appeal on the basis that the claimant was 16, even if she was only 15 at the date of the Secretary of

State's decision. The approach taken was different from that in *CDLA/ 3848/01* (mentioned in the main work), but the result was the same on the facts of the case. In *C12/03–04(DLA)*, a Commissioner in Northern Ireland expressly disagreed with *CDLA/3848/01* and concluded that the Secretary of State was not entitled to refuse benefit at all until the date from which the renewal claim would have been effective. A tribunal, faced with an appeal against a disallowance of a renewal claim made before the date from which a new award would have been effective, therefore had no power to do more than set aside the Secretary of State's decision as having been made without jurisdiction, leaving the Secretary of State to make a new decision. A Tribunal of Commissioners is to consider in February in 2004 whether the same approach should be taken in Great Britain.

pp.219–220, Social Security Act 1998, annotation to s.13(3)

Where a legally qualified panel member has erred in failing to set aside a decision under s.13(3), a Commissioner should usually remedy the defect by setting the decision aside under s.14(7), at any rate where the parties consent and there are no compelling reasons for not doing so (*C24/02–03(DLA)*). 4.025

pp.224–225, Social Security Act 1998, annotation to s.14(1)

In *Moyna v Secretary of State for Work and Pensions* [2003] UKHL 44, [2003] 1 W.L.R. 1929 (also reported as *R(DLA) 7/03*), the House of Lords have reversed the decision of the Court of Appeal that is mentioned in the main work. Lord Hoffmann, with whom the other members of the House agreed, said: 4.026

> "In any case in which a tribunal has to apply a standard with a greater or lesser degree of imprecision and to take a number of factors into account, there are bound to be cases in which it will be impossible for a reviewing court to say that the tribunal must have erred in deciding the case either way: see *George Mitchell (Chesterhall) Ltd v. Finney Lock Seeds Ltd* [1983] 2 A.C. 803, 815–816."

This reaffirms the approach traditionally taken by Commissioners.

It is not necessarily a breach of the rules of natural justice for a tribunal's decision to refer to Commissioners' decisions that were not mentioned during the course of the proceedings before the tribunal. The question is whether the proceedings were unfair and that depends on whether it might reasonably be considered that the case has been decided on a basis that could not have been anticipated by the parties (*Sheridan v Stanley Cole (Wainfleet) Ltd* [2003] EWCA Civ 1046; [2003] 4 All E.R. 1181).

The decision of the Tribunal of Commissioners in *CSDLA/1019/99* (mentioned in the main work) has been reversed on appeal by the Court of Session in *Secretary of State for Work and Pensions v Gillies* [2004] S.L.T. 14. The Commissioners had allowed an appeal against a decision of a disability appeal tribunal, the medically qualified member of which, 4.026a

"Dr. A", also acted on behalf of the Benefits Agency as an examining medical practitioner. The Court distinguished *Lawal v Northern Spirit Ltd* [2003] UKHL 35; [2003] I.C.R. 856 (mentioned in the main work) on the ground that the critical feature in that case was the relationship between the part-time judge and the wing members whereas there was no relationship of lay to professional or of subordinate to superior in *Gillies* itself.

"[38] That being so, one returns to the proposition that the association of Dr. A with other EMPs would be sufficient to give rise in the mind of the reasonable and well-informed observer to an apprehension of bias. Such an observer would surely be blessed with the knowledge that Dr. A and the other EMPs were independent expert advisers in carrying out the work of examining and reporting to the Benefits Agency. If so, why should they not be regarded as independent of each other when it came to the assessment of, and adjudication between, competing medical opinions before the tribunal? There was considerable force in the submission made by the Dean of Faculty that there is a danger that, if Dr. A should be regarded as disqualified in the present type of case, the same objection could be based simply on the membership of a professional body. This is not, of course, the basis which the Tribunal of Commissioners adopted for their decision. However, it does highlight the need to consider whether pointing to a subset of certain professionals involves a distinction without a difference. . . . Having considered the factual circumstances, we are of the view that the fact that Dr. A carried out examinations and provided reports for the Benefits Agency as an EMP would not be sufficient to raise in the mind of the reasonable and well-informed observer an apprehension as to her impartiality as a member of a disability appeal tribunal. The mere fact that the tribunal would require to consider and assess reports by other doctors who acted as EMPs would not be such as to raise such an apprehension."

4.026b   It by no means follows that the appeal that has been brought by the Secretary of State against the decision of the Deputy Commissioner in *CSDLA/444/02* (mentioned in the main work) will also succeed. That case is less readily distinguishable from *Lawal v Northern Spirit Ltd*, notwithstanding the fact that the Deputy Commissioner managed to distinguish the decision of the Court of Appeal in *Lawal* before it was reversed by the House of Lords.

p.228, *Social Security Act 1998, annotation to s.14(8)*

4.027   If a decision of a tribunal has been superseded while an appeal against a Commissioner's decision has been pending, it is necessary to consider the effect of the supersession on the appeal or *vice versa*. If the supersession was under regulation 6(2)(c) (ignorance of, or mistake as to, fact), there may be circumstances in which the appeal to the Commissioner should be treated as having lapsed, particularly if the supersession has given the claimant all that he or she seeks on the appeal. If the appeal is not treated as having lapsed and is allowed, then the supersession is likely to lapse when the tribunal's decision is set aside under subs.(8), whatever the ground on which the supersession was made (*CDLA/ 1317/02*).

However, in practice, the supersession decision is generally allowed to stand, and the decision to be made by a Commissioner or another tribunal following the setting aside of the first tribunal's decision is made in respect of a period ending immediately before the supersession took effect. This approach was held in *CDLA/2968/03* to be justifiable where the parties are content with the outcome of the supersession or where it is plain that supersession would have been appropriate whatever the outcome of the appeal because there had been an obvious change of circumstances or, perhaps, new medical evidence justifying supersession under reg.6(2)(g) of the Social Security and Child Support (Decisions and Appeals) Regulations 1999 in an incapacity benefit case. In *CDLA/ 2968/03*, the claimant had both appealed against and applied for supersession of a decision of a tribunal. The appeal was successful and a Commissioner had referred the case to another tribunal. The application for supersession had failed and the claimant's appeal came before the same tribunal as the remitted appeal. The new tribunal made an award on the remitted appeal and did not limit it on account of the failed supersession application. No award was made on the supersession appeal. On further appeals, the Commissioner held that that was the correct approach where, as in that case, the application for supersession had been under reg.6(2)(c) (error of fact). He advanced three rules:

"1. An application for supersession that results in a refusal to supersede the original decision does not terminate the period under consideration on an appeal against the original decision.

2. Live proceedings arising out of an application for supersession based on ignorance of, or a mistake as to, a material fact lapse when the decision to be superseded is set aside on appeal (provided that there is no further appeal in respect of the original decision).

3. Live proceedings arising out of an application for supersession based on a change of circumstances do not lapse when the decision to be superseded is set aside on appeal (but the application may have to be treated as an application for supersession of a different decision or, perhaps, as a new claim, depending on the circumstances)."

The second and third rules arise because a tribunal or Commissioner hearing an appeal against the original decision must correct any error of fact in the original decision but, by virtue of s.12(8)(b), must not take account of any subsequent change of circumstances.

p.228, *Social Security Act 1998, annotation to s.14(10)*

Where a Commissioner refuses leave to appeal against a decision of a tribunal, no appeal lies against the refusal of leave but it may be challenged by way of an application for judicial review (*Bland v Chief Supplementary Benefit Officer*) [1983] 1 W.L.R. 262 (also reported as *R(SB) 12/83*). It has been made plain in relation to refusals by circuit judges of

4.028

leave to appeal against decisions of district judges that applications for permission to apply for judicial review of refusals of leave to appeal should generally be dismissed summarily on the ground that Parliament has put in place an adequate system for reviewing the merits of district judge's decisions (*R. (Sivasubramaniam) v Wandsworth County Court (Lord Chancellor's Department intervening)* [2003] 1 W.L.R. 475). That decision was given against the background of the Access to Justice Act 1999 but, by analogy (see *Cooke v Secretary of State for Social Security* [2001] EWCA Civ 734 (reported as *R(DLA) 6/01*)), the same approach is likely to be taken in relation to refusals of leave to appeal by Commissioners in the absence of a clear error of law on the part of the tribunal.

pp.229–230, *Social Security Act 1998, annotation to s.15*

It was made plain in *McAllister v Secretary of State for Work and Pensions* [2003] S.L.T. 1195 that, before allowing an appeal against a decision of a person or body exercising statutory powers, the Court of Session in Scotland requires to be satisfied that there are proper grounds for doing so. Therefore a written argument must be submitted, on the basis of which the Court will decide whether the case should be listed for hearing. In England and Wales, the Court of Appeal readily allows appeals by consent, without considering their merits. It is arguable that that is not appropriate in public law cases and that the Court of Session's approach is preferable. There have been a small number of instances when Commissioners' decisions have been set aside by the Court of Appeal without the Court considering the merits of the appeal. Although such a decision given by the Court of Appeal is not binding on anyone other than for the purposes of that particular case (*R(FC) 1/97*), it can create difficulties because the fact that the Commissioner's decision has been set aside plainly means that that too cannot be regarded as binding, although the Commissioner's reasoning may still be regarded as persuasive. The law is thus left uncertain.

In a different context, the Court of Appeal took a robust approach in *Secretary of State for Work and Pensions v H* [2004] EWCA Civ 16. They refused to consider on its merits an opposed appeal, brought by the Secretary of State on grounds that had not been advanced before the Commissioner despite the Commissioner having given a clear opportunity by indicating his provisional views. The Court said that the case did not appear to raise any new point of principle and that, in a case concerned with the mere application of established principles, it was "of the utmost value, on an appeal from a specialist tribunal, to have the considered views of the points at issue of that specialist tribunal before testing them on appeal". They were not impressed by the argument that the Commissioner's decision would remain as an unfortunate precedent, saying that if the issue was that important it was because there were many other similar cases and therefore the Secretary of State would be able to find another case in which to advance his arguments before a Commissioner and, if necessary, the Court.

pp.233–234, *Social Security Act 1998, annotation to s.17*

The Court of Appeal's decision in *Secretary of State for Work and Pensions v Whalley* [2002] EWCA Civ 166 (reported as *R(I) 2/03*), mentioned in the main work, was considered in *CI/1605/02*, in which it was held that the reason that a finding as to a date of onset is conclusive lies in reg. 6(1) of the Social Security (Industrial Injuries) (Prescribed Diseases) Regulations 1985 rather than in s.17. It was pointed out that in *Whalley* the issue had been whether a finding that the claimant was *not* suffering from a prescribed disease so that there was *no* date of onset was conclusive and that that had turned on the finality of a decision on a diagnosis question under the pre-1998 Act system of adjudication, which in turn had precluded a finding in a later claim for disablement pension that there had been an earlier date of onset. While a finding that a claimant has been suffering from a prescribed disease from a particular date is conclusive as to the date of onset by virtue of reg.6(1) of the 1985 Regulations, it remains doubtful that a finding that the claimant has *not* been suffering from a prescribed disease is conclusive under the 1998 Act, rather than merely being final in respect of the period up to the date of the decision in which the finding was made.

4.029

p.237, *Social Security Act 1998, annotation to s.20*

CDLA/3967/02 has been reported as *R(DLA) 5/03*.

In *CSI/146/03*, the Commissioner commented that s.20(2) is rather less helpful to tribunals than the repealed s.53 of the Social Security Administration Act 1992, which allowed tribunals to refer a case for report by any "expert". While medical practitioners were always regarded as "experts", the power to refer cases to experts other than medical practitioners has been lost. She observed that s.7 of this Act, under which a panel member may be instructed as an expert witness, does not fill the gap. It is helpful only in a case where a report is required from either a medical practitioner or an accountant and even then there may be issues of perceived bias if the witness is known to the tribunal (see *CSDLA/444/02* mentioned in the annotation to s.14(1) in the main work and in the supplemental annotation above).

4.030

p.252, *Social Security Act 1998, annotation to s.29*

Where the Secretary of State has decided that a claimant has not suffered an industrial accident and the claimant appeals against that decision, a tribunal may exercise the power conferred by subs. (3) to refuse to decide the issue on the ground that it is unlikely to be relevant to any claim to benefit (*CI/1297/02*). That refusal to decide the issue must replace the Secretary of State's decision, and will make an important difference if the tribunal is wrong and there ever is a claim for benefit, because the Secretary of State's decision would have been conclusive by virtue of subs. (4).

4.031

Administration, Adjudication and the European Dimension

pp.276–278, *Welfare Reform and Pensions Act 1999, s.72 addition of new paragraph*

4.032　With effect from July 5, 2003, a new paragraph is added after s.72(3)(a) by the Employment Act 2002, s.53 and Sch.7, para.55 which reads as follows, (aa) section 2AA of the Administration Act,

pp.338–341, *Claims and Payments Regulations, reg.2; insertion of new definition*

4.033　With effect from October 5, 1999, reg.3(c) of the Tax Credits (Claims and Payments) (Amendment) Regulations 1999 (SI 1999/2572) inserts the following definition in the list of definitions,

" "the Board" means the Commissioners of Inland Revenue; and references to "the Board" in these regulations have effect only with respect to working families tax credit;"

With effect from November 29, 1999 the definition of "adjudicating authority" is omitted; and the following definition is inserted: Social Security Act 1998, Sch.6,

" "relevant authority" means a person within section 72(2) of the Welfare Reform and Pensions Act 1999;"

With effect from April 7, 2003, reg.3 of the State Pension Credit (Consequential, Transitional and Miscellaneous Provisions) Regulations 2002 (SI 2002/3019) inserts the following new definitions at the appropriate point in the list of definitions:

" "the 2002 Act" means the State Pension Credit Act 2002"
"advance period" means the period specified in regulation 4E(2)"
" "guarantee credit" is to be construed in accordance with sections 1 and 2 of the 2002 Act;"
" "qualifying age" has the same meaning as in the 2002 Act by virtue of section 1(6) of that Act;"
" "state pension credit" means state pension credit under the 2002 Act;"

and the words "state pension credit" are inserted into para.(2)(b) after the words "income support"
and a new paragraph (4) is added as follows,

"(4) In these Regulations references to "beneficiaries" include any person entitled to state pension credit."

pp.344–347, *Claims and Payments Regulations, reg.4: insertion of new para.(10)*

4.034　With effect from April 7, 2003, reg.4 of the State Pension Credit (Consequential, Transitional and Miscellaneous Provisions) Regulations 2002 (SI 2002/3019) inserts a new paragraph (10) as follows,

Administration, Adjudication and the European Dimension

"(10) This regulation shall not apply to a claim for state pension credit."

With effect from July 21, 2003, The Social Security (Claims and Payments and Miscellaneous Amendments) Regulations 2003 (SI 2003/1632), reg.2(2)(a), amends reg.4 by adding the words "Subject to paragraphs (6A) to (6D)," at the beginning of para.(6), and adding new paragraphs (6A) to (6D) as follows,

"(6A) Paragraphs (6B) and (6C) apply in relation to a person—
  (a) who has attained the qualifying age and makes a claim for—
    (i) an attendance allowance, a bereavement benefit, a carer's allowance, a disability living allowance or incapacity benefit; or
    (ii) a retirement pension of any category for which a claim is required or a winter fuel payment for which a claim is required under regulation 3(1)(b) of the Social Fund Winter Fuel Payment Regulations 2000;
  (b) who has not yet attained the qualifying age and makes a claim for a retirement pension in advance in accordance with regulation 15(1); or
  (c) who has attained the qualifying age and makes a claim for income support in respect of a period before 6th October 2003.

(6B) A person to whom paragraph (6A) applies may make a claim by sending or delivering it to, or by making it in person at—
  (a) an office designated by the Secretary of State for accepting such claims; or
  (b) the offices of—
    (i) a local authority administering housing benefit or council tax benefit;
    (ii) a person providing to such an authority services relating to housing benefit or council tax benefit; or
    (iii) a person authorised to exercise any function of a local authority relating to housing benefit or council tax benefit,
if the Secretary of State has arranged with the local authority or person specified in head (ii) or (iii) for them to receive claims in accordance with this sub-paragraph, provided that the claim is made on a form which is approved by the Secretary of State for the purpose.

(6C) Where a person to whom paragraph (6A) applies makes a claim in accordance with paragraph (6B)(b), on receipt of the claim the local authority or other person specified in that sub-paragraph—
  (a) shall forward the claim to the Secretary of State as soon as reasonably practicable;
  (b) may receive information or evidence relating to the claim supplied by—
    (i) the person making, or who has made, the claim; or
    (ii) other persons in connection with the claim,
and shall forward it to the Secretary of State as soon as reasonably practicable;

4.035

(c) may obtain information or evidence relating to the claim from the person who has made the claim, but not any medical information or evidence except for that which the claimant must provide in accordance with instructions on the form, and shall forward the information or evidence to the Secretary of State as soon as reasonably practicable;

(d) may record information or evidence relating to the claim supplied or obtained in accordance with sub-paragraphs (b) or (c) and may hold the information or evidence (whether as supplied or obtained or as recorded) for the purpose of forwarding it to the Secretary of State; and

(e) may give information and advice with respect to the claim to the person who makes, or who has made, the claim.

(6D) The benefits specified in paragraph (6A) are relevant benefits for the purposes of section 7A of the Social Security Administration Act 1992."

The same provision inserts the words "in an appropriate office, or other office specified in paragraph (6B) where that paragraph applies," after the words "when it is received".

pp.353–354, *Claims and Payments Regulations, reg. 4B amendment*

4.036   With effect from April 7, 2003, reg.4 of the State Pension Credit (Consequential, Transitional and Miscellaneous Provisions) Regulations 2002 (SI 2002/3019) inserts the words "or for state pension credit." at the end of para.(1)(b).

p.354, *Claims and Payments Regulations, insertion of new regs 4D, 4E and 4F*

4.037   With effect from April 7, 2003, reg.4 of the State Pension Credit (Consequential, Transitional and Miscellaneous Provisions) Regulations 2002 (SI 2002/3019) inserts the following new regulations after reg.4C,

"Making a claim for state pension credit

4D.—(1) A claim for state pension credit need only be made in writing if the Secretary of State so directs in any particular case.

(2) A claim is made in writing either—

(a) by completing and returning in accordance with the instructions printed on it a form approved or provided by the Secretary of State for the purpose; or

(b) in such other written form as the Secretary of State accepts as sufficient in the circumstances of the case.

(3) A claim for state pension credit may be made in writing whether or not a direction is issued under paragraph (1) and may also be made by telephone to, or in person at, an appropriate office or other office

Administration, Adjudication and the European Dimension

designated by the Secretary of State for accepting claims for state pension credit.

(4) A claim made in writing may also be made at the offices of—
  (a) a local authority administering housing benefit or council tax benefit;
  (b) a person providing [¹ to such an authority services relating to housing benefit or council tax benefit]; or
  (c) a person authorised to exercise any function of a local authority relating to housing benefit or council tax benefit [¹ if the Secretary of State has arranged with the local authority or person specified in sub-paragraph (b) or (c) for them to receive claims in accordance with this paragraph].

(5) Any claim made in accordance with paragraph (4), together with any information and evidence supplied in connection with making the claim, shall be forwarded as soon as reasonably practicable to the Secretary of State by the person who received the claim.

(6) A claim for state pension credit made in person or by telephone is not a valid claim unless a written statement of the claimant's circumstances, provided for the purpose by the Secretary of State, is approved by the person making the claim.

(7) A married or unmarried couple may agree between them as to which partner is to make a claim for state pension credit, but in the absence of an agreement, the Secretary of State shall decide which of them is to make the claim.

(8) Where one member of a married or unmarried couple ("the former claimant") is entitled to state pension credit under an award but a claim for state pension credit is made by the other member of the couple, then, if both members of the couple confirm in writing that they wish the claimant to be the other member, the former claimant's entitlement shall terminate on the last day of the benefit week specified in paragraph (9).

(9) That benefit week is the benefit week of the former claimant which includes the day immediately preceding the day the partner's claim is actually made or, if earlier, is treated as made.

(10) If a claim for state pension credit is defective when first received, the Secretary of State is to provide the person making it with an opportunity to correct the defect.

(11) If that person corrects the defect so that the claim then satisfies the requirements of paragraph (2) and does so within 1 month of the date the Secretary of State last drew attention to the defect, the claim shall be treated as having been properly made on the date
  (a) the defective claim was first received by the Secretary of State or the person acting on his behalf; or
  (b) if regulation 4F(3) applies, the person informed an appropriate office [¹ or other office specified in regulation 4F(3)] of his intention to claim state pension credit.

(12) Paragraph (11) does not apply in a case to which regulation 4E(3) applies.

(13) State pension credit is a relevant benefit for the purposes of section 7A of the Social Security Administration Act 1992.

4.038

AMENDMENT

4.039 1. The Social Security (Claims and Payments and Miscellaneous Amendments) Regulations 2003 (S.I. 2003 No. 1632) reg.2, (July 21, 2003).

Making a claim before attaining the qualifying age

4.040 **4E.**—(1) A claim for state pension credit may be made, and any claim made may be determined, at any time within the advance period.

(2) The advance period begins on the date which falls 4 months before the day on which the claimant attains the qualifying age and ends on the day before he attains that age.

(3) A person who makes a claim within the advance period which is defective may correct the defect at any time before the end of the advance period.

Making a claim after attaining the qualifying age: date of claim

4.041 **4F.**—(1) This regulation applies in the case of a person who claims state pension credit on or after attaining the qualifying age.

(2) The date on which a claim is made shall, subject to paragraph (3), be—
 (a) where the claim is made in writing and is not defective, the date on which the claim is first received—
   (i) by the Secretary of State or the person acting on his behalf; or
   (ii) in a case to which regulation 4D(4) relates, in the office of a person specified therein;
 (b) where the claim is not made in writing but is otherwise made in accordance with regulation 4D(3) and is not defective, the date the claimant provides details of his circumstances by telephone to, or in person at, the appropriate office or other office designated by the Secretary of State to accept claims for state pension credit; or
 (c) where a claim is initially defective but the defect is corrected under regulation 4D(11), the date the claim is treated as having been made under that regulation.

(3) If a claimant—
 (a) informs an appropriate office [¹, or other office designated by the Secretary of State for accepting claims for state pension credit or the office of the person specified in regulation 4(D)] of his intention to claim state pension credit; and
 (b) subsequently makes the claim in accordance with regulation 4D within 1 month of complying with sub-paragraph (a), or within such longer period as the Secretary of State may allow,
the claim may, where in the circumstances of the particular case it is appropriate to do so, be treated as made on the day the claimant first informed [¹ an office specified in subparagraph (a)] of his intention to claim the credit."

AMENDMENT

1. The Social Security (Claims and Payments and Miscellaneous Amendments) Regulations 2003 (S.I. 2003 No. 1632) reg.2, (July 21, 2003). 4.042

GENERAL NOTE

The amendments to reg.4 of the Claims and Payments Regulations are significant in that they may provision for much greater co-operation between the Department and local authorities in relation to the receipt of claims for benefits administered by these agencies. To date the only developments under the new arrangements heralded by s.7A of the Administration Act 1992 (added by the Welfare Reform and Pensions Act 1999) has been the introduction of ONE office. 4.043

The new arrangements only apply to claims by those who have attained the age of 60 to retirement pension, incapacity benefit, bereavement benefits, carer's allowance, attendance allowance, disability living allowance, winter fuel payments and income support. Claims by this group to these benefits may be directed to an office designated by the Secretary of State for accepting such claims. In relation to benefits administered by the Department, the party receiving the claim is under a duty to forward the claim to the Department as soon as reasonably practicable.

p.355, *Claims and Payments Regulations, reg. 6: addition of new para. (1ZA)*

With effect from July 21, 2003, The Social Security (Claims and Payments and Miscellaneous Amendments) Regulations 2003 (SI 2003/1632) reg.2, adds new paragraph (1ZA) after paragraph (1) as follows, 4.044

"(1ZA) In the case of a claim made in accordance with regulation 4(6B)—
(h) paragraph (1) shall apply in relation to a claim received at an office specified in that regulation as it applies in relation to a claim received at an appropriate office; and
(i) paragraph (1A) shall apply in relation to an office specified in that regulation as it applies in relation to an appropriate office."

The same regulation substitutes the words "paragraphs (8A) and (8B)" for the words "paragraph (8A) in paragraph (8)," and inserts new paragraph (8B) after paragraph (8A) as follows,

"(8B) In the case of a claim for disability living allowance or attendance allowance made in accordance with regulation 4(6B), paragraphs (8) and (8A) shall apply in relation to an office specified in that regulation as they apply in relation to an appropriate office."

pp.376–378, *Claims and Payments Regulations, reg. 7, insertion of new paras (1A) to (1C)*

With effect from April 7, 2003, reg.5 of the State Pension Credit (Consequential, Transitional and Miscellaneous Provisions) Regulations 4.045

2002 (SI 2002/3019), inserts new paras (1A) to (1C) after para.(1) as follows,

"(1A) A claimant shall furnish such information and evidence as the Secretary of State may require as to the likelihood of future changes in his circumstances which is needed to determine—
  (a) whether a period should be specified as an assessed income period under section 6 of the 2002 Act in relation to any decision; and
  (b) if so, the length of the period to be so specified.
(1B) The information and evidence required under paragraph (1A) shall be furnished within 1 month of the Secretary of State notifying the claimant of the requirement, or within such longer period as the Secretary of State considers reasonable in the claimant's case.
(1C) In the case of a claimant making a claim for state pension credit in the advance period, time begins to run for the purposes of paragraphs (1) and (1B) on the day following the end of that period."

and in para.(4) substitutes the words "jobseeker's allowance or state pension credit" for the words, "or jobseeker's allowance".

pp.383–384, *Claims and Payments Regulations, reg.13 amendment*

4.046   With effect from April 7, 2003, reg.6 of the State Pension Credit (Consequential, Transitional and Miscellaneous Provisions) Regulations 2002 (SI 2002/3019), inserts the words "state pension credit" after the words "disabled person's tax credit" in para.(3).

p.386, *Claims and Payments Regulations, annotation to reg.13C*

GENERAL NOTE

In *CDLA/4331/02*, it was held that, when hearing an appeal from a decision on a renewal claim effective from the claimant's 16th birthday, a tribunal is required to determine the appeal on the basis that the claimant was 16, even if she was only 15 at the date of the Secretary of State's decision. The approach taken was different from that in *CDLA/3848/01*, but the result was the same on the facts of the case. In *C12/03–04(DLA)*, a Commissioner in Northern Ireland expressly disagreed with *CDLA/3848/01* and concluded that the Secretary of State was not entitled to refuse benefit at all until the date from which the renewal claim would have been effective. A tribunal, faced with an appeal against a disallowance of a renewal claim made before the date from which a new award would have been effective, therefore had no power to do more than set aside the Secretary of State's decision as having been made without jurisdiction, leaving the Secretary of State to make a new decision. A Tribunal of Commissioners are to consider early in 2004 whether the same approach should be taken in Great Britain.

Another Tribunal of Commissioners is to rule in *CDLA/5141/2002* whether the power to revise in sub-para.(3) is a free-standing one which may be carried out on any ground or whether the provisions of reg.3 of the Decisions and

Administration, Adjudication and the European Dimension

Appeals Regulations still have to be satisfied before a decision on a renewal claim may be changed.

p.387, *Claims and Payments Regulations, insertion of new reg.13D*

With effect from April 7, 2003, reg.6 of the State Pension Credit (Consequential, Transitional and Miscellaneous Provisions) Regulations 2002 (SI 2002/3019), inserts new reg.13D after reg.13C as follows,   4.047

> **"Advance claims for and awards of state pension credit**
>
> **13D.**—(1) Paragraph (2) applies if—
> (a) a person does not satisfy the requirements for entitlement to state pension credit on the date on which the claim is made; and
> (b) the Secretary of State is of the opinion that unless there is a change of circumstances he will satisfy those requirements—
>   (i) where the claim is made in the advance period, when he attains the qualifying age; or
>   (ii) in any other case, within 4 months of the date on which the claim is made.
> (2) Where this paragraph applies, the Secretary of State may—
> (a) treat the claim as made for a period beginning on the day ("the relevant day") the claimant—
>   (i) attains the qualifying age, where the claim is made in the advance period; or
>   (ii) is likely to satisfy the requirements for entitlement in any other case; and
> (b) if appropriate, award state pension credit accordingly, subject to the condition that the person satisfies the requirements for entitlement on the relevant day.
> (3) An award under paragraph (2) may be revised under section 9 of the Social Security Act 1998 if the claimant fails to satisfy the conditions for entitlement to state pension credit on the relevant day."

pp.389–390, *Claims and Payments Regulations, reg.16 amendment*

With effect from April 7, 2003, reg.7 of the State Pension Credit (Consequential, Transitional and Miscellaneous Provisions) Regulations 2002 (SI 2002/3019), inserts the words "state pension credit" after the words "income support" in para.(4).   4.048

p.391, *Claims and Payments Regulations, insertion of new reg.16A*

With effect from April 7, 2003, reg.7 of the State Pension Credit (Consequential, Transitional and Miscellaneous Provisions) Regulations 2002 (SI 2002/3019), inserts new reg.16A after reg.16 as follows,   4.049

"**Date of entitlement under an award of state pension credit for the purpose of payability and effective date of change of rate**

16A.—(1) For the purpose only of determining the day from which state pension credit is to become payable, where the credit is awarded from a day which is not the first day of the claimant's benefit week, entitlement shall begin on the first day of the benefit week next following.

(2) In the case of a claimant who—
(a) immediately before attaining the qualifying age was entitled to income support or income-based jobseeker's allowance and is awarded state pension credit from the day on which he attains the qualifying age; or
(b) was entitled to an income-based jobseeker's allowance after attaining the qualifying age and is awarded state pension credit from the day which falls after the date that entitlement ends,

entitlement to the guarantee credit shall, notwithstanding paragraph (1), begin on the first day of the award.

(3) Where a change in the rate of state pension credit would otherwise take effect on a day which is not the first day of the claimant's benefit week, the change shall take effect from the first day of the benefit week next following.

(4) For the purpose of this regulation, "benefit week" means the period of 7 days beginning on the day on which, in the claimant's case, state pension credit is payable in accordance with regulation 26B."

p.391, *Claims and Payments Regulations, reg.17 amendment*

With effect from April 7, 2003, reg.8 of the State Pension Credit (Consequential, Transitional and Miscellaneous Provisions) Regulations 2002 (SI 2002/3019), inserts the following words at the beginning of reg.17,

"Except in the case of claims for and awards of state pension credit,"

pp.395–397, *Claims and Payments Regulations, reg.19*

Amendments made to reg.17 by The Tax Credits Schemes (Miscellaneous Amendments No. 4) Regulations 2000 (SI 2000/2978) which entered into force on November 28, 2000 have been overlooked. They make the following changes to reg.19(7):

(a) for sub-para.(e) substitute—
"(e) in the case of a claim for working families' tax credit, the claimant had previously been entitled, or the partner of the claimant had previously been entitled in relation to the claimant, to income support or jobseeker's allowance and the claim for working families' tax credit was made within one month of—

Administration, Adjudication and the European Dimension

        (i) the expiry of entitlement to income support ignoring any period in which entitlement resulted from the person entitled not being treated as engaged in remunerative work by virtue of regulation 6(2) and (3) of the Income Support (General) Regulations 1987; or

        (ii) the expiry of entitlement to jobseeker's allowance;";

(b) for sub-para.(h) substitute–

"(h) in the case of a claim for disabled person's tax credit, the claimant had previously been entitled to income support, jobseeker's allowance, incapacity benefit or severe disablement allowance and the claim for disabled person's tax credit was made within one month of—

        (i) the expiry of entitlement to income support ignoring any period in which entitlement resulted from the claimant not being treated as engaged in remunerative work by virtue of regulation 6(2) and (3) of the Income Support (General) Regulations 1987; or

        (ii) the expiry of entitlement to jobseeker's allowance, incapacity benefit or severe disablement allowance;

(ha) in the case of a claim for disabled person's tax credit, the partner of the claimant had previously been entitled in relation to the claimant to income support or jobseeker's allowance, and the claim for disabled person's tax credit was made within one month of—

        (i) the expiry of entitlement to income support ignoring any period in which entitlement resulted from the partner of the claimant not being treated as engaged in remunerative work by virtue of regulation 6(2) and (3) of the Income Support (General) Regulations 1987; or

        (ii) the expiry of entitlement to jobseeker's allowance;".

4.051 With effect from April 7, 2003, reg.8 of the State Pension Credit (Consequential, Transitional and Miscellaneous Provisions) Regulations 2002 (SI 2002/3019), adds the following sub-para.(ff) after para. (2)(f),

"(ff) state pension credit;"

p.415, *Claims and Payments Regulations, insertion of new reg.26B*

4.052 With effect from April 7, 2003, reg.9 of the State Pension Credit (Consequential, Transitional and Miscellaneous Provisions) Regulations 2002, SI 2002/3019, inserts new reg.26B after reg.26A as follows,

"State pension credit

26B.—(1) Except where paragraph (2) applies, state pension credit shall be payable on Mondays, but subject, where state pension credit is payable in accordance with paragraph (3)(a), to the provisions of regulation 21 (direct credit transfer).

(2) State pension credit shall be payable—

(a) if retirement pension is payable to the claimant, on the same day as the retirement pension is payable; or
(b) on such other day of the week as the Secretary of State may, in the particular circumstances of the case, determine.

(3) Payment of state pension credit shall be made either—
(a) in accordance with regulation 21 (direct credit transfer); or
(b) by means of an instrument of payment or an instrument for benefit payment at such place as the Secretary of State, after enquiry of the claimant, may from time to time specify.

(4) State pension credit paid in accordance with paragraph (3)(b) shall be paid weekly in advance.

4.053

(5) Where the amount of state pension credit payable is less than £1.00 per week, the Secretary of State may direct that it shall be paid at such intervals, not exceeding 13 weeks, as may be specified in the direction.

(6) Where state pension credit is—
(a) paid by means of a book of serial orders; and
(b) increased or reduced by an amount which, when added to any previous such increase, is less than 50 pence per week,
the Secretary of State may defer payment of that increase or disregard the reduction until either—
  (i) the termination of entitlement; or, if earlier,
  (ii) the expiration of one week from the date specified for payment of the last order in that book.

(7) Where state pension credit is—
(a) paid by means of a book of serial orders; and
(b) the amount of state pension credit payable to a third party under Schedule 9 is increased so that the amount of the credit payable to the claimant is reduced by an amount which, with any previous reduction, is less than 50 pence per week,
the Secretary of State may make the payment to the third party and disregard the reduction in the claimant's state pension credit for the remainder of the period to which the book relates."

pp.416–418, *Claims and Payments Regulations, reg.30 amendment*

4.054 With effect from April 7, 2003, reg.10 of the State Pension Credit (Consequential, Transitional and Miscellaneous Provisions) Regulations 2002 (SI 2002/3019), inserts the words "state pension credit" after the words "income support".

pp.421–422, *Claims and Payments Regulations, reg.32 amendment and insertion of new para.(6)*

4.055 With effect from April 7, 2003, reg.11 of the State Pension Credit (Consequential, Transitional and Miscellaneous Provisions) Regulations 2002 (SI 2002/3019), inserts the words "state pension credit" after the words "income support" in para.(3), and adds new para.(6) after para.(5) as follows,

"(6) This regulation shall apply in the case of state pension credit subject to the following modifications—
  (a) at the end of an assessed income period, the information and evidence required to be notified in accordance with this regulation includes information and evidence as to the likelihood of future changes in the claimant's circumstances needed to determine—
    (i) whether a period should be specified as an assessed income period under section 6 of the 2002 Act in relation to any decision; and
    (ii) if so, the length of the period to be so specified; and
  (b) except to the extent that sub-paragraph (a) applies, changes to an element of the claimant's retirement provision need not be notified if an assessed income period is current in his case."

With effect from July 21, 2003, The Social Security (Claims and Payments and Miscellaneous Amendments) Regulations 2003 (SI 2003/1632) reg.2, renumbers a mis-numbered (originally inserted as (1A)) amending paragraph inserted by The Social Security (Claims and Information) Regulations 1999 (SI 1999/3108) as paragraph (1C) as follows,

"(1C) In the case of a person who made a claim for benefit in accordance with regulation 4A(1), a change of circumstances may be notified to a relevant authority at any office to which the claim for benefit could be made in accordance with that provision."

p.426, *Claims and Payments Regulations, reg.34A amendment*

With effect from April 7, 2003, reg.12 of the State Pension Credit (Consequential, Transitional and Miscellaneous Provisions) Regulations 2002 (SI 2002/3019), replaces the words "In relation to cases to which section 51C(1) of the Social Security Act 1986" with the words "In relation to cases to which section 15A(1) or (1A) of the Social Security Administration Act 1992". 4.056

pp.428–429, *Claims and Payments Regulations, reg.35A amendment*

With effect from April 7, 2003, reg.13 of the State Pension Credit (Consequential, Transitional and Miscellaneous Provisions) Regulations 2002 (SI 2002/3019), inserts the words "except that it does not include state pension credit" after the words "paragraph 1" in the definition of "specified benefit". 4.057

pp.452–463, *Claims and Payments Regulations, Sch.9 amendments*

With effect from April 7, 2003, reg.14(1) of the State Pension Credit (Consequential, Transitional and Miscellaneous Provisions) Regulations 2002 (SI 2002/3019), amends Sch.9 as follows, 4.058

(a) in paragraph 1, in sub-paragraph (1)—
  (i) in the definition of "family", at the end, add "and for the purposes of state pension credit "a family" comprises the claimant, his partner, any additional partner to whom section 12(1)(c) of the 2002 Act applies and any person who has not attained the age of 19, is treated as a child for the purposes of section 142 of the Contributions and Benefits Act and lives with the claimant or the claimant's partner;"
  (ii) in the definition of "housing costs", at the end, add—
    "(c) Schedule II to the State Pension Credit Regulations but—
      (i) excludes costs under paragraph 13(1)(f) of that Schedule (tents and sites); and
      (ii) includes costs under paragraphs 13(1)(a) (ground rent and feu duty) and 13(1)(c) (rent charges) of that Schedule but only when they are paid with costs under paragraph 13(1)(b) of that Schedule (service charges);"

4.059
  (iii) in the definition of "mortgage payment", after head (b), insert—
    "or
    (c) Schedule II to the State Pension Credit Regulations in accordance with paragraph 7 of that Schedule (housing costs to be met in state pension credit) on a loan which qualifies under paragraph 11 or 12 of that Schedule, but less any amount deducted under paragraph 14 of that Schedule (non-dependant deductions),";
  (iv) in the definition of "personal allowance for a single claimant aged not less than 25 years", after the words "amount specified" insert "in connection with income support and state pension credit" and for the words "as the case may be" substitute "in connection with jobseeker's allowance";
  (v) in the definition of "specified benefit", after head (c), insert—
    "(d) state pension credit which is either paid alone or paid together with any retirement pension, incapacity benefit or severe disablement allowance in a combined payment in respect of any period;"
(b) in paragraph 3—
  (i) in sub-paragraphs (1) and (2A)(a), after the words "applicable amount" wherever they occur insert "or appropriate minimum guarantee";
  (ii) in sub-paragraph (2A), after the words "Jobseeker's Allowance Regulations" in both places in which they occur, insert "or paragraph 5(9) or (12) or paragraph 14 of Schedule II to the State Pension Credit Regulations";

4.060
(c) in paragraph 5 after sub-paragraph (5) insert—
  "(5A) In the case of state pension credit, a determination under this paragraph shall not be made without the consent of the beneficiary

if the aggregate amount determined in accordance with sub-paragraphs (3) and (6) exceeds a sum equal to 25 per cent. of the appropriate minimum guarantee less any housing costs under Schedule II to the State Pension Credit Regulations which may be applicable in the particular case.";

(d) in paragraph 6—
   (i) in sub-paragraph (1), for the words "Subject to sub-paragraph (6)", substitute "Subject to sub-paragraphs (6) and (6A)";
   (ii) after sub-paragraph (6), insert—
   "(6A) Subject to paragraph 8, in the case of state pension credit, a determination under this paragraph shall not be made without the consent of the beneficiary if the aggregate amount calculated in accordance with sub-paragraph (2) exceeds a sum equal to 25 per cent. of the appropriate minimum guarantee less any housing costs under Schedule II to the State Pension Credit Regulations which may be applicable in the particular case.";

(e) in paragraph 7, after sub-paragraph (8), add—
   "(9) Subject to paragraph 8, in the case of state pension credit, a determination under this paragraph shall not be made without the consent of the beneficiary if the aggregate amount calculated in accordance with sub-paragraphs (3), (4), (5) and (6) exceeds a sum equal to 25 per cent. of the appropriate minimum guarantee less any housing costs under Schedule II to the State Pension Credit Regulations which may be applicable in the particular case.";

(f) in paragraph 8, after sub-paragraph (2), insert—
   "(2A) In the case of state pension credit, the maximum aggregate amount payable under paragraphs 3(2)(a), 5, 6, and 7 shall not, without the consent of the beneficiary, exceed a sum equal to 25 per cent. of the appropriate minimum guarantee less any housing costs under Schedule II to the State Pension Credit Regulations which may be applicable in the particular case.".

4.061

pp.463–467, *Claims and Payments Regulations 1987, Sch.9A amendments*

With effect from April 7, 2003, reg.14(2) of the State Pension Credit (Consequential, Transitional and Miscellaneous Provisions) Regulations 2002 (SI 2002/3019), amends Sch.9A as follows,

4.062

(a) in paragraph 1, in the definition of "relevant benefits", at the end of sub-paragraph (c), insert—
   "and
   (d) state pension credit which is either paid alone or paid together with any retirement pension, incapacity benefit or severe disablement allowance in a combined payment in respect of any period;";
(b) in paragraph 2 for the words from the beginning of sub-paragraph (a) to "is determined", substitute—
   "the amount to be met under—
      (i) Schedule 3 to the Income Support Regulations; or

(ii) Schedule 2 to the Jobseeker's Allowance Regulations; or

(iii) Schedule II to the State Pension Credit Regulations,";

4.063   (c) in paragraph 3—
(i) after sub-paragraph (1), insert—
"(1A) Subject to the following provisions of this paragraph, the part of state pension credit which, as determined by the Secretary of State in accordance with regulation 34A, shall be paid directly to the qualifying lender, is a sum equal to the amount of mortgage interest to be met under paragraph 7 of Schedule II to the State Pension Credit Regulations.";
(ii) in sub-paragraph (3)—
(aa) after the words "or income-based jobseeker's allowance" insert "or a relevant beneficiary's appropriate minimum guarantee in state pension credit" and for the words "sub-paragraph (1)" substitute "sub-paragraph (1) or (1A)";
(bb) in head (b), after the words "as the case may be" insert "paragraph 5(9) or (12) or paragraph 14 of Schedule II to the State Pension Credit Regulations or";
(cc) in the value "A", after the words "as the case may be" insert "paragraph 1 of Schedule II to the State Pension Credit Regulations or";
(dd) in the value "B", after the words "as the case may be" insert "paragraph 7 of Schedule II to the State Pension Credit Regulations or";
(ee) in the value "C", after the words "as the case may be" insert "paragraph 5(9) or (12) or paragraph 14 of Schedule II to the State Pension Credit Regulations or";
(iii) in sub-paragraph (4), at the beginning, insert "Except where the relevant benefit is state pension credit,";
(iv) after sub-paragraph (9), add—
"(10) In sub-paragraph (1), the relevant benefits do not include in the case of state pension credit so much of any additional amount which is applicable in the claimant's case under Schedule II to the State Pension Credit Regulations (housing costs) in respect of a period before the decision awarding state pension credit was made.";

4.064   (d) in paragraph 4, in sub-paragraph (2)(a), after the words "as the case may be" insert "paragraph 9 of Schedule II to the State Pension Credit Regulations or";
(e) in paragraph 10—
(i) for sub-paragraph (2), substitute—
"(2) Subject to sub-paragraph (4), the information referred to in heads (a), (b), (c) and (d) of sub-paragraph (1) shall be provided at the request of the Secretary of State when a claim for—
(a) income support or income-based jobseeker's allowance is made and a sum in respect of mortgage interest is to be

Administration, Adjudication and the European Dimension

brought into account in determining the applicable amount; or
  (b) state pension credit is made and a sum in respect of housing costs is applicable in the claimant's case in accordance with regulation 6(6)(c) of the State Pension Credit Regulations.";
(ii) in sub-paragraph (3), in head (a), after the words "income support" insert ", state pension credit".

With effect from October 6, 2003, reg.2 of The Social Security (Third Party Deductions and Miscellaneous Amendments) Regulations 2003 (SI 2003/2325) amends Sch.9 as follows,

(1) In paragraph 4 (miscellaneous accommodation costs)— **4.065**
(a) in sub-paragraph (1) for "or jobseeker's allowance" substitute, "jobseeker's allowance or state pension credit";
(b) in sub-paragraph (1)(a);
  (i) before "is made" insert "in the case of income support"; and
  (ii) for "as the case may be," substitute "in the case of jobseeker's allowance";
(c) for sub-paragraph (1)(b) substitute—
  "(b) is made—
    (i) in the case of an award of income support, to a person who is in residential accommodation within the meaning of regulation 21(3) of the Income Support Regulations; or
    (ii) to person who is in accommodation provided under section 3(1) of, and Part II of the Schedule to, the Polish Resettlement Act 1947 (provision by the Secretary of State of accommodation in camps) except where that person is in receipt of state pension credit; or
    (iii) in the case of an award of jobseeker's allowance, to a person who is in residential accommodation within the meaning of regulation 85(4) of the Jobseeker's Allowance Regulations; or
    (iv) in the case of an award of state pension credit, to a person who is in accommodation provided within the meaning of regulation 15(7) of the State Pension Credit Regulations,";
(d) in sub-paragraph (1)— **4.066**
  (i) for "hereafter in this paragraph referred to as "miscellaneous accommodation costs" "substitute" or to a person who is only temporarily absent from such accommodation";
  (ii) after "to whom the charges in respect of that accommodation are payable" insert "hereafter in this paragraph referred to as "miscellaneous accommodation costs" "; and
  (iii) for "except in a case to which paragraph 13A of Schedule 7 to the Income Support Regulations apply" substitute "except in a case where accommodation is provided under section

3(1) of, and Part II of the Schedule to, the Polish Resettlement Act 1947";

4.067 (e) for sub-paragraphs (2) and (3) substitute—

"(2) Subject to sub-paragraphs (3) and (3A), the amount of any payment of income support, jobseeker's allowance or state pension credit to a third party determined under sub-paragraph (1) shall be—

(a) in a case where the beneficiary is not in accommodation—
   (i) as specified in sub-paragraph (1)(b)(i) or (iii); or
   (ii) as specified in regulation 15(7)(d) of the State Pension Credit Regulations,

an amount equal to the award of income support, jobseeker's allowance, or guarantee credit payable to the claimant but excluding an amount, if any, which when added to any other income of the beneficiary as determined in accordance with regulation 28 of the Income Support Regulations, regulation 93 of the Jobseeker's Allowance Regulations or regulation 17 of the State Pension Credit Regulations will equal the amount prescribed in respect of personal expenses in sub-paragraph (2A); and

(b) in any other case, the amount of the award of income support, jobseeker's allowance or guarantee credit, excluding the amount allowed by sub-paragraph (2A) in respect of personal expenses.

(2A) The amount in respect of personal expenses where a beneficiary is in accommodation referred to in paragraphs 4(1)(a) or (b) shall be—

(a) for a single person the sum of £17.50;
(b) for a couple where both members of the couple are in such accommodation, £17.50 for each member;
(c) for a member of a polygamous marriage where more than one member is in such accommodation, £17.50 for each member in such accommodation.

(3) This sub-paragraph shall apply where an award is made of—

(a) income support calculated in accordance with Part VII of the Income Support Regulations (calculation of income support for part-weeks); or
(b) jobseeker's allowance calculated in accordance with Part XI of the Jobseeker's Allowance Regulations (part-weeks); or
(c) state pension credit for a period of less than a week calculated under regulation 13A of the State Pension Credit Regulations (part-weeks), or a part week payment of state pension credit calculated otherwise.

(3A) Where sub-paragraph (3) applies then the amount of any payment to a third party determined under sub-paragraph (1) shall be an amount calculated in accordance with sub-

paragraph (2)(a) or (b) as appropriate except that in respect of—
  (a) the income of the beneficiary, if any; and
  (b) the amount allowed for personal expenses by sub-paragraph (2A) above,
the amount shall be the amount used in the calculation under the provisions listed in sub-paragraph (3)(a), (b) or (c), divided by 7 and multiplied by the number of days in the part-week and no payment shall be made to a third party where the Secretary of State certifies it would be impracticable to do so in that particular case.";
  (f) in sub-paragraph (4) for "(2) or (3)" substitute "(2) or (3A)".

pp.469–471, *Claims and Payments Regulations 1987, Sch.9B amendment*

With effect from April 7, 2003, reg.14(3) of the State Pension Credit (Consequential, Transitional and Miscellaneous Provisions) Regulations 2002 (SI 2002/3019), amends Sch.9B by inserting in paragraphs 2(1), 3(1), 5(1) and 6(1), after the words "income support" the words ", state pension credit". 4.068

p.498, *Commissioners Procedure Regulations 1999, annotation to reg.23*

The European Convention on Human Rights does not require a second tier tribunal such as a Commissioner to hold an oral hearing where there has been an opportunity to have an oral hearing before the first tier tribunal (*Hoppe v Germany* [2003] F.L.R. 384). 4.069

p.511, *Decisions and Appeals Regulations 1999, reg.1(3)*

A new definition of "out of jurisdiction appeal" is substituted by the Social Security and Child Support (Miscellaneous Amendments) Regulations 2003 (SI 2003/1050), reg.3(1) with effect from May 5, 2003: 4.070

" "out of jurisdiction appeal" means an appeal brought against a decision which is specified in—
  (a) Schedule 2 to the Act or a decision prescribed in regulation 27 (decision against which no appeal lies); or
  (b) paragraph 6(2) of Schedule 7 to the Child Support, Pensions and Social Security Act 2000 (appeal to appeal tribunal) or a decision prescribed in regulation 16 of the Housing Benefit and Council Tax Benefit (Decisions and Appeals) Regulations 2001 (decision against which no appeal lies);".

This cures a lacuna in the Regulations, which prevented child support, housing benefit and council tax benefit appeals from being struck out under reg.46(1)(a) for want of jurisdiction. It is presumably intended that reg.36 of the Child Benefit and Guardian's Allowance (Decisions and Appeals) Regulations 2003 (SI 2003/916) should continue to have the effect that "regulation 27" is replaced by "regulation 25 of the Child Benefit and Guardian's Allowance (Decisions and Appeals) Regulations 2003" for the purposes of child benefit or guardian's allowance cases.

p.513, *Decisions and Appeals Regulations 1999, annotation to reg.1(3)*

4.071   Adjudication officers under the pre-1998 Act system of adjudication were "officers of the Department . . . acting as such" and so an error by an adjudication officer can constitute an "official error" (*CCS/3553/02*, not following *R(I) 5/02*).

p.518, *Decisions and Appeals Regulations 1999, reg.3(9)(a)*

4.072   The words "had effect" are substituted for the words "was made" by the Social Security and Child Support (Miscellaneous Amendments) Regulations 2003 (SI 2003/1050), reg.3(2) with effect from May 5, 2003. If, on reconsidering the original decision, the Secretary of State takes the view that there was a change of circumstances between the date from which the original decision was effective and the date on which it was made, there must usually be a supersession, with the usual limits as to the date from which the supersession may be effective, rather than a revision.

p.520, *Decisions and Appeals Regulations 1999, annotation to reg.3*

Regulation 3 does not provide an exhaustive list of powers of revision. In *CIB/4751/02*, the Tribunal of Commissioners held that reg.13C(3) of the Social Security (Claims and Payments) Regulations 1987 provides a freestanding power of revision. Similar powers are to be found in regs 13(2), and 13A(3), which also deal with advance awards of benefit, but there is no express power to revise to be found in s.65(6) of the Social Security Contributions and Benefits Act 1992 in relation to an advance award of attendance allowance.

p.521, *Decisions and Appeals Regulations 1999, annotation to reg.3(5)*

A Tribunal of Commissioners is to decide in *CIS/4/03* whether it is possible to challenge by way of appeal a refusal to revise under reg.3(5)(a) for official error. The difficulty is explained in the supplemental annotation to reg.31(2), below.

pp.524 to 525, *Decisions and Appeals Regulations 1999, reg.6(2)*

4.073   The words "had effect" are substituted for the words "was made" in reg.6(2)(i) by the Social Security and Child Support (Miscellaneous Amendments) Regulations 2003 (SI 2003/1050), reg.3(3) with effect from May 5, 2003. This reflects the amendment made to reg. 3(9)(a) and also removes the anomaly that was identified in *CDLA/2050/02* (mentioned in the main work).

The same Regulations also delete the superfluous "or" and "and" after paragraphs (2)(d) and (2)(g) respectively and substitute a new paragraph (2)(c):

"(c) is a decision of an appeal tribunal or of a Commissioner—
  (i) that was made in ignorance of, or was based upon a mistake as to, some material fact; or

Administration, Adjudication and the European Dimension

(ii) that was made in accordance with section 26(4)(b), in a case where section 26(5) applies;".

The new head (ii) must be read with the new reg.7(33) (see below) and is introduced because there was previously no provision to prevent s.10(5) of the Social Security Act 1998 from determining the date from which any supersession under s.26, following the determination of a test case, was to be effective. That was plainly unsatisfactory.

A new para.(2)(m) is inserted by reg.5(2) of the State Pension Credit (Transitional and Miscellaneous Provisions) Amendment Regulations 2003 (SI 2003/2274) with effect from October 6, 2003:

"(m) is a relevant decision for the purposes of section 6 of the State Pension Credit Act in a case where—
  (i) the information and evidence required under regulation 32(6)(a) of the Claims and Payments Regulations 1987 has not been provided in accordance with the time limits set out in regulation 32(6)(c) of those Regulations;
  (ii) the Secretary of State was prevented from specifying a new assessed income period under regulation 10(1) of the State Pension Credit Regulations; and
  (iii) the information and evidence required under regulation 32(6)(a) of the Claims and Payments Regulations 1987 has since been provided."

pp.527–534, *Decisions and Appeals Regulations 1999, annotation to reg.6*

In *CDLA/2115/03*, the Commissioner emphasised that a decision "can only be superseded if there has, in fact, been a change of circumstances which is relevant to the decision under which benefit was awarded, in the sense that the changed circumstances would have called for serious consideration by the authority which made the decision awarding benefit and might well have affected the decision". Although he did not express disagreement with *R(A) 2/90* (mentioned in the main work on pp. 529 and 531), to which he referred, his decision is inconsistent with that decision. He held that there were no grounds for supersession because the change of circumstances claimed by the Secretary of State to be material, which was the claimant having moved to a ground floor flat, might have been relevant to her attention requirements but not to her requirements for supervision and watching over which arose out of her mental condition and which were the basis of her award of both the highest rate of the care component and the lower rate of the mobility component of disability living allowance. He followed *CDLA/3875/01* (mentioned in the main work on p. 532) in pointing out the importance of the Department keeping adequate records of the basis on which awards are made. 4.074

A Tribunal of Commissioners has now taken the same approach in *CIB/4751/02*. They held, at paragraph 10(4) that it followed from *Wood v Secretary of State for Work and Pensions* [2003] EWCA Civ 53 (reported as *R(DLA) 1/03* and mentioned in the main work) that: 4.074a "(a) there can be no supersession under Section 10 unless one of the grounds for supersession specified in Regulation 6 is actually found to exist, and

(b) the ground which is found to exist must form the basis of the supersession in the sense that the original decision can only be altered in a way which follows from that ground."

They, too, did not refer to *R(A) 2/90* but it appears fairly plain that that decision is no longer to be followed. They also disapproved *CSIB/1268/00* (mentioned on p.530 of the main work) and held that tribunals could cure most defects in supersession decisions but they adopted much the same approach as in *CDLA/4217/01* (mentioned on p.529) in relation to the date from which a supersession unfavourable to a claimant is effective. See the supplemental annotation to s.12 of the Social Security Act 1998 for a more detailed note on the case.

In *CIB/4751/02*, blessing was also given to the traditional approach in relation to renewals of awards of one component of disability living allowance where there is a subsisting indefinite award of the other component. The renewal must be by way of an application for supersession, rather than a new claim, and the mere fact that it is found that the claimant continues to satisfy the conditions of entitlement of the component sought is evidence of a change of circumstances for the purposes of reg.6(2)(a) (see paras 146 and 152(d) of the Tribunal's decision). This is based on the premise that an award for a definite period implies a finding that the claimant will not satisfy the conditions of entitlement after the end of that period. In reality, there is often no such finding because an award for a definite period is made merely because the prognosis is uncertain. It seems unlikely that the Tribunal intended that indefinite awards should always be made unless there was some evidence suggesting that the claimant's condition would—rather than might—improve, even though that might be the logical conclusion to be drawn from their decision. It is suggested that their decision should be read as an attempt to make the adjudication system work in circumstances where a person continues to be entitled to the component sought precisely because there has in fact been no change in his or her circumstances.

4.075 In *CIB/313/02*, the Commissioner suggested that reg.6(2)(g) was applicable only where the award to be superseded was based on a personal capability assessment and that where, for instance, it was based on deemed incapacity under reg.28 of the Social Security (Incapacity for Work) (General) Regulations 1995, the proper basis for supersession was reg.6(2)(a)(i). However, in neither case was the point determined because the result would have been the same whichever provision was applied. This is, though, another illustration of the need for a tribunal to be provided with some history of the claimant's award.

In *CIB/4331/01*, the claimant had been awarded the higher rate of the mobility component of disability living allowance on the basis that he was virtually unable to walk but a tribunal considering an appeal from a personal incapability assessment found the claimant to be able to walk at least 800 metres without stopping or severe discomfort. The claimant had specifically relied on the award of the mobility component, which had been made following a report made by an examining medical practitioner, and the Commissioner held that the tribunal was not in a position fairly to decide the incapacity appeal without ensuring that the evidence used for the disability living allowance decision was put before it. In the light of this decision, officers are now instructed to obtain information relating to another benefit when a claimant specifically refers to it. The reverse position arose in *CDLA/2998/03*, where a report prepared for incapacity benefit purposes was relevant to entitlement to disability living allowance and appears to have been relied upon by the Secretary of State. The Commissioner cited *CIB/4331/01* with approval and was critical of the Secretary of State for not informing a tribunal about an appeal against the incapacity benefit decision, although it appears that the claimant did do so.

pp.534–540, *Decisions and Appeals Regulations 1999, reg.7*

Reg.3(5)(a) to (d) of the Social Security and Child Support (Miscellaneous Amendments) Regulations 2003 (SI 2003/1050) makes the following amendments with effect from May 5, 2003. 4.076

In reg.7(1)(a), for "paragraph (2)(b), there is substituted "paragraphs (2)(b), (29) and (30)".
In reg.7(2), for "was made" there is substituted "had effect".
In reg.7(5), after "regulation 6(2)(c)", there is inserted "(i)".
A new reg.7(9)(a) is substituted:

"(a) where the decision is made on the Secretary of State's own initiative—
  (i) the date on which the Secretary of State commenced action with a view to supersession; or
  (ii) subject to paragraph (30), in a case where the relevant circumstances are that there has been a change in the legislation in relation to attendance allowance or disability living allowance, the date on which that change in the legislation had effect;".

In paragraph (29), "Subject to paragraphs (29A) and (29B), a" is substituted for "A" by reg. 5(3) of the State Pension Credit (Transitional and Miscellaneous Provisions) Amendment Regulations 2003 (SI 2003/2274) with effect from October 6, 2003.

The same provision inserts new paragraphs (29A) to (29C) with effect from October 6, 2003:

"(29A) A decision to which regulation 6(2)(1) applies, where— 4.077
  (a) the decision is advantageous to the claimant; and
  (b) the information and evidence required under regulation 32(1) of the Claims and Payments Regulations 1987 has not been provided within the period allowed under that regulation,
shall take effect from the day the information and evidence required under that regulation is provided if that day is the first day of the claimant's benefit week, but, if it is not, from the next following such day.

(29B) A decision to which regulation 6(2)(1) applies, where—
(a) the decision is disadvantageous to the claimant; and
(b) the information and evidence required under regulation 32(1) of the Claims and Payments Regulations 1987 1987 has not been provided within the period allowed under that regulation,

shall take effect from the day after the period allowed under that regulation expired.

(29C) Except where there is a change of circumstances during the period in which the Secretary of State was prevented from specifying a new assessed income period under regulation 10(1) of the State Pension Credit Regulations, a decision to which regulation 6(2)(m) applies shall take effect from the day on which the information and evidence required under regulation 32(6)(a) of the Claims and Payments Regulations 1987 1987 was provided."

Reg. 3(5)(e) of the Social Security and Child Support (Miscellaneous Amendments) Regulations 2003 (SI 2003/1050) inserts new paragraphs (30) to (33) with effect from May 5, 2003.

4.078
"(30) Where a decision is superseded in accordance with regulation 6(2)(a)(i) and the relevant circumstances are that there has been a change in the legislation in relation to a relevant benefit, the decision under section 10 shall take effect from the date on which that change in the legislation had effect.

(31) Where a decision is superseded in accordance with regulation 6(2)(a)(ii) and the relevant circumstances are that—
(a) a personal capability assessment has been carried out in the case of a person to whom section 171C(4) of the Contributions and Benefits Act applies; and
(b) the own occupation test remains applicable to him under section 171B(3) of that Act,

the decision under section 10 shall take effect on the day immediately following the day on which the own occupation test is no longer applicable to that person.

(32) For the purposes of paragraph (31)—
(a) "personal capability assessment" has the same meaning as in regulation 24 of the Social Security (Incapacity for Work) (General) Regulations 1995;
(b) "own occupation test" has the same meaning as in section 171B(2) of the Contributions and Benefits Act.

(33) A decision to which regulation 6(2)(c)(ii) applies shall take effect from the date on which the appeal tribunal or the Commissioner's decision would have taken effect had it been decided in accordance with the determination of the Commissioner or the court in the appeal referred to in section 26(1)(b)."

The new para.(30) is self-explanatory. Paras (31) and (32) are required because personal capability assessments are now carried out before the own occupation test ceases to apply to the claimant. Para.(33) enables s.26 to work properly.

pp. 567–568, *Decisions and Appeals Regulations 1999, annotation to reg. 28(1)*

The principle that time for appealing does not start to run until the claimant has been properly notified of his rights of appeal has been reiterated in *CDLA/3440/03*. Its application in social security cases was not doubted in *CCS/5515/02*, but it was said that different considerations apply in child support cases because there is a third party whose interests must be taken into account and who may be entitled to rely on a defective decision.

CSIB/1268/00 has been disapproved by the Tribunal of Commissioners in *CIB/4751/02*, although they did not accept the distinction between errors of form and errors of substance drawn in *CSIB/1266/00* (see the supplemental annotation to s.12(1) of the Social Security Act 1998, above).

4.078a

p. 571, *Decisions and Appeals Regulations 1999, reg. 31(2)*

The words "or 3A(1)" are inserted after "regulation 3(1) or (3)" by regulation 2(5) of the Child Support (Miscellaneous Amendments) Regulations 2002 (SI 2002/1204), with effect from March 3, 2002 (see the Child Support, Pensions and Social Security Act 2000 (Commencement No.12 Order 2003 (SI 2003/192).

Regulation 3A itself is concerned only with child support decisions and is therefore not reproduced in this work. The insertion is nonetheless interesting because reg.3A(1) is much broader in its scope than reg.3(1) and includes revision for "official error" which, in social security cases, falls under reg.3(5)(a). The consequence is that, in child support cases to which reg.3A applies, the time limit for appealing against a decision that has not been revised for "official error" is extended under reg.3192) but the same is not true in social security cases. In *CCS/5515/02*, the Commissioner suggested that it followed that there was no way of challenging a refusal to revise in a social security case, if it was too late to appeal against the original decision. Whether that is correct is to be considered by a Tribunal of Commissioner in *CIS/4/03*, but the Tribunal held in *CIB/4751/02* that, if there is a right of appeal against the original decision following a refusal to revise, the appeal can succeed only if it can be shown that the decision should have been revised. Otherwise, as was pointed out in *CCS/5515/02*, late appeals could easily be brought by making entirely unmeritorious applications for revision.

4.078b

pp. 581–582, *Decisions and Appeals Regulations 1999, annotation to reg. 36(6)*

CSDLA/1019/99 (incorrectly referred to as *CSDLA/1019/00* in one place in the annotation) has been reversed on appeal in *Secretary of State for Work and Pensions v Gillies* [2004] S.L.T. 14 (see the supplemental annotation to s.14(1) of the Social Security Act 1998, above). The Secretary of State has also appealed against *CSDLA/444/02* but it by no means follows from *Gillies* that that appeal will be successful.

4.078c

In *CSI/146/03*, the Commissioner said that there was no obligation on the President to ensure that a medically qualified panel member sitting on any particular case was a specialist in the field of medicine relevant to the case. It was pointed out that there is not always such a specialist on the panel and, in any event, even if a case is unusual, any medically qualified panel member will ordinarily be able to deal adequately with competing views. If a specialist's report is necessary, it is open to a tribunal to ask the parties to obtain a relevant opinion or to obtain one themselves under s.20 of the Social Security Act 1998.

p.584, *Decisions and Appeals Regulations 1999, annotation to reg.39*

4.079   In *CIS/4248/01*, the Commissioner held that an oral hearing should have been directed in a case where an apparently unrepresented claimant had opted for a paper hearing of an appeal against a decision that income support amounting to some £10,000 had been overpaid and was recoverable from her, in circumstances where the claimant had put forward a case that was tenable if she was believed.

> "A very great deal of money was at stake. Oral evidence would have assisted the tribunal's assessment of honesty, which was central to the case. She had not, as far as could be seen, had the benefit of advice from anyone with experience of tribunals. Those are all factors that suggest that justice required an oral hearing in this case."

In *CIB/2751/02 and CS/3202/02*, the Commissioner considered the difficulties that arise on a request for a domiciliary hearing, where a refusal to allow such a hearing may require the determination of the very issues that arise on the appeal itself. He said that fairness may require that a claimant who is refused a domiciliary hearing is given a further opportunity to provide evidence, perhaps by being visited by an expert appointed under s.7(4) of the Social Security Act 1998, who could then give evidence to the tribunal under reg.50. It is suggested, however, that the reality may be that a domiciliary hearing would not be refused where the legally qualified panel member believed that the claimant might not be able to attend a hearing at an ordinary venue. Virtual inability to walk does not usually preclude travelling in a car, perhaps driven by a relative, or use of a taxi. The greater need may therefore be that, where a domiciliary hearing is refused, it should be made clear to the claimant that it is considered that he or she could attend a hearing at an ordinary venue and should speak to the clerk about any special arrangements that might be necessary to enable him or her to do so. If it becomes apparent to a clerk that the claimant's difficulties are greater than was originally understood, the issue can always be referred back to the legally qualified panel member.

p.596, *Decisions and Appeals Regulations 1999, annotation to reg.49*

4.080   The new form of para.(6), limiting more precisely the circumstances in which a hearing may take place otherwise than in public, raises questions about domiciliary hearings. In *CIB/2751/02 and CS/3202/02*, the Commissioner suggested that it might be possible to hold a public hearing near a claimant's home rather than actually in it. Given that few people other than those invited by the parties ever watch tribunal hearings, the problems raised may be more theoretical than real but the legislation does require them to be addressed. The answer may be that, where a domiciliary hearing in a claimant's home is necessary, it will always be justifiable to hold the hearing in private in order to protect the claimant's private or family life. Presumably a claimant who has asked for an oral hearing can be taken to have waived his rights to privacy to the extent necessary to allow the hearing to take place with other parties being present.

In *CDLA/2462/03*, the Commissioner has reiterated the point that representatives may also be witnesses.

"8. Tribunals operate less formally than courts. They do not operate rights of audience. They allow, of course, professional legal representation. But they also allow lay representation and assistance from anyone whom the claimant wishes to assist in presenting a case to a tribunal. Given that breadth of representation, it is inevitable that the roles of representative and witness cannot be separated in the way that they would in a court. The same person may wish to put the claimant's case and give evidence in support of that case. The tribunal must take care to distinguish evidence from representation so that the former's provenance is known and can be the subject of questioning by the tribunal and other parties. But, subject to the practicalities of the way in which the taking of evidence is handled, there is no objection in principle to the same person acting in different capacities as a witness and as a representative. Nor is there any reason in principle why the probative value of evidence should depend upon whether or not it came from a representative.

. . .

13. I emphasise that I am concerned here with a representative who wanted to give evidence from his own knowledge. I am not concerned with the different circumstance of a representative who wants to make a statement of the claimant's evidence to the appeal tribunal. Some tribunals refuse a representative the chance to do this. They insist on hearing the evidence from the claimant, allowing the representative to supplement the tribunal's questions to ensure that all the evidence is elicited from the claimant. That is a matter that is within the chairman's control of the procedure under regulation 49(1). Nothing I have written above affects the use of that power by [a] chairman to control the way that the claimant's own evidence is presented."

pp.600–605, *Decisions and Appeals Regulations 1999, annotation to reg. 53(4)*

In *R. (Asha Foundation) v Millennium Commission* [2003] EWCA Civ 66 (*The Times,* January 24, 2003), the Court of Appeal considered the approach Sedley J. had taken in *R. v Higher Education Funding Council Ex p. Institute of Dental Surgery* [1994] 1 W.L.R. 242 to the question of whether there was a duty to give any reasons at all and held that, where there is a duty to give reasons, the same approach should be taken to the question whether reasons were adequate. Sedley J.'s approach required the balancing of a number of considerations, which might vary from case to case. He said:

> "The giving of reasons may among other things concentrate the decision-maker's mind on the right questions; demonstrate to the recipient that this is so; show that the issues have been conscientiously addressed and how the result has been reached or alternatively alert the recipient to a justiciable flaw in the process.
>
> On the other side of the argument, it may place an undue burden on decision-makers; demand an appearance of unanimity where there is diversity; call for the articulation of sometimes inexpressible value judgments; and offer an invitation to the captious to comb the reasons for previously unsuspected grounds of challenge."

In *CSIS/1009/02*, it was held that a delay in providing reasons did not necessarily render a decision erroneous in point of law. The Commissioner followed *CJSA/322/01* and *CJSA/3908/01* (mentioned on p.605 of the main work) and disagreed with some of the views expressed in *CDLA/1761/02* (also mentioned on p.605). She held that a delay in providing reasons may itself amount to a breach of Art.6 of the European Convention on Human Rights (although, if the tribunal's decision was not flawed in any other respect, the remedy for such a breach would presumably be an award of damages by a court) and she also held that a delay may be relevant because it may indicate that the reasons are unreliable, as was suggested in *Nash v Chelsea College of Art and Design* (mentioned on p.604 of the main work). However, in the particular case before her, where the statement of reasons had been requested on July 1, 2002 and was not sent to the parties until October 29, 2002, the Commissioner found there to have been no error of law.

In *CDLA1807/03*, the tribunal chairman produced two statements of reasons for the tribunal's decision, the second because he had forgotten he had already written a statement. The reasons differed. The Commissioner commented that the reasons should be a statement of the *tribunal's* reasons and not the chairman's later rationalisation of the conclusion reached by the tribunal and that at least one of the statements did not accurately reflect the tribunal's reasons. He set aside the tribunal's decision.

pp.616–617, *Decisions and Appeals Regulations 1999, Sch.2*

4.082   In para.5, new sub-paragraphs (bb) and (mm) are inserted by reg.2 of the State Pension Credit (Decisions and Appeals–Amendments) Regulations 2003 (SI 2003/1581) with effect from June 18, 2003:

> "(bb) regulation 4D (making a claim for state pension credit) or 4E (making a claim before attaining the qualifying age);"
>
> "(mm) regulation 26B (payment of state pension credit)".

Administration, Adjudication and the European Dimension

p.620, *Decisions and Appeals Regulations 1999, annotation to Sch.2*

A Tribunal of Commissioners is to consider at the end of January 2004 the validity of para.22 of the Schedule.

p.624, *Decisions and Appeals Regulations 1999, Sch.3A*

In para.4, ", (2) or (3)" is substituted for "or (2)" by reg.5 of the Social Security (Working Tax Credit and Child Tax Credit) (Consequential Amendments) (No. 3) Regulations 2003 (SI 2003/1731) with effect from August 8, 2003. 4.083

p.626, *Decisions and Appeals Regulations 1999, Sch.3B*

A new para.5 is substituted by reg.5(4) of the State Pension Credit (Transitional and Miscellaneous Provisions) Amendment Regulations 2003 (SI 2003/2274) with effect from October 6, 2003: 4.084

> "5. In a case where the relevant circumstances is that the claimant ceased to be a patient, if he becomes a patient again in the same benefit week, the superseding decision in respect of ceasing to be a patient shall take effect from the first day of the week in which the change occured."

The misspelling of what should read as "occurred" occurs in the Queen's Printer's copy of the statutory instrument.

p.642, *General Benefit Regulations, reg.16: increase of sum*

With effect from October 1, 2003, the figure £3,510 is increased to £3,744 by the Social Security (Incapacity) (Miscellaneous Amendments) Regulations 2003 (SI 2003/2262) reg.2. 4.085

p.661, *Jobcentre Plus Interviews Regulations, reg.8 insertion of new para.(3)*

With effect from October 27, 2003, The Social Security (Incapacity Benefit Work-Focused Interviews) Regulations 2003, reg.17, amends reg.8 by adding a new paragraph (3) as follows, 4.086

> "(3) A person who, on the day on which the claim for a specified benefit is made or the requirement to take part in an interview under regulation 4 or 7(2) arises or applies is—
> (j) required to take part in an interview; or
> (k) not required to take part in an interview by virtue of—
> (i) a waiver of a requirement; or
> (ii) a deferment of an interview,
> under the Social Security (Incapacity Benefit Work-focused Interviews Regulations 2003 shall be exempt from the requirement to take part in an interview."

Administration, Adjudication and the European Dimension

pp.694–695, *Payments on account Regulations 1988, reg.1 amendments*

4.087   With effect from October 6, 2003, reg. 24 of the State Pension Credit (Consequential, Transitional and Miscellaneous Provisions) Regulations 2002, SI 2002/3019, amends reg.1 as follows,

(a) in the entry relating to "benefit" for the words "jobseeker's allowance and", substitute "jobseeker's allowance, state pension credit and", and

(b) after the entry relating to "severe disablement allowance" insert the following entries—
"state pension credit" means the benefit payable under the State Pension Credit Act 2002;
"the State Pension Credit Regulations" means the State Pension Credit Regulations 2002

pp.700–701, *Payments on account Regulations 1988, reg.5 amendment*

4.088   With effect from October 6, 2003, reg.24 of the State Pension Credit (Consequential, Transitional and Miscellaneous Provisions) Regulations 2002 (SI 2002/3019) amend reg.5(3) by adding the words "or state pension credit after the words "income support" in each place where they occur.

pp.702–703, *Payments on account Regulations 1988, reg.7*

4.089   With effect from October 6, 2003, reg.24 of the State Pension Credit (Consequential, Transitional and Miscellaneous Provisions) Regulations 2002 (SI 2002/3019), amends reg.7 as follows,

(a) for the words "income support and", substitute "income support, state pension credit and";

(b) in sub-paragraph (a), after the words "Allowance Regulations" insert "or Part III of the State Pension Credit Regulations".

pp.703–704, *Payments on account regulations 1988, reg.8*

4.090   With effect from October 6, 2003, reg.24 of the State Pension Credit (Consequential, Transitional and Miscellaneous Provisions) Regulations 2002 (SI 2002/3019) amends reg.8(2) by adding the words "or state pension credit after the words "income support" in each place where they occur.

pp.706–707, *Payments on account regulations, reg.13*

4.091   With effect from October 6, 2003, reg.24 of the State Pension Credit (Consequential, Transitional and Miscellaneous Provisions) Regulations 2002 (SI 2002/3019) amends reg.13(1)(b) by adding the words "or state pension credit after the words "income support" in each place where they occur.

Administration, Adjudication and the European Dimension

pp. 709–10, *Payments on account regulations 1988, reg. 14*

With effect from October 6, 2003, reg. 24 of the State Pension Credit (Consequential, Transitional and Miscellaneous Provisions) Regulations 2002 (SI 2002/3019) amends reg. 14(1) by adding the words "or state pension credit after the words "income support" in each place where they occur.

4.092

p. 710, *Payments on account Regulations 1988, reg. 15*

With effect from October 6, 2003, reg. 24 of the State Pension Credit (Consequential, Transitional and Miscellaneous Provisions) Regulations 2002 (SI 2002/3019) amends reg. 15(2)(d) by adding the words "or state pension credit after the words "income support" in each place where they occur.

4.093

pp. 711–713, *Payments on account Regulations 1988, reg. 16*

With effect from October 6, 2003, reg. 24 of the State Pension Credit (Consequential, Transitional and Miscellaneous Provisions) Regulations 2002 (SI 2002/3019), amends reg. 16 as follows,

4.094

(a) in paragraph 4A, at the end insert—
"(d) state pension credit.";
(b) in paragraph (6), at the end of sub-paragraph (b), insert—
"or
(c) in the calculation of the income of a person to whom state pension credit is payable, the amount of earnings or other income falling to be taken into account is reduced in accordance with paragraph 1 of Schedule 4 (sums to be disregarded in the calculation of income other than capital), or Schedule 6 (sums disregarded from claimant's earnings) to the State Pension Credit Regulations,";
(c) in paragraph (8)—
(i) for the definition of "personal allowance for a single claimant aged not less than 25" substitute—
" "personal allowance for a single claimant aged not less than 25" means—
(a) in the case of a person who is entitled to either income support or state pension credit, the amount for the time being specified in paragraph 1(1)(e) of column (2) of Schedule 2 to the Income Support Regulations; or
(b) in the case of a person who is entitled to income-based jobseeker's allowance, the amount for the time being specified in paragraph 1(1)(e) of column (2) of Schedule 1 to the Jobseeker's Allowance Regulations;";
(ii) for the definition of "specified benefit", substitute—
" "specified benefit" means—
(a) a jobseeker's allowance;

(b) income support when paid alone or together with any incapacity benefit, retirement pension or severe disablement allowance in a combined payment in respect of any period;
(c) if incapacity benefit, retirement pension or severe disablement allowance is paid concurrently with income support in respect of any period but not in a combined payment, income support and such of those benefits as are paid concurrently;
(d) state pension credit when paid alone or together with any retirement pension, incapacity benefit or severe disablement allowance in a combined payment in respect of any period; and
(e) if retirement pension, incapacity benefit or severe disablement allowance is paid concurrently with state pension credit in respect of any period but not in a combined payment, state pension credit and such of those benefits as are paid concurrently,

but does not include any sum payable by way of child maintenance bonus in accordance with section 10 of the Child Support Act 1995 and the Social Security (Child Maintenance Bonus) Regulations 1996."

p.713, *Payments on account Regulation 1988, reg.17*

4.095   With effect from October 6, 2003, reg.24 of the State Pension Credit (Consequential, Transitional and Miscellaneous Provisions) Regulations 2002 (SI 2002/3019) amends reg.17 by adding the words "or state pension credit after the words "income support" in each place where they occur.

p.759, *Child Benefit and Guardian's Allowance (Administration) Regulations 2003, reg.6*

4.096   With effect from September 3, 2003, reg.6 is amended by The Child Benefit and Guardian's Allowance) (Administration) (Amendment No. 3) Regulations 2003 (SI 2003/2107) to read as follows,

"6(1). The time within which a claim for child benefit or guardian's allowance is to be made is 3 months beginning with any day on which, apart from satisfying the conditions for making the claim, the person making the claim is entitled to the benefit or allowance.
(2) Paragraph (1) shall not apply where—
(l) a person has been awarded child benefit or guardian's allowance while he was present and residing in great Britain, or Northern Ireland;
(m) at a time when payment of the award has not been suspended or terminated (under regulations 18 to 20 of the Child Benefit and Guardian's Allowance (Decisions and Appeals) Regulations 2003 or otherwise), he take up residence in Northern Ireland, or

Great Britain as the case may be ("the new country of residence"); and

(n) a new claim for that benefit or allowance is made in the new country of residence, for a period commencing on the later of—

(iii) the date of the change of residence referred to in sub-paragraph (b), or

(iv) the date on which, apart from satisfying the conditions for making the claim, the person became entitled to the benefit or allowance under the legislation of the new country of residence."

General Note

The social security systems of Great Britain and Northern Ireland are formally separate, though in many respects—and certainly in relation to child benefit and guardian's allowance—identical. A problem arose that claimants moving from Great Britain to Northern Ireland (and the reverse) often continued to cash their Great Britain child benefit. This amendment replaces the three month limit on back-dating of benefit to an unlimited period where such a situation has arisen, so that entitlements can be "balanced out". 4.097

p.906, *Regulation 1612/68, Art.7*

In *CJSA/4065/1999* the Commissioner has referred questions to the Court of Justice. On July 10, 2003, the Advocate General issued his Opinion in Case C–138/02 *Collins v Secretary of State for Work and Pensions.* The case concerns Mr Collins who holds both Irish and American nationality. He had spent about ten months working in the United Kingdom after spending a semester as a student here. In 1998 he returned to the United Kingdom to look for work and shortly afterwards claims an income-based jobseeker's allowance. This was refused because he was not regarded as being habitually resident in the United Kingdom. The Advocate General begins his Opinion by recalling the rights of citizens of the Union under Art.39 EC, but also notes that a person must have the status of actually being a "worker" (as distinct from a "work seeker") before he or she can rely on Art.7(2) of Regulation 1612/68. The Advocate General goes on to note that the habitual residence test is, in principle, indirectly discriminatory since it is easier for United Kingdom nationals to fulfil the requirement than nationals of other Member States. However, the Advocate General considers that a condition as to residence which makes it possible to ascertain the degree of connection with the State and the links which the claimant has with the domestic employment market may be justified in order to avoid the movement of persons with the purpose of taking advantage of non-contributory benefits and to prevent abuses. The Advocate General accordingly proposes that the answer to the questions posed by the Commissioner should be that that Community law as it now stands does not require that an income-based social security benefit be provided to a citizen of the Union who seeks work in a Member State with whose employment market he lacks any connection or link. 4.098

In Case C–413/01 *Ninni-Orasche v Bundesminister für Wissenschaft, Verkehr und Kunst*, Judgment of November 6, 2003, [2003] ECR nyr, the Court was considering a reference from Verwaltungsgerichthof, Austria concerning an Italian national, Franca Ninni-Orasche, who had been married to an Austrian national since January 1993 and had been resident in Austria since November 1993. Ninni-Orasche had been employed as a waitress between July 6 and September 25, 1995; she also had some duties as a cashier and in relation to stock control. She was also undertaking part-time study and subsequently passed examinations qualifying her for admission to an Austrian university. She was refused financial support for her studies. The question was whether she was a worker for the purposes of Art.39 EC, and more particularly Reg. 1612/68, since she would then appear potentially to be entitled to financial support for her studies under Art.7(2) of the Regulation (provided other conditions were satisfied). The Court concluded that the short-term work Ninni-Orasche had undertaken qualified her as a worker under Art.39 EC "provided that the activity performed as an employed person is not purely marginal or ancillary" (para.32). This is an issue to be determined by the national courts. Furthermore, a person would not be treated as voluntarily unemployed merely because the initial contract of employment was for a fixed term which has expired.

p.906, *Regulation 1612/68, Article 42*

Article 42

1. *Omitted*
2. This regulation shall not affect measures taken in accordance with Article 51 of this Treaty.
3. *Omitted.*

GENERAL NOTE

4.099 Following the amendment of the EC Treaty, Art.51 is now Art.42 EC and refers to the adoption of measures in the field of social security.

In *C50/90–00 (DLA)* a Commissioner in Northern Ireland concluded that the effect of Art.42(2) can be to preclude the application of Art.7(2) where the matter is governed by Reg. 1408/71 (a regulation made under Art.51 (now 42) EC). The case concerned a claimant for a disability living allowance on the basis of Community law; the claimant was at all relevant times resident in Ireland. She later claimed a disability living allowance in Northern Ireland where she worked, arguing that Art.7(2) meant that the residence and presence conditions could not be applied to her. The Commissioner upholds the decision of the tribunal that she could not maintain the Art.7(2) right since disability living allowance was a benefit falling within Art.10a of Regulation 1408/71, which alone applied to her situation. She says,

"28. It does not appear to me that Article 42(2) can be given anything other than its plain meaning, ie that Regulation (EEC) 1612/68 is not to affect measures taken under Article 51. The provisions of that regulation cannot have any effect on such measures."

In *CIS/852/2001* a Commissioner in England, while not dissenting from the decision of the Commissioner in Northern Ireland, disagrees with the reasoning, since it is too wide. The Commissioner in England says,

"43. I conclude from both the specific comments of the Court in *EC Commission v. French Republic* and from the absence of the point being taken by or to the Court in other cases that the "plain meaning" attached to Article 42(2) in C 50/99–00 (DLA) is too wide. The right granted by Article 7(2) of Regulation 1612/68 is a fundamental aspect of the freedom of movement of workers—and, perhaps it should now be said, of European citizens. It is one of the essential aspects of the freedom granted by Article 39 (formerly Article 48) of the Treaty, securing the freedom of movement of workers. Regulation 1408/71 is about coordinating social security systems under Article 42 (formerly 51) of the Treaty by adopting "such measures as are necessary to provide freedom of movement of workers". Those Articles pursue parallel aims, and I do not readily read a final provision in Regulation 1612/68 as undercutting those parallel aims so as to reduce a worker's rights under Article 7 of that Regulation unless there is clear reason to do so. The reason to do so, as the European Court reflects, is that there is some provision of Regulation 1408/71 in application which provides a benefit to a worker in a different way to Regulation 1612/68 but, by reason of the purposes of those Regulations, to the same end. In other words, it is an example of what used to be given the Latin tag *specialia generalibus derogant*—a specific rule derogates from a general rule. But, in this context, both rules are concerned with granting rights and not restricting them."

p.1020, *Art.4*

The reference to the decision of the Tribunal of Commissioners in the penultimate paragraph on p.1021 should read *R(JSA) 4/03*. 4.100

p.1022, *Dir. 79/7, art.7(1)(a)*

Article 7(1)(a) should read, 4.101

"(a) the determination of pensionable age for the purposes of granting old-age and retirement pensions and the possible consequences thereof for other benefits;"

p.1029, *Human Rights Act 1998*

With effect from August 19, 2003, The Secretary of State for Constitutional Affairs Order 2003 (SI 2003/1887) (see new legislation for the substance of the order) makes the following amendments to the Act, 4.102

(a) In sections 1 and 14 to 16 of the Human Rights Act 1998, for "Lord Chancellor" in each place substitute "Secretary of State".

(b) In sections 2(3)(a), 7(9)(a) and 20(2) and (4) of that Act, the words "the Lord Chancellor or" are repealed.

p.1038, Human Rights Act 1998, s.4

4.103 On July 10, 2003, the House of Lords ruled on the appeal in *Wilson v Secretary of State for Trade and Industry* [2003] UKHL 40. They reversed the decision of the Court of Appeal to make a declaration of incompatibility in respect of s.127 of the Consumer Credit Act 1974.

Wilson had borrowed £5,000 from First County Trust on the security of her BMW 318 convertible. The loan agreement added a £250 document fee to the £5,000 loan, thus mis-stating the amount of the loan as £5,250. In 1999 Wilson issued a claim in the county court, inter alia, for a declaration that the loan agreement was unenforceable because it did not contain all the prescribed terms. The county court ruled in the lender's favour, but this was reversed in the Court of Appeal, but adjourned to enable Convention rights arguments to be considered. The Secretary of State argued that the Court had no power to make a declaration of incompatibility because the agreement pre-dated October 2, 2000, the date the Human Rights Act 1998 entered into force. However, the Court said that the act which violated Convention rights was not the agreement but any order of the Court making the loan agreement unenforceable. They went on to make a declaration of incompatibility.

The House of Lords has ruled that the Human Rights Act 1998 is not to be applied retrospectively, and so there was no jurisdiction in the Court of Appeal to make the declaration of incompatibility. A statute concerned with Convention rights could not render acts unlawful which were lawful when they were undertaken, since this would impose retrospective liability.

4.104 Their Lordships did go on to consider whether the provisions of s.127 were compatible with Convention rights. The section imposed a mandatory sanction designed to ensure that lenders directed their minds to compliance with their obligations. It was a measure for the protection of the consumer, the weaker party in such transactions. This appeared to be in the view of the court not a violation of Convention rights in relation to the loans covered by the section (up to £25,000). In these circumstances there was no lack of proportionality in the sanction for failure to comply with the requirements of the legislation.

p.1047, Human Rights Act 1998, s.7

4.105 In *CIS/4511/2002* the Commissioner reminds tribunals of the need to address fully arguments based on Convention rights in the following terms,

"13. Finally, it is necessary to consider the adequacy of the tribunal's reasons. I agree with the Secretary of State that a tribunal's lack of any power to make a declaration of incompatibility is not a good reason for not dealing fully with Human Rights issues, particularly since a tribunal may have power in some cases to declare subordinate legislation to have been invalidly made-see *Chief Adjudication Officer v. Foster* [1993] 1 All ER 705. The claimant in this appeal clearly went to considerable trouble to set out his arguments under the Human Rights Act clearly and comprehensively in response to the chairman's direction, and I consider that he was entitled to a much fuller explanation of the tribunal's reasons for rejecting his arguments than the very short passage at the end of the statement of reasons set out above. The reasons for the tribunal's rejection of the claimant's discrimination arguments are not apparent from the statement, and I therefore consider that, in all the circumstances, the tribunal's reasons were inadequate."

p.1059, *Art.6 ECHR*

The discussion of bias at pp. 1072-3 has been advanced with the decision of the House of Lords in *Lawal v Northern Spirit Ltd* [2003] UKHL 35, judgment of June 19, 2003. The House of Lords was considering the "systemic issue" of possible objective bias under a system which permitted counsel appointed as part-time judges of the Employment Appeal Tribunal (EAT) to appear on appeals before that court. Though the opinion of the House of Lords is couched very much in the context of the system of adjudication in employment cases, the broad approach is of more general application stressing the "indispensable requirement of public confidence in the administration of justice" which "requires higher standards today than was the case even a decade or two ago." (para.22.). The House of Lords re-affirms the test of bias set out in *Porter v McGill*: "The question is whether the fair-minded and informed observer, having considered the facts, would conclude that there was a real possibility that the tribunal was biased". The House of Lords says that it is unnecessary to delve into the characteristics to be attributed to the fair-minded and informed observer save that such an observe "will adopt a balanced approach." The conclusion is that the practice of permitting counsel appointed as part-time judges of the EAT to appear before it should be discontinued. 4.106

This more robust approach to the issue of objective bias is certain to influence developments in social security adjudication.

The Court of Session has now handed down its decision in the Secretary of State's appeal against the decision of a Tribunal of Commissioners: see Volume III, para.4.62. 4.106a

The Court of Session in *The Secretary of State for Work and Pensions v Gillies*, (November 28, 2003) has reversed the decision of the Tribunal of Commissioners. The Court of Session concluded,

"Having considered the factual circumstances we are of the view that the fact that Dr. A. carried out examinations and provided reports for the Benefits Agency as an EMP would not be sufficient to raise in the mind of a reasonable and well-informed observer an apprehension as to his or her impartiality as a member of a disability appeal tribunal.

The mere fact that the tribunal would require to consider and assess reports by other doctors who acted as EMPs would not be such as to raise such an apprehension." (para.38).

In coming to this decision, the Court of Session considered the decision of the House of Lords in *Lawal v Northern Spirit Limited*, but appear to have distinguished it on the grounds that the circumstances before the House of Lords were that, in the Employment Appeal Tribunal, lay members "look to the judge for guidance on the law and can be expected to develop a fairly close relationship of trust and confidence with the judge." The Court of Session did not consider that the case before them involved any likelihood of deference, there being "no relationship of lay to professional or of subordinate to superior" (para.37). The Court of Session appear to accept that the Tribunal of Commissioners identified the right test, but applied it incorrectly—and this constituted an error of law. The Court of Session took a different view on the application of the test; they were influenced by the argument that, taken too widely, an objection could be based simply on membership of a particular professional body: did pointing to a subset of certain professionals involve a distinction with a real difference?

4.106b   This leaves the authorities on bias in something of an unsatisfactory state. *Lawal v Northern Spirit Limited* would appear to be more in tune with the Strasbourg authorities in its approach to the issue of the possible perception of bias. It takes a broader view of the notion of the objective bystander; *Gillies* makes distinctions which would probably be lost on the objective bystander. However, support for the approach adopted by the Court of Session can be found in the decision of the Administrative Court in *R. (on the application of PD) v Mersey Care NHS Trust* [2003] EWHC 2469. This concerned the possibility of objective bias resulting from the presence on a mental health review tribunal of a consultant psychiatrist employed by the health authority in a case where that authority had detained the patient. The consultant psychiatrist had had no contact with the patient or with the detaining hospital. There was absolutely no question of his having been *actually* biased. The Administrative Court considered that there were adequate safeguards to avoid any objective bystander apprehending the possibility of bias. The issue is not whether a professional is able to retain his or her independence in a particular set of circumstances, but whether an objective and fair-minded observer would be satisfied as to the independence and impartiality of that decision maker. The Administrative Court appears to have been partly influenced by the potential problems in finding a sufficient number of consultant psychiatrists to serve on the tribunals if consultant psychiatrists employed by the NHS Trust which had detained the patient whose appeal was being heard were excluded. That may be a less pressing issue in relation to medical members of the appeal tribunals. It is also questionable whether resourcing issues are a legitimate consideration under the Strasbourg case law which has always rejected arguments based on practicalities in Contracting Parties fulfilling their obligations under Article 6 (for example, in relation to the giving of judgment within a reasonable time where arguments about shortage of judicial resources have been given short shrift: see *Hentrich v France* (1994) 18 E.H.R.R. 440, para.61 of the judgment).

Though the decision in *Gillies* legitimates current practices within the Appeal Service in the appointment of medical members, it may not be the last word on this important issue.

p.1080, *Art.14 ECHR*

In *CG/734/2003* the Commissioner concluded that there was no breach of the Human Rights Act 1998 by reason of the differential treatment under the Computation of Earnings Regulations of weekly-paid and monthly-paid workers when calculating deemed periods of gainful employment for the purposes of entitlement to an invalid care allowance. 4.107

In *CIS/4511/2002* the Commissioner dismisses as without foundation an argument based on Art.1 of Protocol 1 and 14 ECHR that reg. 42(2A) of the Income Support General Regulations breaches Convention rights in a case where a claimant aged 61 with a personal pension plan did not draw income from it and was deemed to have notional income from that plan which reduced his entitlement to income support. The argument was that reg. 42(2A) interferes with a claimant's ability to leave funds in a pension scheme to accumulate and so hinders a claimant's ability to use and develop his property as he wishes. The provision, it was argued, "discriminates against men because the entitlement of women to a state retirement pension between the ages of 60 and 65 means that a smaller proportion of women than men are on income support, so that a greater proportion of men than women with person pension schemes have to draw income from those schemes before the age of 65." (para.7).

CP/5084/2001 (noted on p.1087) is under appeal to the Court of Appeal as *Lynch v Secretary of State for Work and Pensions* [2003] EWCA Civ 497.

The Court of Appeal decisions in both *Hooper* and *Reynolds* are the subject of petitions to the House of Lords for leave to appeal there. Leave has been granted in the *Carson* case.

Developments in Canada

4.108   In *Nova Scotia (Workers' Compensation Board) v Martin*, Supreme Court of Canada, October 3, 2003, [2003] SCC 54, (see *http:/ /www.lancasterhouse.com/decisions/2000/nov/nsca-martin.htm* or *http:/ /www.lexum.umontreal.ca/csc-scc/en/com/2003/texte/03–10–03.3.txt* for full text) the Supreme Court struck down as being in violation of the Canadian Charter of Rights and Freedoms a distinction made in the workers' compensation scheme in Nova Scotia between those suffering from chronic pain attributable to a work-related injury from other disabilities resulting from work-related injuries. Benefits in respect of chronic pain are excluded from the regular workers' compensation system and a four week "Functional Restoration Program" is all that is available. The Supreme Court also affirmed the ability of tribunals to apply and interpret the Charter of Rights and Freedoms.

The distinction drawn by the Nova Scotia scheme (outlined at *http:/ /www.gov.ns.ca/enla/wcrc/applsys2.pdf*) was found to violate s.15 of the Canadian Charter which provides,

"Equality rights

4.109   15.—(1) Every individual is equal before and under the law and has the right to the equal protection and equal benefit of the law without discrimination and, in particular, without discrimination based on race, national or ethnic origin, colour, religion, sex, age or mental or physical disability.

(2) Subsection (1) does not preclude any law, program or activity that has as its object the amelioration of conditions of disadvantaged individuals or groups including those that are disadvantaged because of race, national or ethnic origin, colour, religion, sex, age or mental or physical disability."

The differential treatment was found to be discriminatory because it does not correspond to the actual needs and circumstances of injured workers suffering from chronic pain, who are deprived of any individual assessment of their needs and circumstances. Justice Gonthier said,

" . . . the denial of the reality of the pain suffered by the affected workers reinforces widespread negative assumptions held by employers, compensation officials and some members of the medical profession, and demeans the essential human dignity of chronic pain sufferers."

Though draft very differently, there may be mileage in mounting similar sorts of arguments based on Art.14 ECHR coupled with Art.8 ECHR on the differential treatment of certain disabilities in the United Kingdom social security system.

PART V

UPDATING MATERIAL
VOLUME IV

TAX CREDITS AND EMPLOYER PAID SOCIAL SECURITY BENEFITS

Tax Credits and Employer Paid Social Security Benefits

p.21, *Taxes Management Act 1970, s.54*

The Inland Revenue have published a code of practice on the settlement of tax credits appeals. See *IR 168: How tax credits settlements are negotiated*. For the application of this section to employers' appeals, see the Tax Credits (Employer Penalty Appeals) Regulations 2003 (SI 2003/1382).

5.001

p.124, *Social Security Contributions and Benefits Act 1992, Sch.11*

With effect from October 1, 2002, paras 2(b) and 4 of Sch.11 have been repealed by the Fixed-term Employees (Prevention of Less Favourable Treatment) Regulations 2002 (SI 2002/2034). The effect is to remove the SSP exemption for contracts of not more than three months.

p.165, *Tax Credits Act 2002: general note*

The Inland Revenue published in November 2003 a general paper "New Tax Credits–Ensuring Compliance" This notes the high level of overpayments estimated to have been made under the working families' tax credits scheme (an estimated 10%–14% of the total of £5.05bn awarded in the year 2000–2001). It sets out the Inland Revenue strategy, using the powers of the TCA 2002, to combat fraudulent claims or provision of information under the Act.

5.002

p.169, *Tax Credits Act 2002, s.1(3)(d)*

The Tax Credits Act 2002 (Child Tax Credit) (Transitional Provisions) Order 2003 (SI 2003/2170) [see Part I above] makes transitional provision, so far as entitlement to child tax credit is concerned, for pensioners with children transferring from income support to state pension credit.

5.003

p.173, *Tax Credits Act 2002, s.3(2)*

The Inland Revenue has accepted that it is appropriate to make protective claims in cases where the claim will lead to a nil award on then current information but where a claimant may later in the year be entitled to tax credits. In such cases, nil awards will be made. See *Tax Adviser, June 2003, p.13*. The Revenue's statistics show that at October 2003 about 130,000 "nil awards" had been made.

5.004

p.179, *Tax Credits Act 2002, s.6*

The Inland Revenue has announced that it will not seek penalties from a taxpayer who has a nil award following a claim and who then fails to make a mandatory notification of a change of circumstances. See *Tax Adviser, June 2003, p.13*.

5.005

p.179, *Tax Credits Act 2002, s.7(10)*

It is understood that the practice of the Revenue is to make all initial decisions on the basis of the previous year's income. Where the claim

5.006

form indicates that the current year's income should be used, the Revenue then make an immediate revision under s.15.

p.190, *Tax Credits Act 2002, s.15*

5.007   It is understood that the practice of the Revenue is to use this power to revise an initial decision based on the previous year's income in cases where the change of circumstances is that the current's year's income, as reported in the claim form.

p.209, *Tax Credits Act 2002, s.29*

5.008   The Inland Revenue has published a code of practice dealing with recovery of overpayments: *COP26–What happens if we have paid you too much tax credit.*

p.213, *Tax Credits Act 2002, s.32*

5.009   The Inland Revenue has announced that, by concession, it will not seek penalties from those who fail to comply with the mandatory provisions listed in s.32(1) when the award to a claimant is a nil award.

p.259, *Income Tax (Earnings and Pensions) Act 2003, General Note*

5.010   Part 7 of ITEPA was entirely repealed and replaced by the Finance Act 2003, s.140 and Sch.22 (Employee securities and options) with effect from April 15, 2003.

It is no longer outside the scope of tax credits cases, following the amendment of reg.4 of the Tax Credits (Determination and Calculation of Income) Regulations 2002 (SI 2002/2006). See the note to that regulation.

p.267, *Income Tax (Earnings and Pensions) Act 2003, s.48*

5.011   It was thought that the provisions of Ch.8 of Part 2 of ITEPA were within the scope of tax credits because of the definition of "employed" in the Working Tax Credit (Entitlement and Maximum Rate) Regulations 2002 (SI 2002/2005), reg.2. That regulation was amended by the Tax Credits (Miscellaneous Amendments No.2) Regulations 2003 (SI 2003/2815), reg.13, to clarify the intended policy that payments under these provisions are not within the scope of tax credits. Sections 48–61 of ITEPA are therefore no longer of relevance to this work.

p.364, *Working Tax Credit (Entitlement and Maximum Rate) Regulations 2002: amendment of reg.2 (definition of "employed")*

5.012   With effect from November 26, 2003, reg.13 of the Tax Credits (Miscellaneous Amendments No.2) Regulations 2003 (SI 2003/2815) amended the definition of "employed" in reg.2 by adding at the end:

"otherwise than by reason of Chapter 8 of Part 2 of that Act (deemed employment in respect of arrangements made by intermediaries)."

For the reason behind this amendment, see ITEPA s.48 (p.267, above).

p.377, *Working Tax Credit (Entitlement and Maximum Rate) Regulations 2002: amendment of reg. 9(3)*

With effect from November 26, 2003, reg.14(2) of the Tax Credits (Miscellaneous Amendments No.2) Regulations 2003 (SI 2003/2815) amended reg.9(3) to read:

5.013

"(3) Case B is where, for at least one day in the preceding 182 days, the person has been a person [for whom at least one of the following benefits has been payable and for whom the applicable amount] included a higher pensioner or disability premium [in respect of him] determined—
 (a) in the case of income support, in accordance with [paragraphs 10(1)(b) or (2)(b) or 11, and where applicable 12,] of Part III of Schedule 2 to the Income Support (General) Regulations 1987;
 (b) in the case of income-based jobseeker's allowance, in accordance with [paragraphs 12(1)(a), or (b)(ii), or (c), or 13, and where applicable 14 of Part 3 of] Schedule 1 to the Jobseeker's Allowance Regulations 1996;
 (c) in the case of housing benefit, in accordance with [paragraphs 10(1)(b) or (2)(b) or 11, and where applicable, 12] of Part III of Schedule 2 to the Housing Benefit (General) Regulations 1987;
 (d) in the case of council tax benefit, in accordance with [paragraphs 11(1)(b) or (2)(b) or 12, and where applicable, 13] of Part III of Schedule 1 to the Council Tax Benefit (General) Regulations 1992.
For the purposes of this Case "the applicable amount" has the meaning given by section 135 of the Contributions and Benefits Act."

p.378, *Working Tax Credit (Entitlement and Maximum Rate) Regulations 2002: amendment of reg. 9(8)*

With effect from November 26, 2003, reg.14(3) of the Tax Credits (Miscellaneous Amendments No.2) Regulations 2003 (SI 2003/2815) amended reg.9(8) to read:

5.014

"(8) Case G is where the person was entitled, [for at least one day in the preceding 56 days], to the disability element of working tax credit or to disabled person's tax credit by virtue of his having satisfied the requirements of Case A, B, E or F at some earlier time.

For the purposes of this Case a person is treated as having an entitlement to the disability element of working tax credit if that element is taken into account in determining the rate at which the person is entitled to a tax credit."

p.386, *Working Tax Credit (Entitlement and Maximum Rate) Regulations 2002: amendment of reg.14(2)(a)(iii)*

5.015 With effect from November 26, 2003, reg.15 of the Tax Credits (Miscellaneous Amendments No.2) Regulations 2003 (SI 2003/2815) amended the reg.14(2)(a)(iii) to read:

"(iii) in respect of any period between his eighth birthday [and the last day he is treated as a child for the purposes of this regulation,] where the care is provided out of school hours, by a school on school premises or by a local authority; or"

p.392, *Working Tax Credit (Entitlement and Maximum Rate) Regulations 2002: amendment of reg.18(3)*

5.016 With effect from November 26, 2003, reg.16(2) of the Tax Credits (Miscellaneous Amendments No.2) Regulations 2003 (SI 2003/2815) amended reg.18(3) as follows:

"(3) A claimant satisfies this paragraph if—
[(a) he is aged at least 50; and
(b) he starts qualifying remunerative work; and]
(c) he undertakes qualifying remunerative work for at least 16 hours per week; and
(d) he satisfies the condition in paragraph (4), (6), (7), (8) or (9)."

p.393, *Working Tax Credit (Entitlement and Maximum Rate) Regulations 2002: amendment of reg.18(4), (6), (7) and (9)*

5.017 With effect from November 26, 2003, reg.16(3) of the Tax Credits (Miscellaneous Amendments No.2) Regulations 2003 (SI 2003/2815) amended reg.18(4)(a), (b), (6) and (7) so as to insert "qualifying remunerative" between "starting" and "work" in each paragraph. Regulation 16(4) of SI 2003/2815 also substituted "carer's" for "invalid care" in reg.18(9)(a).

p.408, *Tax Credits (Determination and Calculation of Income) Regulations 2003: amendment of reg.2 (definition of "joint claim")*

5.018 With effect from November 26, 2003, reg.3 of the Tax Credits (Miscellaneous Amendments No.2) Regulations 2003 (SI 2003/2815) amended the definition of "joint claim" in reg.2 by substituting "section 3(8)" for "section 4(6)".

p.411, *Tax Credits (Determination and Calculation of Income) Regulations 2003: amendment of reg.3(1)*

5.019 With effect from November 26, 2003, reg.4(2) of the Tax Credits (Miscellaneous Amendments No.2) Regulations 2003 (SI 2003/2815) inserted at the end of reg.3(1):

"Any trading loss in the year not set off as a result of the calculations in Steps One to Four above due to an insufficiency of income may be carried forward and set off against trading income (if any) of the same trade, profession or vocation in subsequent years (taking earlier years first) for the purposes of calculation of income under this regulation."

pp.411–412, *Tax Credits (Determination and Calculation of Income) Regulations 2003: amendment of reg.3(4)*

With effect from November 26, 2003, reg.4(3) of the Tax Credits (Miscellaneous Amendments No.2) Regulations 2003 (SI 2003/2815) amended reg.3(4) to read:

"(4) Paragraph (5) applies in the case of a claimant who is—
(a) resident but neither ordinarily resident nor domiciled in the United Kingdom, [. . .]
(b) resident and ordinarily resident but not domiciled in the United Kingdom [or]
[(c) resident but neither ordinarily resident nor domiciled in the United Kingdom.]"

5.020

p.412, *Tax Credits (Determination and Calculation of Income) Regulations 2003: amendment of reg.3(7)*

With effect from November 26, 2003, reg.4(4) of the Tax Credits (Miscellaneous Amendments No.2) Regulations 2003 (SI 2003/2815) amended reg.3(7) to omit "and" at the end of sub-para.(b), to add "and" at the end of sub-para.(c)(iii), and to add after sub-para.(c) the following:

"(d) any contribution made by the claimant, or in the case of a joint claim, by either or both of the claimants, if made in accordance with Inland Revenue Extra Statutory Concession A9."

5.021

p.412, *Tax Credits (Determination and Calculation of Income) Regulations 2003: insertion of new reg.3(8)*

With effect from November 26, 2003, reg.4(5) of the Tax Credits (Miscellaneous Amendments No.2) Regulations 2003 (SI 2003/2815) added after reg.3(7):

"(8) If—
(a) a claimant has sustained a loss in relation to a Schedule A business or an overseas property business; and
(b) the relief to which he is entitled in accordance with section 379A(2) and (3) of the Taxes Act exceeds the amount of his property income or foreign income for tax credits purposes, for the year in question;
the amount of his total income for tax credit purposes, computed in accordance with the preceding provisions of this regulation, shall be reduced by the amount of the excess.

5.022

In this paragraph "Schedule A business" and "overseas property Business" have the same meanings as they have in the Taxes Act."

These various amendments to reg.3 follow representations to the Inland Revenue about income tax provisions considered relevant to tax credits but not included in the Regulations as first made.

p.414, *Tax Credits (Determination and Calculation of Income) Regulations 2003: amendment of reg.4(1)*

5.023   With effect from November 26, 2003, reg.5(2) of the Tax Credits (Miscellaneous Amendments No.2) Regulations 2003 (SI 2003/2815) amended reg.4(1) to add after sub-para.(k) the following:

"(l) any amount charged to income tax for that year under Part 7 of ITEPA."

This amendment follows the amendments to ITEPA Part 7 in the Finance Act 2003.

p.415, *Tax Credits (Determination and Calculation of Income) Regulations 2003: amendment of reg.4(3)*

5.024   With effect from November 26, 2003, reg.5(3) of the Tax Credits (Miscellaneous Amendments No.2) Regulations 2003 (SI 2003/2815) substituted a new reg.4(3) to read:

"(3) This paragraph applies if (apart from section 64 of ITEPA) the same benefit would give rise to two amounts ("A" and "B")—
  (a) "A" being an amount of earnings from a claimant's employment as defined in section 62 of ITEPA, and
  (b) "B" being an amount to be treated as earnings under any provision of Chapter 10 of Part 3 of ITEPA.
In such a case, the amount to be taken into account in computing the claimant's employment income is the greater of A and B, and the lesser amount shall be disregarded."

pp.415–417, *Tax Credits (Determination and Calculation of Income) Regulations 2003: amendment of Table 1*

5.025   With effect from November 26, 2003, reg.5(4) of the Tax Credits (Miscellaneous Amendments No.2) Regulations 2003 (SI 2003/2815) made the following amendments to Table 1:

"(a) in item 11D, for "Part 4 of ITEPA" to the end of the sentence, substitute "Part 3 of ITEPA, by virtue of any provision of Chapter 6 of Part 4 of ITEPA",
  (b) after item 14B, insert—
    "14C. The discharge of any liability of an employee in connection with a taxable car if no liability to income tax arises by virtue of section 239(1) of ITEPA.
    14D. A benefit connected with a taxable car if no liability to income tax arises by virtue of section 239(4) of ITEPA."

(c) in item 16, for "Project" substitute "Scheme";
(d) after item 16 insert—
"17. The payment or reimbursement of reasonable additional household expenses incurred by an employee who works from home, within the meaning of section 316A of ITEPA.
18. The payment or reimbursement of retraining course expenses within the meaning of section 311 of ITEPA."

p.417, *Tax Credits (Determination and Calculation of Income) Regulations 2003: amendment of reg.4(5)*

With effect from November 26, 2003, reg.5(4) of the Tax Credits (Miscellaneous Amendments No.2) Regulations 2003 (SI 2003/2815) inserted "231 to 232" after "provision of sections".   5.026

These various amendments to reg.4(3) and (5) and Table 1 adjust the extent to which the employment income provisions of ITEPA apply to tax credits.

The Inland Revenue have confirmed that the previous amendments to this regulation (by SI 2003/732) extend the definition of employment income to include all termination payments taxable under Ch.3 of Pt 6 of ITEPA. But at the same time the recipient of a payment in lieu of notice (PILON) is not regarded as continuing at work. The intention is to include the income but not to make the period available for a working tax credit claim during the period of notice, following the income tax treatment, where those payments are taxable. However, under general income tax rules, there is no tax on the first £30,000 of such payments: ITEPA s.403.

p.432, *Tax Credits (Determination and Calculation of Income) Regulations 2003: amendment of reg.7*

With effect from November 26, 2003, reg.6 of the Tax Credits (Miscellaneous Amendments No.2) Regulations 2003 (SI 2003/2815) amended Table 3, Item 24 in reg.7 by replacing the words from "housing benefit" to the end by "or housing benefit".   5.027

This corrects the existing text.

p.436, *Tax Credits (Determination and Calculation of Income) Regulations 2003: replacement of reg.8 (student income)*

With effect from November 26, 2003, reg.7 of the Tax Credits (Miscellaneous Amendments No.2) Regulations 2003 (SI 2003/2815) replaced the text of reg. 8 with the following: 5.028

Student Income

"8. "Student income" means, in relation to a student—
(a) in England and Wales, any grant—
(i) under regulation 15 of the Education (Student Support) Regulations 2002 other than a grant under paragraph (1)(c) or (8) of that regulation or

(ii) under regulation 15 of the Education (Student Support) (No.2) Regulations 2002 other than a grant for Parents Learning Allowance as defined in regulation 15(7) of those Regulations;

(b) in Scotland, any dependant's grant payable under regulation 4(1)(c) of the Students' Allowances (Scotland) Regulations 1999; and

(c) in Northern Ireland, any grant which corresponds to income treated as student income in England and Wales by virtue of paragraph (a)."

p.441, *Tax Credits (Determination and Calculation of Income) Regulations 2003: replacement of reg.10 (investment income)*

5.029   With effect from November 26, 2003, reg.8(2) of the Tax Credits (Miscellaneous Amendments No.2) Regulations 2003 (SI 2003/2815) amended Table 4 in reg.10 by adding, after Item 11:

12. A purchased life annuity to which section 656 of the Taxes Act applies.	The capital element of the annuity as defined and calculated in section 656 of the Taxes Act.

This corrects an error in the original regulations.

p.437, *Tax Credits (Determination and Calculation of Income) Regulations 2003: amendment of reg.11 (property income)*

5.030   With effect from November 26, 2003, reg. 9 of the Tax Credits (Miscellaneous Amendments No.2) Regulations 2003 (SI 2003/2815) amended para.(1) by substituting "qualifications" for "qualification" and adding after para.(2):

"(3) Where a Schedule A business (as defined within Schedule A set out in section 15 of the Taxes Act) makes a loss to which the relief provisions of section 379A of the Taxes Act apply, then such relief as may arise under subsection (1) of that section shall be applied in calculating property income for the purposes of this regulation."

Section 379A of the Taxes Act 1988 deals with Schedule A losses—that is, losses derived from the business of exploiting land in the UK.

p.447, *Tax Credits (Determination and Calculation of Income) Regulations 2003: amendment of reg.12 (foreign income)*

5.031   With effect from November 26, 2003, reg.10 of the Tax Credits (Miscellaneous Amendments No.2) Regulations 2003 (SI 2003/2815) amended reg.12 by adding at the end:

"(4) Where an overseas property business (within the meaning of the Taxes Act) makes a loss to which the relief provisions of section

379A of the Taxes Act apply, by virtue of section 379B of that Act, then such relief as may arise under section 379A(1) shall be applied in calculating foreign income for the purposes of this regulation."

Section 379A deals with Schedule A losses (see the note immediately above). Section 379B applies section 379A in relation to an overseas business as it applies to a Schedule A business.

pp.456–458, *Tax Credits (Determination and Calculation of Income) Regulations 2003: amendment of reg.19 (general disregards)*

With effect from November 26, 2003, reg.11 of the Tax Credits (Miscellaneous Amendments No.2) Regulations 2003 (SI 2003/2815) amended reg.19 to substitute the following for Items 9 and 14 of Table 6: 5.032

"9. Any payment by way of foster care receipts to the extent that those receipts qualify for relief under Schedule 36 to the Finance Act 2003.

14. Any payment under the Community Care (Direct Payments) Act 1996, section 57 of the Health and Social Care Act 2001, section 12B of the Social Work (Scotland) Act 1968, Article 15A of the Health and Personal Social Services (Direct Payments) (Northern Ireland) Order 1996 or section 8 of the Carers and Direct Payments Act (Northern Ireland) 2002."

In addition, the same amending regulation amends Item 11(a) to read:

"(a) to adopters which is exempt from income tax by virtue of section 327A of the Taxes Act;"

These amendments follow the introduction in the Finance Act 2003 of new measures dealing with tax relief on payments to adopters and foster carers. Section 175 of the 2003 Act introduces from April 6, 2003 a new section 327A (Payments to adopters) to the Taxes Act 1988. This makes statutory a previous extra statutory concession exempting payments to adopters from income tax. This applies to payments under the Adoption Act 1976 but not the Adoption of Children Act 2002 for adoption support services. Section 176 of the 2003 Act introduces Sch.36 to that Act (foster carers) with effect from April 6, 2003. The Schedule makes provision for the exemption from income tax, subject to limits, of income received by foster parents for their fostering services.

p.465, *Child Tax Credit Regulations 2002: amendment of reg.2 (definition of advanced education)*

With effect from November 26, 2003, reg.17 of the Tax Credits (Miscellaneous Amendments No.2) Regulations 2003 (SI 2003/2815) amended the definition of "advanced education" in reg.2(1) to read: 5.033

" "advanced education" means full-time education for the purposes of—

(a) a course in preparation for a degree, a diploma of higher education, a higher national diploma, a higher national diploma or higher national certificate of Edexcel or the Scottish Qualifications Authority, or a teaching qualification; or

(b) any other course which is of a standard above ordinary national diploma, a national diploma or national certificate of Edexcel [. . .], a general certificate of education (advanced level), [or Scottish national qualifications at higher or advanced higher level];"

p.479, *Tax Credits (Income Thresholds and Determination of Rates) Regulations 2002, reg.4*

5.034 With effect from November 26, 2003, reg.18 of the Tax Credits (Miscellaneous Amendments No.2) Regulations 2003 (SI 2003/2815) inserted at the end of reg.4 the following further prescribed benefit:

"(d) state pension credit within the meaning of the State Pension Credit Act 2002 or the State Pension Credit Act (Northern Ireland) 2002."

p.498, *Tax Credits (Claims and Notifications) Regulations 2002, reg. 8(2)(c)*

5.035 With effect from November 26, 2003, reg.20 of the Tax Credits (Miscellaneous Amendments No.2) Regulations 2003 (SI 2003/2815) amended reg.8(2)(c) to read:

"(c) the reason for that decision was that the person or any of the persons did not satisfy paragraph [(1)(c)] of regulation 9 of the Working Tax Credit Regulations;"

p.498, *Tax Credits (Claims and Notifications) Regulations 2002, reg.26*

5.036 With effect from November 26, 2003, reg.21 of the Tax Credits (Miscellaneous Amendments No.2) Regulations 2003 (SI 2003/2815) substituted the word "credit" for "element" in reg.26(2)(b) and the phrase "regulation 9(1)(c)" for "regulation 9(2)" in both reg. 26(2)(c) and reg. 26(3)(c).

p.515, *Tax Credits (Claims and Notifications) Regulations 2002, reg.33*

5.037 With effect from November 26, 2003, reg.22 of the Tax Credits (Miscellaneous Amendments No.2) Regulations 2003 (SI 2003/2815) amended reg.33 to read:

"Dates to be specified in notices under section 17 of the Act

33. In a notice under section 17 of the Act—
(a) the date which may be specified for the purposes of subsections (2) and (4) of that section shall not be later than 6th July

following the end of the tax year to which the notice relates [or 30 days after the date of the notice, if later];
(b) the date which may be specified for the purposes of subsection (8) of that section shall not be later than 6th July following the end of the tax year after the tax year to which the notice relates [or 30 days after the date of the notice, if later]."

p.601, *Statutory Sick Pay (General) Regulations 1982, reg.9(2)*

The layout of reg.9(2), but not the actual wording, is incorrect. It should read as follows:

5.038

"(2) In any case where—
(a) a decision has been made by an insurance officer, local tribunal or Commissioner in proceedings under Part I that an employee is entitled to an amount of statutory sick pay; and
(b) the time for bringing an appeal against the decision has expired and either
　　(i) no such appeal has been brought; or
　　(ii) such an appeal has been brought and has been finally disposed of,
that amount of statutory sick pay is to be paid within the time specified in paragraph (3)."

PART VI

FORTHCOMING CHANGES AND UP-RATING OF BENEFITS

PART VI

FORTHCOMING CHANGES

6.001 This section aims to give users of Social Security Legislation 2003 some information on significant changes coming into force between November 24, 2003—the date to which this Supplement is up to date—and mid-April 2004, the date to which the 2004 edition of the main work will be up to date. This section reflects our understanding of sources available to use at January 26, 2004. Users should be aware that there are likely to be further legislative amendment between then and April 2004. This section of the Supplement should at least enable users to access the relevant legislation on the TSO website—
http://www.legislation.hmso.gov.uk/legislation/uk.htm

The Social Security (Electronic Communications) Carer's Allowance) Order 2003

6.002 The Social Security (Electronic Communications) Carer's Allowance) Order 2003 (SI 2003/2800), which enters into force on December 1, 2003 amends the Claims and Payments Regulations 1987 and the Notification of Change of Circumstances Regulations so as to make provision for claims for, and the notifying of a change of circumstance relevant to an award of, carer's allowance, to be made electronically.

Article 2 amends the Claims and Payments Regulations 1987. Article 2(1) amends reg.2 of those regulations inserting new definitions into that regulation. Art.2(2) inserts a new regulation 4ZC, which authorises the use of electronic communication to make a claim for, and to provide any certificate, notice, information or evidence connected with a claim for carer's allowance subject to the provisions set out in Sch.9ZC. Art.2(3) inserts a new regulation 32ZA, which provides for the giving of information in relation to carer's allowance to be given by means of an electronic communication subject to the provisions set out in Schedule 9ZC. Article 2(4) inserts a new Sch.9ZC; this Schedule authorises the Secretary of State to use electronic communications in connection with claims for, and awards of, carer's allowance. It also sets out the conditions to be satisfied where a claim for carer's allowance is made by means of electronic communication and makes other provisions which apply to any electronic communication made in connection with carer's allowance.

Article 3 adds a new paragraph (1ZA) to reg.5 of the Notification of Change of Circumstances Regulations to provide that where a change of circumstances is notified in respect of carer's allowance for the purposes of s.111A(1A) to (1G) and 112(1A) to (1F) of the Administration Act 1992, by an electronic communication, the provisions set out in Sch.9ZC to the Claims and Payments Regulations 1987 1987 apply to that notification.

6.003 Article 4 revokes the Social Security (Electronic Communications) (Child Benefit) Order 2002 (SI 2002/1789) ("the Child Benefit Order"). The provisions inserted into the Claims and Payments Regulations 1987 by the Child Benefit Order have been revoked by the Child Benefit and Guardian's Allowance (Administration) Regulations 2003 (SI 2003/492).

The Social Fund Cold Weather Payments (General) Amendment (No.2) Regulations 2003 (SI 2003/3023)

6.004 These Regulations amended, with effect from November 28, 2003, the Social Fund Cold Weather Payments (General) Regulations 1988 (SI 1988/1724) ("the principal Regulations") in relation to the list of weather stations and applicable postcode districts in Sch.1 to those Regulations.

Regulation 2 amended Sch.1 to the principal Regulations by substituting Dyce (Aberdeen Airport) for Craibstone Weather Station and Ringway (Manchester Airport) for Woodford Weather Station as Craibstone and Woodford weather stations are unable to provide the temperature data required.

The Social Security (Notification of Change of Circumstances) Regulations 2003 (SI 2003/3209)

6.005 With effect from January 6, 2004, these Regulations amended the Social Security (Claims and Payments) Regulations 1987 ("the 1987 Regulations") and the Social Security (Notification of Change of Circumstances) Regulations 2001 ("the 2001 Regulations") in respect of notification of changes of circumstances by benefit recipients.

Regulation 2 amended the 1987 Regulations to provide that changes of circumstances affecting the continuance of entitlement to benefit or the payment of benefit shall be notified to the Secretary of State in writing or by telephone (unless he requires the person to give written notice or accepts another means of notification) or, if he so requires in a class of case, the changes shall be notified in writing unless he accepts another means of notification in any particular case.

Regulation 3 amended the 2001 Regulations to make similar provision for the purpose of offences relating to failure to notify such changes of circumstances.

Forthcoming Changes

The Tax Credits (Claims and Notifications) (Amendment) Regulations 2003 (SI 2003/3240)

These Regulations amended, with effect from January 1, 2004, the Tax Credits (Claims and Notifications) Regulations 2002 (SI 2002/2014: "the principal Regulations"). Regulation 1 provides for citation, commencement, and effect. Regulation 2 introduces the amendments to the principal Regulations. Regulations 3 and 4 amend regs 8 and 26 of the principal Regulations respectively, making minor corrections of a clerical and drafting nature. **6.006**

This instrument replaces the provisions contained in regulations 19 to 21 of S.I. 2003/2815, which were purportedly made by HM Treasury under powers conferred on the Commissioners of Inland Revenue.

The Social Security (Child Maintenance Premium) Amendment Regulations 2004 (SI 2004/98)

These Regulations amended the Income Support (General) Regulations 1987 (SI 1987/1967) ("the Income Support Regulations"), the Jobseeker's Allowance Regulations 1996 (SI 1996/207) ("the Jobseeker's Allowance Regulations") and the Social Security (Child Maintenance Premium and Miscellaneous Amendments) Regulations 2000 (SI 2000/3176) ("the Child Maintenance Premium Regulations"). **6.007**

Regulation 1 provides for citation, commencement and interpretation. Regulations 1 and 4 apply from February 16, 2004. Regulations 2 and 3 apply— **6.008**

- from February 16, 2004 in relation to a case in respect of which s.23 of the Child Support, Pensions and Social Security Act 2000 ("the 2000 Act") has before February 16, 2004 come into force (s.23 relates to the abolition of the child maintenance bonus) (reg.1(3)(a));
- where reg.1(3)(a) does not apply, from the date on which s.23 of the 2000 Act is commenced for different types of cases (reg.1(3)(b));
- from February 16, 2004 in respect of a person who, on or after that date, makes a claim for income support or an income-based jobseeker's allowance and on or after that date receives a payment of child maintenance made voluntarily (reg.1(3)(c));
- in respect of a person who, on February 16, 2004, is entitled to income support or an income-based jobseeker's allowance and on or after that date first receives a payment of child maintenance made voluntarily whilst he is entitled to that benefit, from February 16, 2004 if the first such payment of child maintenance is received on that date, or from the day on which the first such payment of child maintenance is received if it is received after that date (reg.1(3)(d)).

6.009 The Income Support Regulations and the Jobseeker's Allowance Regulations are amended to make it clear that when more than one payment of child maintenance is made—

- in respect of more than one child or young person, or
- by more than one person in respect of a child or young person,

all such payments which are to be taken into account in any week shall be aggregated and treated as a single payment of child maintenance (regs 2 and 3).

6.010 The Income Support Regulations and the Jobseeker's Allowance Regulations are also amended to ensure that when payments of child maintenance are made otherwise than weekly the child maintenance premium disregard is applied to each weekly equivalent amount of child maintenance paid (regs 2 and 3).

Regulation 4(1) substitutes a new regulation for reg.1 of the Child Maintenance Premium Regulations (citation and commencement) to ensure that those Regulations apply—

- from February 16, 2004 in respect of a person who, on or after that date, makes a claim for income support or an income-based jobseeker's allowance and on or after that date receives a payment of child maintenance made voluntarily; or
- in respect of a person who, on that date, is entitled to income support or an income-based jobseeker's allowance and on or after February 16, 2004 first receives a payment of child maintenance made voluntarily whilst he is entitled to that benefit, from February 16, 2004 if the first such payment of child maintenance is received on that date, or from the day on which the first such payment of child maintenance is received if it is received after that date.

Regulation 4(2) omits reg.2(1)(b) and (2)(b) of the Child Maintenance Premium Regulations as a consequence of the amendments made by regs 2 and 3 of these Regulations.

The Social Security (Hospital In-Patients) Amendment Regulations 2004 (SI 2004/101)

6.011 These Regulations altered, with effect from January 26, 2004, the Social Security (Hospital In-Patients) Regulations 1975. They amended the amount of benefit payable to a beneficiary's dependant after the beneficiary has received 52 weeks of free in-patient treatment in a hospital and then has his benefit adjusted so that the first 20% only of the basic pension is payable. They provide that the next 38%, instead of 40%, of the basic pension is not payable and any excess over 58%, instead of 60%, of the basic pension is payable to the dependant.

Forthcoming Changes

NEW BENEFIT RATES FROM APRIL 2004

(Benefits covered in Volume I)

	April 2003 £ pw	April 2004 £ pw
Disability benefits		
Attendance allowance		
higher rate	57.20	58.80
lower rate	38.30	39.35
Disability living allowance		
care component		
highest rate	57.20	58.80
middle rate	38.30	39.35
lowest rate	15.15	15.55
mobility component		
higher rate	39.95	41.05
lower rate	15.15	15.55
Carer's allowance	43.15	44.35
Severe disablement allowance		
basic rate	43.60	44.80
age related addition—higher rate	15.15	15.55
age related addition—middle rate	9.70	10.00
age related addition—lower rate	4.85	5.00
Maternity benefits		
Maternity allowance		
standard rate	100.00	102.80
Widow's benefit and retirement pensions		
Widowed parent's allowance or widowed mother's allowance	77.45	79.60
Bereavement allowance or widow's pension		
standard rate	77.45	79.60
Retirement pension		
Category A	77.45	79.60
Category B (higher)	77.45	79.60
Category B (lower)	46.35	47.65
Category C (higher)	46.35	47.65
Category C (lower)	27.70	28.50
Category D	46.35	47.65

6.012

Forthcoming Changes

	April 2003 £ pw	April 2004 £ pw
Incapacity benefit		
Long-term incapacity benefit		
basic rate	72.15	74.15
increase for age—higher rate	15.15	15.55
increase for age—lower rate	7.60	7.80
invalidity allowance—higher rate	15.15	15.55
invalidity allowance—middle rate	9.70	10.00
invalidity allowance—lower rate	4.85	5.00
Short-term incapacity benefit		
under pension age—higher rate	64.35	66.15
under pension age—lower rate	54.40	55.90
over pension age—higher rate	72.15	74.15
over pension age—lower rate	69.20	71.15
Dependency increases		
Adult		
carer's allowance	25.80	26.50
severe disablement allowance	25.90	26.65
maternity allowance	33.65	34.60
retirement pension	46.35	47.65
long-term incapacity benefit	43.15	44.35
short-term incapacity benefit under pension age	33.65	34.60
short-term incapacity benefit over pension age	41.50	42.65
Child	11.35*	11.35*
Industrial injuries benefits		
Disablement benefit		
aged 18 and over or under 18 with dependants		
—100%	116.80	120.10
90%	105.12	108.09
80%	93.44	96.08
70%	81.76	84.07
60%	70.08	72.06
50%	58.40	60.05
40%	46.72	48.04
30%	35.04	36.03
20%	23.36	24.02
aged under 18 with no dependants		
—100%	71.55	73.55
90%	64.40	66.20

Forthcoming Changes

	April 2003	April 2004
	£ pw	£ pw
80%	57.24	58.84
70%	50.09	51.49
60%	42.93	44.13
50%	35.78	36.78
40%	28.62	29.42
30%	21.47	22.07
20%	14.31	14.71
unemployability supplement		
basic rate	72.15	74.15
increase for adult dependant	43.15	44.35
increase for child dependant	11.35*	11.35*
increase for early incapacity—higher rate	15.15	15.55
increase for early incapacity—middle rate	9.70	10.00
increase for early incapacity—lower rate	4.85	5.00
constant attendance allowance		
exceptional rate	93.60	96.20
intermediate rate	70.20	72.15
normal maximum rate	46.80	48.10
part-time rate	23.40	24.05
exceptionally severe disablement allowance	46.80	48.10
Reduced earnings allowance		
maximum rate	46.72	48.04
Death benefit		
widow's pension		
higher rate	77.45	79.60
lower rate	23.24	23.88
widower's pension	77.45	79.60

Benefits in respect of children

	April 2003	April 2004
Child benefit		
only, elder or eldest child (couple)	16.05	16.50
only, elder or eldest child (lone parent)	17.55	17.55
each subsequent child	10.75	11.05
Child's special allowance	11.35*	11.35*
Guardian's allowance	11.35*	11.35*

* These sums payable in respect of children are reduced if payable in respect of the only, elder or eldest child for whom child benefit is being paid (see reg.8 of the Social Security (Overlapping Benefits) Regulations 1979).

Forthcoming Changes

NEW BENEFIT RATES FROM APRIL 2004

(Benefits covered in Volume II)

		April 2003 £ pw	April 2004 £ pw
Contribution-based jobseeker's allowance			
personal rate—aged under 18		32.90	33.50
aged 18 to 24		43.25	44.05
aged 25 or over		54.65	55.65
Income support and income-based jobseeker's allowance			
personal allowances			
single person—aged under 18 (usual rate)		32.90	33.50
aged under 18 (higher rate)		43.25	44.05
aged 18 to 24		43.25	44.05
aged 25 or over		54.65	55.65
lone parent aged under 18 (usual rate)		32.90	33.50
aged under 18 (higher rate)		43.25	44.05
aged 18 or over		54.65	55.65
couple both aged under 18		32.90	33.50
both aged under 18, one disabled		43.25	44.05
both aged under 18, with a child		65.30	66.50
one aged under 18, one aged 18 to 24		43.25	44.05
one aged under 18, one aged 25 or over		54.65	55.65
both aged 18 or over		85.75	87.30
child—birth to September following 16th birthday		38.50	42.27
September following 16th birthday to under 19		38.50	42.27
premiums			
family—*ordinary*		15.75	15.95
lone parent		15.90	15.95
breavement		22.80	23.95
pension—*single person (JSA only from October 2003)*		47.45	49.80
couple		70.05	73.65

	April 2003 £ pw	April 2004 £ pw
enhanced pensioner	70.05	73.65
higher pensioner—*single person (JSA only from October 2003)*	47.45	49.80
couple	70.05	73.65
disability—*single person*	23.30	23.70
couple	33.25	33.85
enhanced disability—*single person*	11.40	11.60
couple	16.45	17.08
child	16.60	16.75
severe disability—*single person*	42.95	44.15
couple (one qualifies)	42.95	44.15
couple (both qualify)	85.90	88.30
disabled child	41.30	42.49
carer	25.10	25.55

	October 2003 £ pw	April 2004 £ pw

Pension credit

Standard minimum guarantee		
single person	102.10	105.45
couple	155.80	160.95
Additional amount for severe disability		
single person	42.95	44.15
couple (one qualifies)	42.15	44.15
couple (both qualify)	85.90	85.90

Forthcoming Changes

NEW TAX CREDIT RATES 2004–05

6.014

	2003–04 £ pa	2004–05 £ pa
Working tax credit		
Basic element	1,525	1,570
Couple and lone parent element	1,500	1,545
30 hour element	620	640
Disabled worker element	2,040	2,100
Severe disability element	865	890
50+ Return to work payment (under 30 hours)	1,045	1,075
50+ Return to work payment (30 or more hours)	1,565	1,610
Child tax credit		
Family element	545	545
Family element, baby addition	545	545
Child element	1,445	1,625
Disabled child element	2,155	2,215
Severely disabled child element	865	890
Income thresholds		
Income disregard	2,500	2,500
First threshold	5,060	5,060
First threshold for those entitled to child tax credit only	13,230	13,480
First withdrawal rate—37%		
Second threshold	2,500	2,500
Second withdrawal rate—6.67%		